PENGUIN ANANDA

CONVERSATIONS WITH DADA VASWANI

A devotee of Sai Baba of Shirdi, Ruzbeh N. Bharucha in one of the most influential spiritual writers of our times. He is the author of fourteen books, including the bestselling Fakir trilogy, which has been translated into several languages. In 2014, *Rabda: My Sai . . . My Sigh*, published by Penguin Books, was an instant bestseller.

Formerly a journalist, he is also a documentary film-maker. His documentary *Sehat . . . Wings of Freedom*, on AIDS and HIV in Tihar Jail, was selected and screened in the XVII International AIDS Conference in 2008. His collaboration with Zambhala—India's yoga, music and life spirit festival, the first of its kind—gave birth to a series of powerful videos called 'Ramblings with Ruzbeh Bharucha'. His articles have been published in the *Times of India*, *Free Press Journal*, *Indian Express*, *Maharashtra Herald*, *Sunday Observer*, *Jam-e-Jamshed* and *Afternoon*.

His book *My God Is a Juvenile Delinquent* has been included in the reading list of all judicial academies.

Ruzbeh is the 110th Master for the 'Speaking Tree', where he writes an immensely popular blog on spirituality.

His Facebook page has reached out to thousands in a very short span of time. The daily affirmations and messages are a source of inspiration to many. He lives with his family in Pune.

You can reach him here:
Facebook: www.facebook.com/ruzbehbharucha
Twitter: @ruzbehnbharucha
Website: www.ruzbehbharucha.net
Youtube: www.youtube.com/channel/UCo-rFxiF7R9qaMMWdpj5fJQ

A young Dada Vaswani seated at the feet of His Master, Sadhu Vaswani.

Conversations with DADA VASWANI

A Perfect Disciple, A Reluctant Master

RUZBEH N. BHARUCHA

PENGUIN
ANANDA

PENGUIN ANANDA

USA | Canada | UK | Ireland | Australia
New Zealand | India | South Africa | China

Penguin Ananda is part of the Penguin Random House group of companies whose addresses can be found at global.penguinrandomhouse.com

Published by Penguin Random House India Pvt. Ltd
7th Floor, Infinity Tower C, DLF Cyber City,
Gurgaon 122 002, Haryana, India

First published in Penguin Ananda by Penguin Random House India 2016

10 9 8 7 6 5 4 3 2

The views and opinions expressed in this book are the author's own and the facts are as reported by him which have been verified to the extent possible, and the publishers are not in any way liable for the same.

ISBN 9780143426660

Typeset in Adobe Caslon Pro by Manipal Digital Systems, Manipal
Printed at Replika Press Pvt. Ltd, India

www.penguin.co.in

To

The Universal Mother Goddess and our Creator
Sai Baba of Shirdi
All Divine, Perfect, Ancient, Ascended Masters
Archangels and Angels
Celestial, Terrestrial, Physical Warriors of Light
The Oneness Family

And to Saina, whom I am sure of . . .

Author's Note

There are innumerable books by Dada Vaswani and on Dada Vaswani. I had no intention of writing another book on the saint. Thus, I tried my best to not accept the invitation to pay a visit to Dada's Mission and also to meet the Master. Two months later, it was Saina, my wife, who, out of sheer exasperation, convinced me to go and meet Dada.

Once you enter the Mission, you cannot miss the Samadhi of Sadhu Vaswani, a Perfect Master and the Guru of Dada Vaswani.

Bowing at the Shrine, I felt I was back in Shirdi in front of my Master, Baba Sai. Thus, it was in the Holy Shrine of Sadhu Vaswani that I decided to write this book. I was also quite certain that I would not write another biography of Him. The problem with biographies is that either the book sounds condescending or it looks as though you are besotted or sucking up to the focus of your attention.

I just wanted to write a book on spirituality and get answers to questions about life, and the paranormal and illusionary stuff associated with the spirit world. I wanted the book to be a conversation between a sage and a seeker. I wanted the book to help anybody interested in spirituality or to enable the person to keep his/her head above water in the face of adversities. I hope this book helps all those who are striving to walk the path.

I wanted to bring out a documentary along with this book, but due to personal reasons, after having filmed more than a hundred hours, I decided that maybe the time wasn't right. Hence, the book first.

I interviewed Dada over a period of a few months. Met Him innumerable times. Each time I realized that it must be due to some good karma in some past life of mine that I had been given the opportunity to spend some truly spiritual time with the Saint. I had a great time talking to Dada. We laughed and talked and wanted to spend more time with each other, but when you are a spiritual Master, you have lots of responsibilities and thus Dada could spare only an hour and a half every day. Every time we would end the interview, He would tell one and all around Him that He wanted to spend more time conversing about various things.

Being with Dada was like reconnecting with my grandparents and elders. There are two qualities about Dada that I doubt I have encountered in anybody else.

The first and foremost is that Dada is truly a disciple. I will not use an adjective to describe a disciple. There are no comparative grades for being a disciple. Either you are a disciple or you are not. When you meet Dada, you come back with the fragrance of Sadhu Vaswani. You sometimes even forget Dada. That is Dada's greatest strength and His most profound quality—His love for His Guru, Sadhu Vaswani.

Many people wonder that why there aren't any truly great Gurus like these who were present in the past. That is probably because there are no real disciples. You have followers and devotees and very often disillusioned people who spend their lives fooling themselves and their loved ones about following the spiritual path when in reality all they are doing is hiding or running away from reality. Then there are those who are on a perpetual spree of spiritual shopping—but disciples are rare.

Dada is a disciple.

I love Him for that.

If I could be blessed with one tenth of the love my Guru has for His Master, I think the burden of my existence on Mother Earth will be lightened. If you are a Guru reading this emotional twaddle, then pray you have one disciple like Dada in your noisy flock.

Being a disciple, Dada becomes the most humble man I have ever met. I have met powerful sages, great human beings, leaders and truly good and noble individuals, but I doubt if I have ever met a more humble person than Dada Vaswani. I guess because He doesn't consider Himself as a Master and only operates and lives and breathes as a disciple, humility comes naturally to Him and flows through His very breath. You try to touch His feet and He tries to dive for yours. He receives all accolades on behalf of His Master. He is untouched by pride. Even articles on Him written four decades ago talk about this aspect of His humility.

He fell down at the age of ninety-two while playing a game with kids and has since then been on a wheelchair. He is ninety-eight years old now. Not once has He complained to anybody including Himself. Furiously independent, He now has to be dependent on others for a lot of things. Most importantly, He can no longer have his privacy. But He does not complain. Somebody who was always outdoors, on His feet, now sits quietly, working, meeting people, talking, attending satsangs and painful physiotherapy sessions. He does it happily, without complaining. This Man, this disciple, this Master, goes about His life making His Master happy and proud of Him. Dada's humility and surrender to His Master is humbling.

Dada and I shared a lot of laughter. He is one of the wittiest and most humorous people I have ever met. His humour is never disparaging. He never puts people down. He always likes to ignore the ninety-nine flaws and focus on that one good quality in people. I will truly miss those days.

When I am breathing my last and reliving all the heartwarming moments I have gone through, my time with Dada Vaswani will certainly stand out among them.

This book will hold a special place in my heart. Not because of Dada Vaswani the Saint, but because of Dada Vaswani the disciple.

I pray the Divine Mother bless you always.

Jai Baba. Jai Maa.

1

Sadhu Vaswani Mission is in the heart of Pune, but the moment you enter, it is like stepping into another world. I know this sounds clichéd, but trust me, it is another world. You forget you are in the city. There is an aura of calmness to the whole place. The security guards smile at you. Unlike other places where they usually look at me as if I was something left after an intergalactic waste management programme. It is a truly calm place. There are beautiful trees. It is spotless. A huge, old-fashioned, wide building greets you, which was owned earlier by a Zoroastrian family or trust. It certainly looks it. The ground floor is a long, huge hall where I guessed there would be satsangs or spiritual gatherings, meditation classes and devotional music get-togethers held. And then to left is Sadhu Vaswani's Samadhi.

Naresh Singhani from the Mission had been corresponding with me for the past few months. I had written an article on Sadhu Vaswani, which was published in *The Perfect Ones*, and I was informed that it was liked by many in the Mission, and Sister Krishna, wanted to meet me.

'Hello, Ruzbehji.'

'For God's sake, you make me sound like some respected *mithaiwalla.* Drop the ji.'

Naresh didn't know what to say, so he shook my hand with great vigour.

Sadhu Vaswani's Samadhi is the first thing you notice when you look around the Mission. A marble enclave with Sadhu Vaswani's statue and His last mortal remains have been encased in the rectangular marble slab. There is a narrow carpet, of about thirty-odd feet, laid down so one can remove one's footwear to reach the Samadhi. I knelt and said a short prayer. Then I looked up at Him.

'I have a feeling I might be told to write a book on Dada Vaswani. You will have to decide if I should take it up. If yes, then let us make it very clear, you and Sai Baba of Shirdi will have to write the book. I am sorry, my name will be on the cover. You both decide how to go about it as I have no clue how this book or the documentary . . . Oh yes . . . You and Baba will be making a documentary film too . . . It will be written or filmed. If, for whatever reason, dear Sadhu Vaswani, You or Baba Sai of Shirdi, are unable to give your collective precious time, then don't let this project take off. I love You all. Naresh is standing on one foot now, impatient. I am meeting Dada and Sister Krishna, please try Your best that I don't put my illustrious foot in mouth, a talent I could truly live without. Jai Baba. Jai Gurudev.'

So I was taken upstairs and Naresh, along with his wife, Anita, sat with me and we had tea. The sun beams entered the veranda and it was a peaceful moment. Birds chirping. Cool wind blowing. I realized I had forgotten my shoes near the Samadhi. Anyway, I looked around. There is an open kitchen facing the terrace on which we sat. I could see many women hard at work there, somebody cooking, somebody on the computer, phone ringing . . . And then Krishna entered. She is in her mid-fifties. You could make out that she must have been on her feet all day. Krishna has lived in the Mission since she was three years old and she serves Dada round the clock. She has taken care of everything related with the Mission and since Dada has physically been on the wheel chair, Krishna's role has become all the more important as now she is the catalyst for the world to reach Dada.

'When Dada had the fall, how old was He?' I asked Krishna.

'It was on 7 May 2010. He will turn ninety-eight on 2 August 2016, so He was in His early nineties.'

'How did he fall? What happened?'

'As you know, every moment with Him is a revelation. We were at a *Sadhana* Camp in Panama, that day we had travelled and Dada said, "I am so tired after the inaugural session; I will skip the cultural programme that they are having in the night." So we said fine Dada, it's okay. They will do it on their own. Suddenly He finishes eating His dinner and He says, "I am being called. I want to go for the Cultural Programme." Actually, we had already told everyone that Dada would not be coming. We informed Dada this, but Dada insisted. As if He was aware of what was to happen. We followed Dada downstairs and there, before entering the hall, children were playing table tennis. So Dada, wherever He is, whenever He sees children playing, it is an opportunity for Him to join in and He can never miss out such joy. He is one with them. He will cry with them; He will talk with them; He will laugh with them.'

'He becomes like them basically.'

'Exactly, He becomes a child. So that child spirit in Him is the most visible of His human traits . . . even in His day-to-day behaviour, even in His sickness. Like yesterday, He was down with a fever and in His child spirit, He was whispering, "Oh Mother, you have given me this beautiful gift!" So the child spirit in Him is a quality that keeps Him going. Dada also says, "I regard God as my Mother. So whenever I have any problem, any difficulty which people pass on to me, I immediately pass it on to my Mother and then I completely forget about it because I know my Mother will take care of it." So, as I said, Dada was playing with the children and He was so enthusiastic. The boy He was playing with lobbed the ball at Dada and Dada was jumping here and there with his shawl. Then, in third or fourth shot, Dada's foot got entangled in His shawl and He fell down. And, at that time also, there was such a Divine smile on His face, even as He fell down with a great thud. We all didn't know what to do, but He was smiling and he said, "Nothing to worry, don't panic, don't panic. Everything will be alright." He lay down flat, you know, like He fell on his back. Incidentally, all the injuries – the shoulder, the femur bone, are on the right side of His body.'

I remembered Avatar Meher Baba, who once injured the right side of His body and, in another accident, His left side. Both times, the other side was untouched.

'And Dada knew that He had broken His bones because He is virtually a doctor Himself. He couldn't move any part of His body. He was in excruciating pain, but to make sure we did not panic He kept saying He was not in pain. He lay on His back and told me, "I know there are many bones that are broken, but you all don't panic. Everything will become okay." So we immediately called for an ambulance and we were at a resort, which was an hour and a half away from the main town. The ambulance came after such a long time and by then, you know, the word spread around the camp. Somebody was doing *mantra japa*, somebody was crying, but Dada smiled in spite of the pain. We told him to take an analgesic, but He refused saying, "If I am not touched or moved there is no pain."'

'So He was lying down for nearly two hours in pain?'

'Yes, He lay on the floor because we didn't want to shift Him. I could feel from the position of his big toe that He had fractured His femur bone for sure. So He said, "You all don't move me, you all don't touch me; let the people come and we will go to the hospital." But for the entire hour and a half, He was so peaceful. In fact He sang a song while lying down. He even composed a song. Then the ambulance arrived and we experienced the worst possible ride in the ambulance because the road was so rocky and uneven.' Krishna grimaced, he eyes gleaming with pain. She shook her head in resignation.

'And at every jerk, Dada was in such agonizing pain I cannot describe it. We were ourselves having so much difficulty just sitting down, but He was calm and kept chanting, "Ram, Ram!" His mind was completely with Sadhu Vaswani. Him chanting "Ram, Ram" meant He was in terrible agony. And in Panama, the medical facilities are limited. We kept requesting those people to do something, but it was an uphill task. First, there was a huge language problem. They speak only Spanish. Of course, we had a lot of Spanish people with us; whatever we had to communicate we had to tell our people and they would communicate it to them. So, in the night, we went to a hospital in Panama. They administered him first-aid, but we decided that we would fly him by air-ambulance to Chicago, where our doctors were present. They know his system, they know everything. Dada is no stranger to pain and illness.'

'How far is Panama from Chicago?'

'It took us half a day because it was a chartered flight. We left at nine, then it had to stop somewhere for re-fuelling and then we reached Chicago in the afternoon.'

'So, basically, he was not really touched till he reached Chicago? They were giving him painkillers?'

'They just gave him painkillers and they put in a plinth because after x-rays it was clear Dada had broken His bones. Even a slight movement was giving Him a lot of pain. They all recommended we do the surgery in Panama, but we wanted our doctors to be with Dada. Also, the language barrier was a huge problem. But the strange part was that Dada had no problem in talking to the Spanish doctors and the staff, and making them laugh. So the doctors would wonder why we were so worried about Dada as He seemed perfectly at ease and was joking with them. Little did they realize how much pain He was in. He is always calm and cool about pain.'

'How long was the operation?'

'On 9 May, they did His hip surgery and it lasted for four to five hours, but it was successful. In fact, the day after the surgery, the patient cannot walk. When they came to check on Him the next day, they said that He doesn't have pain. So the physiotherapist even made him take a few steps. They said they would keep a period of one week between the two surgeries, because the surgeries are major and the time involved was very long, so they didn't want Dada to stay under anaesthesia for a long time. He was on blood thinners already. So they postponed the elbow surgery for a week later. But you know after they made Him walk, to prepare Him for the elbow surgery they had kept his elbow in traction for for six days. It is a very painful and uncomfortable experience, but still Dada didn't have a frown on His face. In fact, He would tell us every time, "Can you see who is coming from the window? Can you see He has come to protect me? He has come to take care of me." All the time, his mind was on His Master and His Gods. He had so many visions during that week; He used to be awake through full nights. He used to be singing as if He was conversing with somebody, and, though the windows were shut all the time as it was snowing outside, He would say, "Look at this window. Can't you see Him? See there is Gurudev. There is Krishna."

'He was very lucid and would hold conversations, but then, once again, go into a trance-like state. For that entire week, it was as if Dada was not really with us. Though physically, He was with us, but it was as if He was in some other realm all the time. But with the doctors and all those who would attend to Him, He would give them proper responses. As a patient the only issue is to make Him eat.'

'He doesn't eat properly, you mean?'

'Very poor eater. Like even now He has a fever from yesterday, but He refuses to eat anything. He will just drink a little soup or something. We will force him, force him, force him, but He says no.'

'But He is a poor eater even in the best of conditions, isn't that true? I mean, He hardly eats.'

'Very frugal. His eating habits are very frugal. So little that one wonders how His body copes and where He gets his energy from.'

'So, after all the surgeries, how much time did it take for him to start moving about?'

'He walked few hours after His first surgery, but then during the elbow surgery He had a stroke. The strange thing is that it was Dada who informed the doctor that all was not well. The elbow surgery went on for about seven hours. The surgery was event-free in itself, but in the recovery room He had a stroke. The doctors didn't realize it. Dada knew. He opened His eyes, and the doctor told Him, "Everything went well. You are fine." And Dada just told the doctor, "No." He just shook His head indicating all was not well. We were wondering why Dada was insisting that all was not well. So they brought Him in the room. Then, at night, when the surgeon came to examine Him, it was he who realized that Dada had had a stroke. The left side of His body had been affected.'

So the fall affected the right side of His body and the stroke affected the left side of His body. Like Meher Baba, Dada too had two mishaps— each time one part of his body had been affected.

'The left side of His body was partially paralyzed?'

'Yes. That's why He cannot walk. It wasn't the fall and the fractures, it was the stroke. His recovery from the stroke is due to His will power and His surrender to Sadhu Vaswani. The doctors have all wondered how could Dada look forward towards the physiotherapist and his gruelling sessions. Usually patients have to be coaxed into doing their therapy. And here was a ninety-year-old man who would look forward to the physiotherapists and He used to tell them, "What is the new thing you are going to teach me today?" Each step was so painful. The physiotherapists told us that many patients would tell them that they preferred to live a crippled life than go through this whole process. But Dada was anxious to begin being independent; more anxious than all of them, in fact.'

'Has the fall and the stroke changed his quality of life?'

'Dada is a very independent person. He never likes to be dependent. He can, with help, still move about with the wheelchair for a short period of time; in the room or on the veranda. He is a lover of silence. Before the fall, his door was always closed. He would be writing, reading, praying, working, meditating in silence. Only when He needed us, He would ring the bell. So, by nature, He is the most independent person. But He never complains. He has accepted His lot most gracefully and I am not saying this because of the love I or those who serve Him have for Him. Whoever interacts with Him feels the same way.'

I couldn't begin to understand what the fall and the stroke must have done to Dada. For ninety years of your life, you have been an independent and a private person. Now to be dependent and have people in your space all the time must be suffocating and claustrophobic. In all my meetings with Dada, only once did He refer to His situation. We had finished our interview and I knelt down, and He held my hand, and I told Him, 'Dada, I will see you tomorrow.' And I remember He looked at me and said, 'Yes, Ruzbeh, come whenever you want, I am going nowhere. I am a cripple now.'

And then after a few seconds, He smiled and said, 'This body is a cripple.'

'Even now, He will never ask us to do anything He can do on His own. We will keep telling Him, "Dada, can we do this?" He will say no. "I can do it. As long as I can do it on my own I don't want any help." So if you ask if there has been a change, then yes, this aspect has changed, but otherwise there is no other change. He is just the same—His writing, reading, reactions, meeting people, His spirit of adventure, all remain the same. Even now, when we went on a holiday to Goa, we saw people paragliding there. And He said, "I want to go paragliding." One look at Him and we all were certain that if He didn't have this problem, we would have had a hard time stopping Him. He is extremely young at heart; very, very, very young.'

'He is still continuing with his physiotherapy, right?'

'Every day.'

'And what is the purpose of that?'

'Because there is no circulation after a stroke, it's necessary to get proper exercise. So if he doesn't exercise even for two days, it makes a lot of difference.'

'Has He lost all sensation in His foot?'

'No, sensation is still very much present. Earlier there wasn't, but now He can move His toes because of his physiotherapy.'

'Does He have a daily routine?'

'Now it is a little different. You want His routine since the fall or His earlier usual routine?'

'Both.'

'His earlier routine was different. He used to get up between 2.00 and 2.30 a.m. Because I used to sleep in the next room, I used to see the bathroom light on. And He used to sleep on the floor in His room. All His life, He has slept on the floor, but after the attack, the doctors insisted that He begin sleeping on a special bed. He used to sleep on a plank of wood with just one thin cloth-like thing called *farasi*. Not a carpet, but we call it farasi. It's made of cotton, a little thick. It was just that and a white sheet on top.'

'All His life He slept on that?'

'All His life He has slept on that. And He would meditate till 6.00 or 6.30 a.m.'

'From 2.30 to 6.30 a.m.?'

'Yes, and then He would do a little exercise. He would proceed to do a lot of writing, reading, whatever He wanted. His door would be shut; we could never access him till around 9.30 a.m. He would always lock His door. Even when He slept, the door would be locked. He liked His privacy and when at work or meditating, He would not want to be disturbed. Afterwards, when He started falling ill, we told him we will never enter your room and please keep it shut, but don't lock the door. He obliged like He always does.'

'So around 9.30 a.m. He would come out of His room and then?'

'He would come to the *Kutiya*, where Sadhu Vaswani passed the last six years of His life. Dada would spend some time at the Kutiya and then He would meet people and have His breakfast. Around 10.30 a.m., He would go for a walk. Every day. Every single day. He never missed His walk.'

'I have heard He used to walk very briskly.'

'Very fast. We had to run sometimes behind Him. And if you don't start the walk with Him, then we would to take a rickshaw or a scooter ride to catch up with Him. He was that fast and that focused; so focused on his walk, O God!'

The look on Krishna's face made me realize how much she and all of Dada's inner circle must miss those days. There was sheer love and nostalgia for the days gone by.

'Then, after the walk usually, He would visit one or the other institution that He has begun. Sometimes He would go to the Inlaks Hospital and there He would go and meet the patients, speak to them, enquire after them, ask them if they were facing any problems and how could we help them. Or sometimes there were some devotees who were sick at home, so He would go to meet them; or if there's a wedding, He would go to see if any help was needed. He was very, very accessible. If there was a death in the family, Dada would go for the cremation; He would go for all the ceremonies and comfort the families.'

'Was this His routine till He had the fall?'

'Yes, till He had the fall. That's why our full *sangat* is used to that one-to-one-contact with Dada. He was that accessible. Anyway, thus till 1.00 p.m. in afternoon, He would be out and only then come home. But from the moment He would enter the Mission, it would take Him an hour to reach His room as there would always be people around, who wanted to speak to Him, or something or the other would come up. Then He would have His lunch and take a nap for half an hour or a maximum forty minutes. He has always taken this power nap in the afternoon.'

'That is because He would wake up at 2.30 a.m. every day.'

'Yes. Then He would wake up and prepare for His talk or do some writing work because He does a lot of writing and then, every evening, there would be a spiritual gathering, a satsang, where devotees gather for meditation or bhajans or a talk. After the satsang we would meditate at the Samadhi and then there would be meetings with different people or Mission work. I cannot begin to tell you how many meetings there used to be. And then, at night, He would have dinner and then He would just relax. And sleep late. He hardly slept and even now he hardly sleeps.'

'Now what is His routine?'

'He gets up very early. Like last night He was up at 3.15 a.m. Then He sits in meditation. He sits in silence. Then, after that, He again lies down for some time. Then He takes His walk on the terrace. He takes three rounds in the morning; it takes him twenty–twenty-five minutes.'

'When you say He takes a walk, what does that mean?'

'We hold Him from both sides, one–one hand each and He does three rounds from His room till the terrace and back. Earlier, He would take seven rounds, but because He has developed knee pain, He has been advised to reduce that walking too. Earlier, He would walk for about forty minutes. Now it is getting difficult because of the lack of strength. Even if the doctor tells Him, "You have knee pain, Dada, You take rest, avoid the walk tomorrow morning." He will obey the doctor and not walk in the morning, and then, by afternoon time, He will tell us, "Now I have taken rest, so let me try. One round let me try taking. I will feel better." So that is His spirit.'

'He must be really missing his interaction with one and all?'

'I guess so, but He says everything happens at the right time. "So now is the time for me to be more with myself and with God, and to write more."'

'He writes a lot even now?'

'A lot. Just yesterday He composed I think four or five songs. Poetry just flows out of Him, in Sindhi especially. Even in English, but more so in Sindhi. So many times we ask Him questions, He will reply in poetry.'

'Tell me, after His morning walk what does He do?'

'So the morning goes in the nitty-gritty's of the body. Then he has a frugal breakfast and after that He comes to the Kutiya and we have a little kirtan session in the morning. After that, He sits down to read and write. Then in the afternoon, a short nap and in the evening also He reads and writes, followed by the daily satsang. Even now if we have to meet people we meet them after the satsang, but not throughout the day.'

'So you all take Him down for the satsang?'

'Every day He comes down. He walks till the elevator. Then He sits on the wheelchair. For a year I think He used to walk down to the satsang hall.'

'Really?'

'Yes. He would walk till the satsang hall downstairs. But now, His knees are giving Him lot of pain.'

'He must love to travel?'

'Oh yes, anything outdoors. Now, in a few months, we will travel to the West. Because He feels He must give as much of Himself as He possibly can.'

Krishna informed me that her grandparents and parents were devotees of Sadhu Vaswani. After partition, when Sadhu Vaswani moved to Mumbai first for a few months and then settled down in Pune, her family moved in with Sadhu Vaswani. Krishna's pregnant mother had a fall and was justifiably concerned about the well-being of her child and she approached Sadhu Vaswani who assured the anxious mother that all was well with the child. This reassurance made Krishna's mother frequently attend the daily satsang.

'So I guess I have been attending satsang and coming to the Mission since I was in my mother's womb. And Dada always says that the child, even if in the womb, absorbs all energies it is surrounded with. Thus, I was very privileged.' I was about to speak further when Krishna shot out of her chair like a rocket and ran.

I sighed. Had I said something which I shouldn't have? I shut my eyes. Did a mental rewind. Does the Mission have a major issue with making documentary films? I mean, why would Krishna leap out of her chair like that? I knew I could drive people up the wall, but even I was getting impressed with my growing prowess of making people fly out of their chairs and run for their lives. I looked at Naresh and Anita.

'If I said something I shouldn't have, I am sorry. If I said something I don't remember, my apologies . . .'

'Oh, nothing like that. Dada rang the bell and thus Krishna Didi went to see if all was well.'

'What bell?'

'The bell.'

'What bell . . .?'

Fortunately for both Naresh and me, Krishna walked in.

'Sorry, Dada wanted something. So will you write the book and make the documentary film?'

I nodded. I made a mental note: Get your blasted ears examined.

Half an hour later, I was taken into another room. Dada entered. He had just turned ninety seven-years old a few weeks ago. His skin did not have a wrinkle. His face radiated a glow. He did not look like a man in his nineties. I made another note to myself: Cut down on the smoking, drinking and swearing. I bent to touch Dada's feet and I nearly had an out-of-body experience as Dada tried to touch my feet.

I looked at Dada and then He smiled. His smile reached His eyes and made them sparkle. I remembered my maternal grandmother who had passed away a few years ago, in her nineties. She had the same mischievous smile.

Dada and I spoke for ten minutes. I took His blessings and, once again, He bent to touch my feet. I made another note: Devise a new technique of touching Dada's feet. Don't let Him bend. Be quick on the draw.

Dada gave me prasad—a bag of chips, which I was certain, Meher, my eight-year-old daughter would enjoy.

I took Dada's leave. Again I paid a visit to Sadhu Vaswani's Samadhi. I remembered to wear my shoes this time. I gave Meher the blessed chips once I returned home.

'Oh, nice! Where did you get them from, dad?' she enquired.

'Dada blessed them and gave them for you.'

'I think I am going to like Dada Vaswani.'

'I am sure.'

'How did the meeting go?'

'He keeps quoting His Master. I wonder how I am going to write a book if Dada keeps saying, "It is all my Master's grace . . . Sadhu Vaswani will decide . . . Sadhu Vaswani knows best" . . . I mean, how am I going to fill three hundred pages . . .'

'You should have told Dada this.'

'I did. I told Dada, "Dada, I truly love Your love and devotion towards Your Master. I hope I feel the same for Baba Sai, but I can't write a book if You leave everything squarely at the feet of Your Master."'

'Good, good.'

'I know, I thought so too . . .'

'No dad, these chips are good.'

I made another note: First talk and then offer an eight-year-old a bag of blessed chips.

~

The next day I returned in the morning to the Mission. Paid my respects to Sadhu Vaswani at the Samadhi. It was around eleven. I was taken to a room in the Kutiya. It was here that Sadhu Vaswani had spent the last six years of His life, virtually on bed. He had fallen down; broken His hip bone. He had refused to get a surgery done. He wanted to go through the pain. For six years, He had barely slept as the pain and his twitching muscles would wake Him up every few minutes. He had passed away in this room. As you entered, there was a beautiful photograph of Sadhu Vaswani hung on the wall. Then, under the photograph, there is the bed on which He had reposed. A lamp burnt, which was kindled by Dada Vaswani at the moment, after His Guru, Sadhu Vaswani, had left His physical body. A painting of Sadhu Vaswani's adopted daughter, Shanti, who passed away four years after Sadhu Vaswani took Samadhi was there too. After He left His body, she had a heart attack. She had never really recovered from His passing.

When I asked Krishna, she told me,

'Shanti was Sadhu Vaswani's adopted daughter. While she was still very young, Shanti had come down with typhoid. It was felt that she would probably succumb to the disease. At that time, Sadhu Vaswani quietly went to the terrace of her house and had begun to pray for her. When He returned to her bedside and stood beside her, she suddenly opened her eyes. From her lips came the words, "I had reached the kingdom of Sri Krishna! Why did You call me back? From now on, I will be with You, under Your care." From then on, this Guru–disciple relationship only grew from strength to strength.

'Shanti was like a mother to the entire household, especially to Dada Jashan, the young Dada Vaswani. He would be so engrossed in service to Sadhu Vaswani that He would pay no attention to His personal needs. His sleep, food and clothes was relegated to the side. It was Shanti who would try to attend to His needs and cater to the necessities. Dada's heart was filled with a deep respect and gratitude for Her unconditional efforts, unending kindness and caring. Before Sadhu Vaswani passed away, He had told Dada, "Shanti is so closely and intricately linked with me that I fear she may not be able to bear the agony of my passing. If anything should happen to me, you please take good care of her."

'Dada was very particular about his routine of going for a brisk walk. One day, He saw that Shanti was quite unwell and decided to forego His walk. Shanti insisted that He should not deprive himself of his daily exercise. Being uneasy about her condition, Dada decided not to go far and instead walked in the campus of the Mission in order to be easily accessible.

'Dada's instincts were correct. Barely had fifteen minutes elapsed before a man came running towards Dada, saying that Shanti had collapsed and he could not feel her pulse. Dada ran to her and the doctor was already there, confirming that Shanti's pulse had stopped. Looking at Shanti, Dada said, "How could you just leave and go away without saying good-bye?" At once, Shanti opened her eyes. While bidding farewell, she uttered the word, 'Jashan (pain)! Jashan, Jashan!' With her head lovingly ensconced in Dada's lap, she breathed her last. Sadhu Vaswani had passed away in 1966 and Shanti in 1970. Shanti's death was a beautiful one, with her head resting on Dada's lap.'

There were a few people sitting in the blessed Kutiya. It's a very serene room. Outside, on the veranda, a cool breeze blows. There are beautiful trees all around us. On the opposite side is the St Mira School, which is run by the Mission itself.

Krishna, along with Piya, both who are always by Dada's side, stood while Dada prayed to His Guru.

Piya, like Krishna, had been blessed by Sadhu Vaswani and Dada Vaswani's presence since her childhood. Unlike Krishna, who was virtually brought up by Sadhu and Dada Vaswani, Piya lives with her family in a house opposite the Mission.

Then the wheel chair was turned around and Dada, with folded arms, greeted those present. After a while, He looked at me and He smiled. His smile was like a child's, no pretence, with true happiness and glee. There is no external paraphernalia around Dada to distract him. He does not like pomp and glamour, and through our interviews His down-to-earth nature always shone through. Krishna once told me that during an interview which required a photo shoot, there was a spot on Dada's shawl. When she went to get another one, Dada told her there was no need. He just turned the shawl inside out and went for the interview. He saw me and smiled, and I knelt and held His hand when He tried to touch my feet. We looked at each other.

'I am happy to see you Ruzbeh. I have begun to go through *The Fakir*. The title is so beautiful, it reminds me of Sadhu Vaswani.'

I nodded. I kissed His hand and took my leave.

2

After a few days we met again at the Kutiya. I could make out Dada was a bit shy. There were three cameras placed around him. Lots of fancy lighting and a backdrop. Both He and I were perplexed. Krishna and Piya helped Dada onto a chair. We sat down and He looked at me.

'I thought it would be a bit more informal,' He whispered.

'Dada, look at me. I am dressed in torn jeans and I am unshaven. That is how informal I thought it was going to be.'

'For a while I felt we had entered a Hollywood set.' Then we both chuckled.

'Tomorrow, I will make sure all this disappears. Just cameras and basic lighting.'

'Yes. That would be good. I got scared coming in.' Again He chuckled and I grinned. His smile, laughter and chuckles are infectious.

Piya made sure the mic was placed properly and not a crease was visible on Dada's shawl. She looked at me. Realizing that there was nothing much she could do to make me look more human, she went and stood behind the camera. She is very particular about how Dada looks, the lighting on Dada, the sound, the surrounding. Everything should be perfect when Dada is concerned. For both her and Krishna, it feels as though nothing else exists for them but Dada. Krishna sat on the floor. Naresh and Anita were present too. I winked at Naresh. He quickly avoided my eyes, but had a grin on his face. The doors were shut. And the fans were off. It felt like a furnace inside, and I looked at Dada and smiled. I sent a quick prayer to Baba Sai and Sadhu Vaswani to begin work on the book and film. Jai Baba.

'Dada, there was a time when You read one book a day. Are you still a voracious reader?'

'Nowadays, I hardly find time to read books. And my beloved Gurudev Sadhu Vaswani taught me that it is better to meditate on the Name Divine than to read books. Once, I happened to be in jail with Gurudev. Those were the days of India's freedom struggle. Gurudev was sentenced to be in prison for fourteen days, for leading a Satyagraha. Sister Shanti, Gurudev's spiritual daughter, came to visit us and to enquire whether there was anything in particular that we needed from home. I requested her to get me a trunk full of books. The very next day, Shanti brought me a whole load of books. Seeing this, the jailer was surprised. He said to me, somewhat sarcastically, "How long is your sentence—fourteen days or fourteen years? Why have you called for so many books? Will you actually manage to read all of them?"

'As it happened, Gurudev Sadhu Vaswani's imprisonment caused an uproar across the whole town (Karachi). People began to agitate; they asked for a no-confidence motion to be passed against the cabinet. Within four days, we were released and my trunk full of books was left in the prison. Gurudev said to me, "You are of the Eternal; the book of the heart sufficeth." On an earlier occasion, Gurudev had said to me, "You are fond of books. When will you start reading the book of all books, the only book that counts—the Book of your Heart?" After all, what do we get from reading books? We read a book, we ponder its contents, we hold discussions and, at the end of it all, what do we achieve? Therefore, let me repeat Gurudev's words: "Read the Book of all books, the Book of the Heart." Reading books may make a man a scholar, but it does not always give him wisdom or true knowledge. The Book of the Heart is with everyone. You do not need to go to a library; it is there with you and within you. The Book of the Heart is the Book of the Self.'

'All that is fine Dada, but have You discontinued reading altogether or do you still read?'

Dada chuckled. He has the most divine smile. Childlike and full of mischief.

'Where is the time? Now I feel happy when I get a new book. I do not read it. I just turn over the pages and if a line strikes me, I stop there and move no further. I try to dive deep into the meaning of that line.'

'Did You and do You have any preference for any particular kind of books?'

'No, therefore I read a variety of books. I used to pick up a book here, a book there. I became a Jack of all trades and master of none.'

'But You used to read one book a day. That must have made you a very busy Jack.'

'That was for a year, when I was in charge of the college library.'

'That is 365 books in a year. You read fiction or was it all heavy duty spirituality stuff?'

'You know, I wanted to write a novel.' He grinned with a twinkle in His eyes. 'Then one night I had a dream. A very wise soul asked me why would I want to waste my time writing a novel, when I could use that time serving those in need. So I went to sleep an aspiring novelist and woke up as aspiring seeker of the Lord.'

Another mental note: Thank my Baba Sai for not giving me such fine dreams.

'Was there any particular book which really made a profound impact on you?'

'*The Prophet* by Khalil Gibran.'

'Why?'

'In all honesty, even I have been wondering all these years why the book made such an impact on me. I don't know, but I read his book over and over again.'

'When was the last time you re-read it?'

'Several years ago. But the last time I saw it was a few weeks ago when I received a copy of its latest edition. And I recalled what Gibran himself had said several years ago. He had given a loan to someone and he wanted the money back. He asked for it repeatedly but got no response. He decided to appeal to a court of law. He was then told clearly by one and all that how could a man who wrote *The Prophet* sue for money? This taught me a lesson. I once heard somebody say, "My father did not tell me how to live. He lived and let me watch him do it." When Benjamin Franklin decided to interest the people of Philadelphia in street lighting, he hung a beautiful lantern at the end of a long bracket attached to the front of his house. He kept the brass brightly polished and carefully lit the wick every evening. Anyone walking on this dark street could see this light from a long way off and come under its warm glow. It was not long before Franklin's neighbours also began placing lamps outside their doors. Soon the entire city followed his example with enthusiasm.'

If Benjamin had hung a beautiful lantern in one of our cities, he would have found it missing the very next day, and being sold in the black market.

'Thus, if books have taught me anything, Ruzbeh, it is that one needs to live life in the most humble and dignified manner and serve one's Masters by serving all creation.'

'You mean don't read The Bhagavadgita; live it?'

'Yes. The day people begin to live their holy and sacred scriptures, the world will witness the Golden Age. The Bhagavadgita is my companion. It is not the kind of a book that you read once and put it down. It takes time, perhaps a lifetime to understand it. It is not as simple as it appears to be. You have to dive into the depths of every sloka. So I used to select a few slokas and concentrate on them. My beloved Master's emphasis was not on reciting the Gita. "The Gita," He said again and again, "is to be lived, is to be assimilated in one's life." My prayer to God has been that I may bear witness to the Gita in daily action—daily yagna to the *Yagneshwar*, the Eternal.

'*Dharmakshetre Kurukshetre Samaveta Yuyutsavaha* . . . thus, Ruzbeh, the very first word of the Gita is the word 'dharma'. The opening word of this magnificent scripture is dharma—the great word of ancient India. Just as beauty was dear to Greece and power was dear to Rome, dharma was close to the soul of India. Our ancient rishis exhorted us to build our life in dharma. Dharma is derived from *dhru* which means "hold". Dharma is the power, the force, the jivan shakti which holds life. Kshetra means "field". Let us, therefore, ask ourselves: "What am I sowing in the field of life—dharma or adharma?" If you are one of the blessed souls who are sowing the seeds of dharma, your life becomes a song, a Gita of the Lord!'

'What have You learnt from The Gita, Dada?'

'Whatever I have learnt is from the Gita and my beloved Master who was a living Gita. The teaching is the same. The Gita, the Bible, the Quran, the Zen Avesta and other scriptures have the same teachings. What we lack is not the teaching but bearing witness to it in deeds of daily living. The scriptures are not a noun, they are a verb. Do it!

'One of the things that comes to mind and which is so applicable to our times is the dictum, "The man who cooks food for himself alone is no better than a thief." In the earlier days, it was a practice among all the people to share their food with others; kings and aristocrats performed *anna daana* as a matter of daily habit, the ordinary householders shared their food with guests. They also offered food to ascetics and beggars who came to their doorstep seeking alms; even beggars shared their food with birds and animals. But today, people store even a tiny roll of left-over dough in the fridge and save it for the next meal. Whatever food remains after the meal, is 'locked' and 'stored' in airtight containers and put away in the fridge. The Gita tells us to share our food with others; the Gita also warns us that stale, left-over, reheated, old food is *tamasic*.'

Dada paused. Very often he would pause for long. Sometimes one could be mistaken into thinking that He has forgotten the flow of conversation, but Dada would then continue from where He had left off. Dada never forgets. Never a name, person, conversation, nothing. He really is something else.

'On both counts, Ruzbeh, we would do well to give away any food that we may have in excess. But what do we see nowadays? There are no guests, no ascetics, no alms-seekers whom we are obliged to feed; all the food which otherwise would have been given away to the hungry, or to birds and stray dogs and cows, is stored in the fridge instead. I must admit that I am often saddened when I see food being taken out of the fridge—for my heart pleads for those starving and hungry ones who could have gratefully eaten the excess food preserved in the refrigerator. Gurudev Sadhu Vaswani shared his food with the underprivileged every day. Before he sat down for lunch, he would take a portion of his meal and personally go out and give it to a beggar on the road. Is this not the very essence of healthy living—sharing whatever we have with those who need it more? For we must never ever forget that everything we possess, all that we have and hold, is left with us in the capacity of a trustee. Sharing what we have with others brings joy and sublimates the mind. It fills man with the joy of expansion; it purifies him and detaches him from the vice-like grip of absolute ownership. Offered in the spirit of yagna or sacrifice, even eating becomes a sacrament—provided we offer our daily food to God and share it with others. "He who eats what is left from the sacrifice, is released from all sins; but the impious one, who cooks food for himself alone, he verily eats sin!"'

I wanted to tell Dada that Lord Krishna did not have to deal with extreme inflation and during those days householders were not so caught up in trying to survive. In this day and age, storing leftovers for the next day has become akin to survival. But I agree. We have become a I-me-myself society. Anyway, enough of my rambling.

'Is it true that Lord Krishna said that those who remember Him at the time of passing away shall go forth to Him? How does that happen? I mean, one could have spent a lifetime of debauchery and then, lo and behold, conveniently remember Lord Krishna and go to Him.'

'One needs to remember that in order to remember the Lord or Master, when one leaves the body, one has to make a practise of remembering Him, through one's life. Let me tell you another story. There was a Sri Krishna disciple who remembered Him all the time, and thus saw and heard only the name of Sri Krishna wherever he went. Once he was travelling through a green forest, which was an abode for thousands of birds. The birds twittered in the trees and he exclaimed, "The birds are praising thee, O Lord. What a feeling! Krishna! Krishna!" A trader, who owned a big grocery shop, happened to meet him. "Swamiji, what is it that excites you so much?" he asked and the disciple said, "Didn't you listen to those birds? They are singing, Krishna, Krishna . . ." The grocer was surprised, but being witty by temperament, he replied, "I can hear only, 'Salt, pepper, chillies, mustard . . .' A local priest specializing in performing birth and death rituals, who also happened to be there, said, "Both of you are wrong, the bird is saying, 'Ladoo, Peda, Jelabi . . . '" Why did each one hear something different? That is because if a man is intoxicated by the Name Divine, he will hear only of his Divine, be it Rama, Sita, Krishna, Zarathustra, Christ, Allah. Whatever fascinates and engages the mind, echoes and vibrates in the mind. The same thoughts repeat in circles. Thus, the sacred scripture tells us to cultivate the soul. Follow the spiritual path. Seek out a Guru and achieve the goal! It is up to man to chart the course of his own spiritual progress. Man is known by the company he keeps. Man certainly has a choice here. The company of the good and virtuous ones keeps him healthy and positive. Bad company makes him miserable and loathsome. Hence, we must choose the company of those who will lead us towards a life which is positive and beautiful. We must seek the company of saints and sages. When we absorb the holy and positive vibrations of their environment, our hearts and souls are energized, our thoughts and aspirations are uplifted and purified. We are well aware that this gross physical body that we wear needs nourishment. Unless we eat healthy, nutritious food at timely intervals, we know we cannot live an active, healthy life. Proxy eating cannot give your body the nutrients it needs. You have to involve the 'self'. In other words, I cannot eat for you when you are hungry! You have to eat your food yourself. The same is true of spiritual sustenance. I cannot cultivate anybody else's soul! You have to work for your own spiritual growth. You may seek out a Guru for guidance and sure enough he will show you the path, but you have to move forward on your own steam. Such an association nourishes and sustains our spiritual evolution and makes it possible for one to be absorbed in the name of one's God, Goddess, Guru. And remember, this philosophy has been espoused by all the Great Ones and all religions. Read the Gita, the Avesta, the Bible, the Koran—they all say the same thing, in different ways and languages. But the essence is the same.

'Thus the chanting of the Name and focus on the Name makes an individual one with the Master? But getting back to Lord Krishna, there are a lot of personalities in the same person.

'Yes, therefore, so many people believe that Krishna is not one Krishna. Some say he appeared 5000 years ago, some say about 6000 years ago, so during all the centuries there have been accretions to his identity. It is natural. We find similar stories in the lives of most of the great ones. But His words are still relevant today.'

'But Lord Krishna seemed to have a very large heart and was full of love as only that would explain how He could manage 16,000 wives. What is that story? I mean, it can't be possible, sensible and healthy to have 16,000 wives?'

'Sixteen thousand wives, that is just a story.'

For Lord Krishna's sake I hope and pray it is just a story.

'So, Dada, what is the symbolism of that story?'

'In those days, there was a man called Narakasura, he had abducted 16,000 girls and kept them prisoners. So they called on to Sri Krishna and beseeched Him to come. And when He did, they told Him, "You have come. Now You must save us, You must liberate us, You must come and set us free." So Lord Krishna goes and fights Narakasura and defeats him, and all the 16,000 girls now tell Him that society is not going to take them back, because once they have lived under the roof of Narakasura, nobody will accept them. So Sri Krishna does what is expected of him. He marries them, in order to give them the security and respect in society . . .'

'Poor Krishna. But, Dada, when the common man hears all this, there is a different perception and they say if the Lord was okay with so many women, why not us?'

'Yes, true. Thus, the common man must be told the entire story. Superficial reading, surface reading will not take us far. The story must be read at a much higher level. And our sages and scholars have explained the story in higher terms—some say that the 16,000 princesses were rishis, siddhas, sages, who had been granted the boon of participating in the Sri Krishna avatar; some say that they were *gopis* who lived, loved and died for Krishna, but never really married Him; some say that the Lord was demonstrating symbolically, the duties of a true householder. Some say that the 16,000 princesses symbolize ragas, musical strains that were mastered by Krishna's flute and so on. The story goes that once, Maharishi Narada came to examine how

Krishna was treating His wives. He visited each of the households and witnessed perfect harmony and absolute domestic bliss. Krishna was taking care of His children, helping His wife with the household chores and so on . . . Narada accepted that in each home he saw a Divine, Supreme Being who was a perfect monogamist. This story is also from the *Bhagavata Purana*. Prophets work and live and speak at a much higher level than the ordinary man, and therefore it is very difficult for a common man to understand them. That is why Meher Baba stopped speaking.'

'Ahhhh, yes, Avatar Meher Baba, but before coming to Meher Baba I want to ask another question about Krishna. In the war, He does not shy from using whatever means to achieve His objectives. To some people it could seem like manipulation or deceit. When a common man does something like this, he is considered to have a very low moral compass.'

'Let me tell you one thing, when young people come and tell me, Krishna went about with gopis, with girls, why do you prevent us from doing so? I tell them, first become Krishna and then you do what He did. Krishna can do it but you are not Krishna.'

'But that is the whole problem, this is exactly what I am trying to tell you that the Gita has gone to millions of people, they are not going to have that kind of perception or wisdom that You have. Is there something else to these stories of Krishna or is this what happened?

'But as I said, we have to be Krishna before we can understand Him. That is why it is said, it is best to have *Sri Rama* as your role model, live like Him, in truth and courage and virtue; but have *Sri* Krishna as your teacher; follow *His* teachings. We get taken in by stories of Krishna and we suit them to our own ends; let me manipulate, let me lie, let me do this and that . . . But as I said, we have to be Krishna, before we set out to imitate Him. But the Gita was preached to mortals like us; we can and must follow its teachings to the extent we can.'

'Apart from Your Guru, Sadhu Vaswani, have You seen normal people bring forth God or Krishna alive in their lives.'

'Oh yes, and many times they are the most humble of all souls—the salt of the earth. Let me tell you a childhood story. When I was a student of class six, I was the guest of a close family friend who had a huge house with several rooms in it. The house was built on a hilltop. The head of the family was called *Kaka*. His son came to receive me at the station and took me to their sprawling home. I was taken to Kaka's room. In spite of the drawn curtains, which made his room appear dark, Kaka's glowing countenance arrested me. Though he appeared arrogant, every member in his family respected him. In the earlier days, reverence for elders was ingrained in every child. Today, this reverence is regretfully lacking. Sadhu Vaswani would often say, "The root of education is reverence and the fruit of education is service."

'After respectfully greeting him, I stood up to leave. My stay there was comfortable; I was pampered by servants who were at our beck and call. The entire day I would be out exploring different parts of the city and would return exhausted. Pleasantly tired, I would quickly slip into deep sleep like a baby.

'A painful spasm in my stomach woke me up one night at 2.30 a.m. I had probably over eaten the previous night. I had overindulged and eaten more kulfi–falooda (a delicacy made of milk and sugar) than I should have. The pain was intense and did not allow me to go back to sleep. I ventured outside in search of some medicine to relieve the pain. In the darkness that enveloped me, I saw a faint flicker of a lantern. As I drew close to it, I could hear the sound of someone praying and sobbing. "Have mercy on me, O Lord! You are the Merciful One!" was the often repeated prayer. I drew closer and found that it was Kaka who was repeating the prayer, accompanied by sobs.

'Kaka's face shone with an unearthly light. The strange gleam in his eyes was akin to a radium clock glowing in the dark. Entranced, I stood there, my stomach ache totally forgotten. Slowly, the scattered rays of the sun seeped into the room and Kaka gradually slipped into sleep, I quietly left the room.

'The next day I was anxious to meet him. Entering his room, I said, "Kaka, last night I was fortunate to spend some time in your room." On hearing this he became furious with me. His rude behaviour did not deter me. Knowingly, I said, "O Revered One, you cannot hide your true self from me."

'On hearing this, Kaka's demeanour changed. Beckoning me to come closer, he started chatting with me. His sweet and appealing voice was like the melody of the flute. I had witnessed his true self and grew immensely fond of him. Though the time of my departure had approached, I just did not feel like leaving him. But I received a letter from my mother saying, "Son Jashan, your school has reopened. It is time to return home soon."

'With a heavy heart, I went to bid farewell to Kaka. I sat by his feet and unbidden tears flowed from my eyes. I requested him to give me a parting message. Looking squarely, yet compassionately, into my eyes, he said, "My child, whatever you do, do it well! Don't attempt to do many things at the same time. Whatever you do, do it to the best of your ability. Do it as an offering to the Lord. Are you a housewife, cooking food? Then cook food with the thought that Sri Krishna Himself will come and partake of it. If you are sewing, do it as if what you are sewing may be worn by the Lord Himself. Offer all your actions to the Lord. Sri Krishna *arpanam*. Such actions will not bind you to this cycle of birth and death."'

'And . . .'

'And means?'

'Any more such stories?'

'You want to hear more.'

'I am trying to write a book, Dada, and the usual process of writing a book about a Master is that the Master talks and I write . . .'

'I am not a Master. I am my Master's disciple.'

'You are Your Master's disciple but You are the Master of many disciples.'

'I don't have any disciples. Only friends.'

'Ya right. And . . .'

So Dada blushed and smiled, and continued.

'Once, I heard the melodious sound of a flute. My steps took me in that direction where I saw a man, oblivious of his surroundings, was playing the flute. I stood still drinking in the sweet melody. When he opened his eyes, he looked at me and greeted me warmly, and I asked him how he had learnt to play the flute so beautifully. He told me that this was a gift bestowed on him and added, "I am incapable of playing the flute at my will. I can only do it when the spirit within me stirs."

'He told me that one day when he was in deep prayer and silence, he heard a voice within him. The voice said, "Dear one, from now on you will be blessed with the gift of playing the flute."'

Saying this Dada lapsed into silence. I sighed. I wish I had a voice tell me such cool things. 'Dear Ruzbeh, henceforth you will write sensibly.' Or 'dear Ruzbeh, henceforth you will become mature.' All I hear is 'Dear one, light up another cigarette.' Hmm.

'So the man told me that "Now I place the flute on my lips and rapturous tunes cascade from it." I was truly humbled being with this simple man. He took me to his hut where we sat and spoke. I asked him if I would ever be able to see the beautiful face of The One who played the flute through him and he said, "Yes, my child, you too can surely see Him if you build your life on this one teaching. Live in this world; enjoy it thoroughly. You do not have to renounce the world and become an ascetic. But do not become a slave to the world. You can drink the water from the river, you can even bathe and swim in the water, but don't ever drown in the water." The man was living the Gita. This simple, humble man, for whom most would not even spare a second glance, was living the Gita.'

There was a long silence. We both seemed lost in our own thoughts. After a while, a divine question popped into my head.

'And?'

'And what?'

'Any more such experiences?'

Dada sighed. There was silence once again.

'I was a professor in college when this incident took place. The college had closed for the Diwali vacation. I longed to spend my holidays in a quiet place in peace and solitude. I loved villages, so I went to a small village named Abrahim Haider which was situated near the ocean. The refreshing evening breeze and the dancing waves provided a perfect ambience. But, reaching there, I experienced a strange pulsating silence. The next day as I was taking a stroll at the seashore, I felt a few drops of rain fall on my face. Soon, it started raining and I ran to seek shelter.

'At a distance, I saw a small hut. This village has many Muslim residents and I was concerned if the hut belonged to a Muslim as I did not know how he would receive me and I did not want to upset anybody.

'I knocked on the door. A sweet voice called out, "Come in, this hut is open to all." The door creaked open and with tentative steps I entered the hut. A Muslim *darvesh* was seated inside. His eyes shone like candles. He looked about forty two years old and he had a well-shaped beard. His welcoming smile beckoned me to Him. Looking squarely at me, He said, "This hut does not belong to me." I naturally thought that probably He too, like me, had come here to seek shelter from the rain.

'More confident now, I asked, "Whom does this hut belong to?" He responded, "This hut belongs to Sri Krishna." I looked at him in wonder. How could this person, who was a Muslim, be talking of Sri Krishna? Seeing my bewilderment, He smiled and said, "I was a fisherman who used to haul in fish for a living. One day, I saw a wondrous being in my hut. It was Sri Krishna with a flute on his lips! I was blessed to see this wondrous sight for several days continuously. Totally absorbed in His wonder, I forgot all about going to fish for my livelihood. I was completely captivated by the glory of Sri Krishna. He became an integral part of my life. Suddenly His figure disappeared before my eyes. I was disconsolate with grief. I came back to the temporal world and set out to search for some work to maintain myself. I decided to resume fishing, so I joined my friends. However, whenever I saw a fish getting caught, I could not bear its suffering. I immediately would rescue it and put it back in the waters. Sri Krishna had touched my heart. I could no longer see anyone in suffering and pain. I then resorted to carpentry to earn a livelihood." I was touched by the darvesh's love for Lord Krishna. It was during this vacation that I learnt carpentry from him. My mother had told me that you have the aspiration to dedicate your life, so if you want to live alone you must learn everything—cooking, stitching, carpentry, ironing.

'In this darvesh, I behold a blend of Peter and Jesus—Peter the fisherman and Jesus the carpenter. When the day to bid farewell arrived, I reluctantly took leave of him. I did not want to return home without a special teaching from him. I, therefore, asked him for a message. "Never be a believer," he said to me emphatically. I was shocked. Seeing my stunned expression, he continued with a smile, "Never be a believer in yourself. Believe only in the grace of God. If you rely only on yourself, you may slip easily. Depend only on God!"

'The second teaching he passed on to me was "Never be overconfident, for temptations can be very powerful. The day you pride yourself on your spiritual progress will probably be the day when your fall can be the greatest."

'The third teaching which he gave me was "Never be judgemental. How can I judge another when I have a basket of faults and failings on my back? The path that leads to the Ultimate is a slippery path. Therefore, tread it carefully." He was truly a blessed soul.'

More silence.

'How was your experience of meeting Meher Baba?

'My experience was wonderful. I felt I was floating in the ocean of love.' He had a faraway look in his eyes. As though He was once again in the presence of Meher Baba.

'What was Your age at that time?'

'I met Him in the forties, but all one could do was simply gaze and gaze and gaze at Him. And you actually felt a stream of love flowing out of Him, pulling us to Him.'

'He must have been in silence at that time?'

'Yes. He rarely came to Poona, but I think whenever He came he used to send me a word that He has come to Poona.'

'How many times did You meet him?'

'Just a few times. Because I was in Poona and He came to Poona very rarely. I never went to Nagar.'

'And was He very strict?'

'In principles, yes; but not in His ordinary behaviour. In principles, He was very strict. With His *mandali*, He was very strict.' Dada, like a child, rolled His eyes.

'Yes, He was like a dictator.'

'He knew human nature. He realized that a human being, if left alone, would defile the very best. Therefore, He pulled them up.'

'What about Mehera Maa? Did you meet Mehera Maa?'

'I did not have occasion to meet Her. When I was with Him, I loved to be with Him for as long as I could.'

'How was Meher Baba's relationship with Sadhu Vaswani?'

'Good. Meher Baba came on one occasion, He gave His darshan in this building.'

'Dada, apart from Ramana Maharshi and Rama Krishna Paramhansa, who were not from this side of the country, one had Meher Baba, Babajan, Sadhu Vaswani, Tajuddin Baba, Narayan Maharaj, Upasini Maharaj, Sai Baba of Shirdi—so many Masters, who were present in the body. There was a collective movement of spirituality especially in Maharashtra.'

'Yes, it was a period of renaissance of spirituality.'

'But there was no mass spiritual evolution or revolution . . . Why?'

'Everybody worked individually. It wasn't a collective movement. Someone like you should have brought them together and Maharashtra would have been the spiritual capital of India.'

Yeah, right.

'You met the revered Ramana Maharshi too?'

'Yes.' Dada's eyes lit up again.

'In which year did you meet Him?'

'1939.'

'You had gone with Sadhu Vaswani?'

'Yes.'

'And what was the teaching of the Maharshi?'

'Sri Ramana Maharshi said that nothing is good or evil. Everything depends on one's mind. Difficulties too are created by the mind. The trained mind is always at peace. It is the mercy of God that we have Gurus and Scriptures to guide us, and indicate to us the way to be truly happy. A question was asked of Him, that what should man do so that he is always walking towards the Lord? And the Maharshi said, "Immediately start to think of the Lord." The more you think of God, the more you will grow in a spirit of detachment. Do not wait for all desires to disappear to be able to live a life of bhakti. He was a man of attainment. The civil surgeon, who operated upon the Maharshi, told me that the Maharshi had a boil on his arm, which was malignant and had to be operated upon. The very first thing that the Maharshi said to him was, "Don't give me an anaesthetic." And the surgeon said to him that such a thing would kill anybody. Ramana Maharshi said, "Don't worry." He had reached that level. He had gone beyond body consciousness.

'Ramana Maharshi is venerated by the devout as "the great sage of Arunachala". A mystic philosopher, He was an inspired devotee of the Lord. He was a simple, saintly soul. He spoke very little, but His profound silence communicated great truths and insights to those who could attune themselves to his vibrations. "The highest form of grace is silence," He taught us. "It is also the highest form of *upadesh*."

'Animals would pass by Him, but they never disturbed Him or harmed Him. He spoke to birds and animals in their language. He was one with nature—one with Mother Earth. All this while, He continued to live in the natural caves on the Arunachala hills, but His devotees established an ashrama, where people would come to have His darshan and seek His blessings. The cow Lakshmi visited the prayer hall every day and came to touch His feet. He too returned her call daily and went to the cowshed to bless her. Ramana Maharshi gave initiation by a look or by silence. His look was piercing and concentrated. It penetrated into the very depths of one's being. This was especially for those who turned to the Maharshi for guidance, but could not make it physically to Tiruvannamalai. One day, Ramana Maharshi was sitting in His hall, surrounded by His devotees. It was time for lunch. Many of the devotees were feeling hungry. They moved to the dining hall. In those days, the Maharshi was suffering from rheumatism in the knees. This caused swelling of the knees and also gave Him great pain. He had to rub His knees before he could get up. He got up, he leaned on his stick and moved towards the dining hall. On the way, He saw a poor villager, a village milkman. The Maharshi recognizes him as a friend from a long time ago and said to him, "Is it you my friend?" "Yes, Maharshi," said the poor villager.

He was wrapped in a cotton shawl. There was a pot of clay hanging from a strap on his shoulder. And the Maharshi said to him, "Have you brought the porridge that I loved to eat in those olden days?" "Yes, Maharshi, I have brought the porridge." And He began to eat the porridge, much to the delight of the village milkman. The milkman's face beamed with joy. His happiness knew no bounds. In the meantime, so many devotees were waiting in the dining hall, many of whom were hungry. One of them came out and, "Swami, this is so unfair. For the sake of a villager, You make us wait. Until You come to the dining hall, until You are served first, we will not get our food. And you are here waiting, talking to a poor villager." The Maharshi became indignant and said, "Why do you think I am here? Am I here only for your sake? Where were you when I spent years on the hills? It was these poor villagers who took care of me, who fed me with their porridge; how can I forget them? I belong to them as much as to anyone of you." He made no distinction between the poor and the rich.

'His compassion reached all. His compassion reached the lowliest of the low. There is an incident in his remarkable life. There was once a poor old beggar with a long beard. He came and took his residence in an old, dilapidated, broken temple very close to the ashram. During the day he would go to the town and beg. He would eat the food that he got by begging. And he was seen to spend hours together gazing and gazing and gazing at the beauteous face of the Beloved Master. One night, a devotee of Ramana Maharshi found him standing in the temple, gazing at Arunachala. And this devotee asked him, "Why are you here at this late hour of the night? What are you doing here?" This poor old beggar says to the devotee, "I sleep here in this temple." "You sleep here in this temple! How could that be so? Do you actually live here in this dilapidated temple, which is in the midst of a thick jungle? Are you not afraid?" And this poor, old beggar said, "How can I be afraid? The Maharshi's mercy reaches me; His mercy takes care of me. All night I feel I am surrounded by a blue radiance. And with the Maharshi's light and love on me how can I be afraid?" The words of this poor, old beggar made the devotee feel humble and he thought to himself, "The Maharshi's light and love reach this poor old beggar, they reach the lowliest of the low. But the Light is denied to so many of us; so many of us, who regard ourselves as the chosen disciples of the Master, the light of Maharshi is denied to us!" Dada lapsed into silence once more.

The Light can only reach the one whose heart is open, pure and without the filth of give and take, I guess. That is why so many of us are denied the Light of the Master.

'Ramana Maharshi's mercy, His compassion was not restricted to human beings only. It moved out to birds and animals. One day, the Maharshi was sitting in the hall when someone brought a wounded dove to him. He looked at the bird with compassion; he placed the wounded dove on the palm of his hand. He looked lovingly at the bird, then turned to his devotees to ask, "Is there anyone ready to take care of this wounded bird until it recovers and flies away?" The Maharshi's question received no answer. Sometime earlier, the Maharani of Baroda had presented to the ashrama a rare white peacock and almost everyone there had been eager to take care of this precious bird. But on that day, no one came forward to take care of this wounded dove. Then Ramana Maharshi turns around, looks into the faces of his devotees; He gazes at the wounded bird and speaks to the frail bird, "O bird, what a pity, you are but a poor useless creature, you are not a white peacock presented by the Maharani! Otherwise, many of them would have come forward to take care of you, to tend you until you recovered and flew away. Now there is no one to take care of you. There is no one to tend to you." And this wounded bird was kept in the ashrama, in a makeshift cage until it recovered and flew away. But this great lesson which the Master gave, the great lesson of equal compassion for all, remains and will remain for the ages to come. In 1939, I had the opportunity to visit this great saint and sit at His lotus feet. I wanted to speak to Him, but those around Him objected and told me that He does not speak much with anyone. But He spent forty minutes with me and we spoke to each other. I asked Him what is the goal of life? He did not speak much English and neither did He understand it. So the interpreter sitting next to Him translated it for me. He answered my question saying, "Self-realization is the goal of life."

'Then I asked Him, "How can I attain it?" And He laughed His memorable laugh that I am not able to forget even today. He said, "Do not worry about the future! Your first duty is to enquire about your own self. Unless you know your own self, why waste time over knowing other things?" "Religion," He would add, "is not a doctrine, but Self-realization." As the end of His pilgrimage in this world drew close, and Maharshi lay on His deathbed, He told His grieving disciples, "You say I am going away. But where can I go? I shall always be here. Do not give importance to the body."

'You must wipe out the ego, in order to read the Book of the Heart. You must conquer the ego self, to arrive at the true knowledge of the Self. Jalal-u-din Rumi was one of the greatest scholars the world has known. He wrote many books, he read many scriptures. His students lived in awe of him. One day, Rumi heard a knock on his door. He opened the door and found a man standing there. His name was Shams-e-Tabriz. Both gazed at each other. Rumi was wonderstruck. He thought, "Who could this man be?" Then the Light of recognition shone in his eyes. At once, Rumi fell at the feet of this man. He could recognize the Guru in Him. Shams-e-Tabriz picked up Rumi's manuscripts and threw them in a river. Rumi was shocked. His hard work of many years was destroyed within a minute. He began to weep. He said, "I loved my books more than my children." Shams-e-Tabriz, seeing the plight of his disciple, consoled him with the words, "Read the 'Book of your Heart'. For You are of the Eternal." This marked the beginning of Rumi's spiritual journey. He went deep within and wrote beautiful, timeless poetry. Centuries have passed, yet Rumi's poetry is read with great fervour and devotion even now. His book *Masnavi* is a marvellous work. I read it sometimes. This book is a rare treasure. We have received this birth to know our true self. We should explore and study the 'Book of our Heart'. For when we go to the other shore, we will leave behind everything, except the knowledge of the Self which is an emanation of the Supreme Self—that for want of a better word we call God. That art Thou! It is this knowledge alone that has any real value.

'Man's heart yearns for a manifestation of God. In this Kali Yuga, as we wait for the final incarnation of the Lord, how can we—millions of us—find His manifestation? Therefore, in this age of strife, disharmony and severe spiritual affliction, God has sent out among us God-souls, men of God, saints and sadhus. In short, the true Gurus. They are here with this sacred mission: To reveal God's love to us, and to lead our erring, wandering souls back to God. In this human birth, we cannot see God in person, but it is our good fortune that we can see the Guru, hear His or Her upadesh (guidance), associate ourselves with daily satsang (spiritual congregation), accept their gracious prasad (holy offerings), indeed, grasp the holy feet firmly, and through Him, all God's blessings and all God's grace will come to us!'

'Dada, who is a Perfect Master? I know nowadays a number of spiritual guides are addressed as a Perfect Master, but I feel they are more like guides and life trainers. They are still grappling with their own inadequacies and destinies, just like us all. So who is a Perfect Master?'

'Selflessness, humility, compassion. These are three common qualities you will find in every Master.'

'Yes, these qualities are mandatory, but that doesn't make one a Perfect Master like our respective Gurus, Sai Baba of Shirdi and Sadhu Vaswani. You have met so many Masters, who is a Perfect Master in this time and age . . .'

'You are a perfect master. I feel My Master in you.'

Yeah, right!

'But then You see Your Master in everybody. Do you think we are moving about in the right way spiritually? The so-called present Masters who are leading their disciples and devotees . . .'

'I believe there is a meaning in everything that happens. Everything happens for a purpose. I believe whatever comes from God, whatever happens to us is for our good; it comes to purify us. Even what some people call deception.'

'True, Dada, everything that happens, happens according to the will of God but . . .'

'Yes, there is a meaning of mercy in everything that happens . . .'

'But then do you just sit back and let things happen?'

'We do our work in our own way. We can't do everything. We can light a candle. That is all. Let us leave the rest to the law of karma. Karma will take care. Suppose I am rude to you, you don't have to react and be rude to me. That is for the law of karma to decide. You have to do your duty, you have to be loving to me.'

I wanted to tell Dada that karma was a strange animal and so many of us have a tendency to place our shortcomings on its shoulders.

'The law of karma has been described as the law of causation—the foundation on which this Universe evolves. It is a universal law, an all-inclusive law which operates on the lives of all of us. It affects all aspects of our existence—spiritual, psychic, physical. It influences our thoughts, intentions, motives and actions. It embraces our past, present and future, linked in a continuous cause–effect relation. The impact of this law is inexorable and inescapable. Its effect, reaction and response are absolutely impartial. We could say that it is the law of karma that upholds dharma, and maintains justice, equity, order and balance in the universe. The law of karma operates on individuals, as well as groups, communities, races and nations.

'Any action, thought or feeling generated by an individual brings with it certain indelible impressions, which are stored in the mind as samskaras. Every act, thought or feeling leaves behind a trace, which has the power to bring joy or sorrow.'

'So the law of karma decides our birth, upbringing, our temperament . . . our virtually everything, Dada?'

'To a large extent, yes. These are karmic residues and they can bring about consequences on three different levels. The first is the very specie of one's next birth; bird, animal, plant or human. Then, one's life span and one's life experiences—pleasurable or painful. Karmic actions lead to results that may affect us in this birth or in the lives to come. Thus, karma is closely linked with the concept of rebirth.

'So, Ruzbeh, you might ask me what happens to us in the interim between death and rebirth? Are all souls condemned to be born again and again—caught in the cycle of birth, death and rebirth?

According to Vedanta wisdom, there are four possibilities open to the soul after death. For one who has attained enlightenment during this life, there is total liberation from the cycle of birth and death. Such a one attains sadyah mukti or instantaneous liberation and is not born again.'

That rules most of us out, I mused.

'For one who has not attained liberation, but achieved purity of mind and devotion to the Creator, whom we call Brahma, there is a force which pushes the soul beyond the pull of this world and towards liberation. This is karma mukti—gradual or sequential liberation. In this process, the soul is led along a path of light and so attains an increasing expansion in consciousness until liberation is attained.'

Out, out, out.

'For one who has tried to live a virtuous life, but is not ready for liberation, there is a finite period of existence on the astral plane, where the astral body experiences pleasurable conditions. This is known as swarga. It is not liberation, but a relative experience of pleasure. This finite period is brought to an end when the soul's good karma is exhausted, and the soul is re-born into a new life.'

Hmm, this could work.

'For one who has accumulated no good karma at all, there is the painful fourth alternative—a period of intense suffering. But this period also comes to a close when the sinful karma is exhausted and the soul is re-born in a new embodiment. Thus, in the first two cases, liberation is attained. In the third and the fourth, the soul must return to the earth for the sake of its further evolution—after a period of heavenly pleasure or hellish suffering. In these cases, karma will determine the soul's next embodiment. For there are residues, remnants of karma that are not exhausted in the life after death state, be it heaven or hell. It is this residue that influences one's rebirth and life experiences. In other words, none of us are born into this world with what is called a clean slate. Even what we consider to be hereditary traits are in reality determined by the karma of previous lives.

'When you understand the concept of karma, you will realize why man has to accept both joy and sorrow. The karma of our previous births determines our destiny in this life. The law of karma is the law of action and reaction. We have all heard of Newton's Third Law: Every action has an equal and opposite reaction. Every action must lead to a reaction. The reaction may be immediate or it may occur in due course of time. But no action can be cancelled. It will, inevitably, lead to a reaction.

'When we bring our hands together, we produce a sound—a clap, as we call it. The sound is the effect; the cause is the coming together of our hands. The law of cause and effect is purely scientific and applies to all actions. What we have done in the past has determined our present life; what we do today, will determine our future.

'Sadhu Vaswani referred to the law of karma as the law of the seed. He said to us, "Go and learn the law of the seed from any farmer, any peasant you meet. Any farmer will tell you that you will only reap what you sow. If you sow apples, you will reap apples. If you sow mangoes, you will reap mangoes. If you sow thorns, you will reap thorns."

'The law of karma is also the law of effort and destiny; the effort of yesterday is the destiny of today. The effort of today will be the destiny of tomorrow. Every effort that I am putting forth today is going to be my destiny tomorrow—maybe in a future life. The efforts that I have put in during my earlier life have become my destiny today.

'We are all subject to this law. You cannot get a reprieve from the law of karma. You can save yourself, however, by improving your karma. The seed you sow today shall grow into a tree and bear fruit; you must eat it, whether the fruit is bitter or sweet. We will have to face the consequences of our own actions. Nothing, no one can save us from the law of karma. So powerful is the law that even Sri Rama could not save his father, King Dasharatha, from the consequences of his karma!'

'I agree with all that you say, Dada. But what about free will? Or is it just an illusion, like the rising and the setting of the sun?'

'The universe gives us a chance again and again—a thousand times. At every step, in every round of life, we have to make a choice. We are free to make a choice.

'So while we all take birth with a karmic residue which determines our personality, we are also born with a certain freedom of choice with which we can succeed in accumulating new, good, positive karma. This choice, this freedom, this ability, is available to every human being, and it is this which gives all of us the possibility of determining our own future destiny—not only for this life, but in the lives to come.

'The law of karma is neither fatalistic nor punitive; nor is man a hapless, helpless victim in its bonds. God has blessed each one of us with reason, intellect and discrimination, as well as the sovereign free will. Even when our past karma inclines us towards evil, we can consciously tune our inclination towards detachment and ego-free action, thus lightening the karmic load.

'A recognition and full awareness of the law of karma can help us to face life with a positive outlook. It can evoke in us the spirit of willing acceptance and thus help us evolve as masters, rather than slaves of circumstances. Above all, we can take control of our own actions and, thereby, shape our own future positively.

'When we begin to understand the concept of karma, we will never ever blame God for anything that happens to us. We will realize that we are responsible for all that happens to us. As we sow, so shall we reap. Rich or poor, saint or sinner, miser or philanthropist, learned or illiterate—as you sow, so shall you reap. This is the Universal Law that applies to individuals, to whole communities, societies, nations and races. As we sow, so shall we reap.

'Sri Ramakrishna Paramahansa was brilliant at illustrating the most profound and complex truths of life by means of beautiful and simple parables. One day, he said to His disciples, "Every day, fishermen cast their wide nets into the sea. A few fish are caught in the net. Many escape. Those that have escaped the net, swim about freely in the ocean; indeed, some fish are never ever caught. But those that are caught in the net, struggle to escape, and some of them actually succeed. They leap so valiantly, that they free themselves from the net, and get back into the vast and deep waters of the sea, where lies their true home. There are other fish caught in the net who also struggle to be free, but in vain. In vain, they seek a way out, for someone to free them from the death-trap that ensnares them. They struggle persistently. But there are a few fish who are blissfully ignorant, happily unaware of their condition. They are content to rest passively in the net that ensnares them, unaware of the terrible and painful fate that awaits them."

'Lord Buddha urged His followers not to waste their time and energy on futile speculations. "How did karma originate? Why are some people rich and others poor? Does God exist? If He exists, where exactly is He?" These are unanswerable questions on which we have no need to dwell. Only realize the truth that you are bound by your karma. All your time and energy and effort must be focused on freeing yourself from the bonds!

'He narrated to His disciples the story of a man whose house had caught fire. The neighbours rushed out to help him. They tried to put out the flames and called out to him, "Come out of the house or you will soon be reduced to ashes!" The foolish man said to them, "I will not leave this house until you answer three questions of mine: First, what caused the fire? Second, what is the exact temperature of the fire? Third, what are the chemical constituents of the fire? Until I get answers to these three questions, I shall not budge from here."

'Incensed by his foolish stubbornness, the people cried, "You idiot! Is this the time or place to ask such questions? Get out of this burning inferno, save your skin. We can discuss these questions and others after we have put the fire out." But the man was adamant. "No way," he shouted. "I shan't leave this house until my questions have been answered."

'Ruzbeh we all are like that man. "Man is burning," The Buddha repeated emphatically. "Some are trapped in the fire of hatred; others in the flames of envy, passion, greed or jealousy, ego and pride. Quench the flames! Quench the flames!"'

'So, basically, it all began with free will and how one used one's free will, and then now it has accumulated into karma. Often the only free will we have is the manner in which one goes through one's karma. So eventually, it means that free will has been the most important thing and karma is just the ramification of free will?' I enquired.

'Yes.'

'But, Dada, what is the purpose of birth? I mean why all this song and dance?'

'The purpose of life, as I think of it, is to become more and more perfect. "Be ye perfect as your Father in heaven is perfect." Those are the words of Jesus. Every experience that comes to me, teaches me a lesson I need to learn. But perfection again I believe is awareness. You become more aware. What is the difference between me and a holy man? The holy man is more aware then I am. What is God? God is awareness.'

Krishna once told me that ever so often when Dada went walking, he would get on His knees to pick up a crawling insect or an ant tenderly, place it away from harm and then resume His walk. If one saw Him cut a fruit you realised that He did so with reverence. He did every single thing with awareness and love.

'The issue is, in this lifetime, let us assume, there is a man or a woman who has reached a certain degree of awareness, but as soon as that individual passes away and is reincarnated, does this awareness still exists within the individual or does one have to start all over again? I would like to believe no effort goes to vain?'

'Nothing goes to vain, Ruzbeh. Nothing. Therefore, we should try to grow in awareness and thus our karma improves. The Lord assures us of this in the Gita. If you have reached a certain level of awareness, of sadhana, it is not wasted when this life ends. You carry it with you to reach the next stage in your evolution . . . "On this path, effort never goes to waste, and there is no failure. Even a little effort towards spiritual awareness will protect you from the greatest fear."— The Bhagavadgita (2:40)'

'So you mean karma and awareness all are in the hands of the individual. But then what about one's Guru? Can the Guru . . . You know . . . sort of . . . tweak the karmic blueprint?'

'Nobody else except the Guru can come between karma and the individual. But the Guru does not like to interfere with my karma because he knows that my karma is not punitive. Karma is reformative.'

'But the Guru can intervene or bail the disciple out?'

'Yes, only the Guru can.'

'That is why the Guru is above the magnificent trio, Lord Brahma, Vishnu, Mahesh. What would be the circumstances which would necessitate a Guru to intervene? Could that also be connect with the past life disciple and the Guru?'

'Not necessarily. But the Guru is compassionate.'

'But the Guru can't be partial, Dada. The Guru cannot choose to intervene at a whim. Then where is the justice of it all?'

'Ruzbeh, the Master's Grace needs no logic and no justification. It is likened to a room that has been in darkness for years. If you light a single matchstick in that room, darkness instantly disappears and the room is filled with light. Grace is the lighting of the matchstick.'

Dada is big on the inexplicable presence of Grace. He is of the opinion that Grace needs no justification or reason or logic. Grace comes about without any explanation. That is why it is called Grace. I still feel that makes God, Goddess, Guru sort of partial. Karma I understand. But to single somebody out due to a sudden gush of love and compassion, is great for the recipient but excludes a large part of the following. Not good. Not good at all.

'Ok so back to the Guru. Let us assume, for whatever reason, the Guru has taken on somebody else's suffering or experience—what happens with the laws of karma? Who pays the karmic bill? Does the Guru have to undergo discomfort, pain?'

'Yes, somebody has to pay for it.'

That somebody is the poor Guru. Told you Grace would lead to trouble.

'But how does the Guru take on the karmic balancing if the Guru is no longer in the body?'

'The Guru also is taking birth after birth. Otherwise it is not necessary for the Guru to enter the cycle of birth and death, but He chooses to take upon Himself the sufferings of others. Meher Baba—how many accidents did He meet? But He smiled through it all. Sadhu Vaswani—for the last six years of His life, He could barely sleep as the painful twitches kept Him awake and He refused to get operated on.'

'So the Guru, once again comes down in the human body just to take on the suffering of all those S/he has taken under the wings and would the Guru remember that? Would the Guru come down with the same Divine consciousness?' I asked.

'There are two Gurus—there is the *drisht* (visible) Guru and then there is the *adrishta* (invisible) Guru. The drisht Guru may not remember everything but the adrishta Guru does. They are two sides of the same coin.'

'Now this is a question that has bothered me, let us say there is a Perfect Master who has taken on the harsh and discomforting experiences of the disciples and has to come down to pay their karmic bill. Now to take on the suffering of His or Her lot, The Guru, will in all probability not be aware of His or Her Divinity, or else how can S/he suffer and thus pay the bill? So the Guru is virtually like a common person, getting the thrashing of his or her life, not knowing why. Could that lead to personal karma being created by the Guru and then the Guru losing His or Her essence?'

'Maybe the Guru does penance and pays off the accumulated karma of His or Her disciples.'

'I get that, but the Guru will not be in an uplifted consciousness. In normal consciousness could the Guru, as a normal human being, become angry, or negative or do something to accumulate personal karma, then what? The Master does not know now why He or She is going through these experiences, who He or She really is?'

'Yes, most often the Guru will not know, but there are times the Guru is aware.'

'What if he does not know? Then what happens? Does S/He comes down with a certain elevated consciousness to be able to go through it calmly or even that need not happen? Because then that takes a very high for the Guru?

'As I think of it, the Guru really does not know whether what S/He is paying is personal karma or the karma of one or more disciples. Though according to the Scriptures, the Guru is aware.

'In all probability, The Master is not aware of His or Her Divinity. Karma could be created. So does that experience create a new karma? Because, at this particular point, the Master may be with the consciousness of an elevated person, but not necessarily with the knowledge of the past, present, future. Would S/He begin to create karma just by going through the karmas of others by His or Her reaction to the situation?'

'No. I do not think the Guru after reaching such an exalted position can be bound by general laws of karma.'

'So the Guru is karmic free from all reactions experienced whilst paying of the karmic debt of His or Her disciples?' That's me again.

'Yes. Karma that has been collected, until the time that S/He became a Master, that continues and it has to be paid. But no new karma is formed.'

'So a Perfect Master, is free of karma.'

'Yes, from manufacturing karma. The Master rises above the law of karma.'

'So the Master rises above the law of karma and may not be aware of this fact, when the Master comes down to pay the debt of the disciples. Is there any kind of a period after which the Guru has to come down or is it conditional to what the Guru wants?'

'Not necessarily, because the Master has broken the confines of space and time. The place of birth, manner of birth, the conditions, environment, everything—the Master is beyond all this. All the Master has to do is pay off the karmic debt of the disciples on behalf S/He intervened.'

'The usual belief is when the Master leaves the body, the Master stays put in the spirit plane. My question, let us say a Perfect Master comes down, the disciples are yet praying to that Master. But a time will come when the Perfect Master has to come down to square the karmic debt owed by the disciples, which the Master has manipulated. Now the devotees and disciples will not know when the Master is going to come down, live in the body, like a normal human being, in all probability unaware of His or Her own powers. But the disciples are praying to that Master, who they are certain is hearing all their prayers and is with them. What happens to those prayers? Where do those prayers go?'

'I told you there are two Gurus; there is the drisht or visible Guru with whom we can come in contact, but there is also the adrishta or invisible Guru, who is always with us, wherever we are.'

'So there is one Guru, who has now manifested Himself into two. One eternal and the other transitory, who comes and goes, to pay off the karmic debt of His or Her disciples. The real Guru, the eternal Guru, is always with us; while the earthly Guru comes down, gets a karmic *dhulai* of a lifetime and then returns to the Original Form. Is that what you are trying to say? It is just energy? So even though the Master is down, the Master is still up. And the prayers of the disciples still reach the Master?'

'I would not say manifested because there are times when both the drishta and the adrishta Guru become one.'

'Now, each Master has both these qualities of being visible and invisible. So when the Master comes down to pay off the karmas of his flock, the adrishta Guru is yet on top and the prayers of the disciples reach him?'

'For the adrishta, there is no here or there.'

Hmm. So this is what I understand. The Perfect Master leaves the body. In the spirit dimension, the Perfect Master is also within each disciple. That Perfect Master takes on the karma of His or Her disciples. A time comes when the karmic credit card bill needs to be paid. The eternal form of the Perfect Master is always there. But somebody has to foot the bill. So from the seed comes the tree and from the tree comes the fruit, and from the fruit comes a seed again. So the Perfect Master manifests Himself or Herself in another body on Mother Earth, pays the karmic bill, most often not aware of His or Her original form. Once the karmic bill is paid, the Master may then leave the body and merge back to His or Her eternal self, or remain in the body and regain His or Her Divine Self-realization and then work for the well-being of all creation. And once the work is done S/He returns back to His or Her eternal form. The Master now in either the spirit plane or the physical plane cannot create new karma but has to complete the karmic debt of all those He or She has intervened on behalf of. That is why Sai Baba of Shirdi has mentioned often that He had taken birth over eighty times. He had come down eighty times to wash His disciples' karmic debt. Each time in another form. The original form of Sai Baba of Shirdi one could never know, but each form belongs to the original Divine Form.

Okay, got it. Or have I?

For instance there are ten avatars of Vishnu. Now, when an individual prays to one of the avatars, does it reach the avatar or reach Lord Vishnu?

I mean, if I were to pray to Lord Rama, an avatar of Lord Vishnu, who came down for karmic purposes and other larger purposes, does it reach Lord Rama or Vishnu directly? I may not have a personal connect with Lord Vishnu, but with His Avatar as Lord Rama, I might have a personal connect. Because there may be a Perfect Master who may have come in various bodies having different physical impressions, like Sai Baba of Shirdi, says He has reincarnated eighty times. I have no idea what the original form of Sai Baba of Shirdi is, but I am praying to the Sai Baba of Shirdi the way I see Him, as His eighty-third incarnation.

'The Sai Baba of yesterday is different from the Sai Baba of today because the body has changed. The body is not the same. Even when in the body, Sai Baba as a child was different from Sai Baba as a young man and different when He took Samadhi. His body changed in one lifetime, but it was the same Sai Baba throughout, irrespective of the physical changes. We do not pray to just the young Sai Baba or the old Sai Baba, but to Sai Baba. The body keeps changing. We think of it as one body but it is not one body. It is a changing body—constantly changing. That which is visible, changes.'

'So what you are saying is that just as Sai Baba remains the same through His physical changes; the Eternal Soul remains the same through the various incarnations and avataric manifestations.'

That could also mean that maybe, just maybe, all the Prophets could have come from one source. I don't mean God or Goddess, everything comes forth from that one source. I mean, what if every Prophet that has ever come to preach and bring forth change and a new religion, could have been just one single Entity, being reborn, time after time after time? Just as Lord Vishnu's ten Avatars are in the end Lord Vishnu, all Prophets could have come forth from the same source. If that was true, then what a fine mess we have created. All of us fighting to prove the superiority of their Prophet and, in reality, all the Prophets are One.

Being reborn through the passage of time to preach the same message in different languages and using different phrases, but eventually the same person saying the same thing to a hilariously daft audience. No wonder The One in various disguises of various Prophets has stopped visiting planet Earth.

After every interview with Dada, after all the cameras were turned off, I would touch Dada's feet and He would try to touch mine . . . He tries to touch the feet of anybody who tries to touch His feet . . . He seeks blessings of all those who come to seek His blessings and His humility embraces you, fills you with warmth and the realization that God hasn't given up on mankind. Dada would bless me with prasad. He would say, 'Please give Ruzbeh prasad, for his daughter, Meher.' It would always be some delicious snack that Meher loved and Dada would never forget. Everyone around would, but not Him. No matter how tired He was, how occupied he was, He never ever forgot. He has never sent me back empty-handed. Chips, chocolate biscuits, cakes, chocolates, sweetmeats and similar delicious blessings, and Meher would say, 'Dada sends all this for me?' I would say, 'Yes, baby. He sends all this for you . . . He says this is for the sweetest baby in all of creation . . .' Meher would smile and say, 'Dada speaks just like you, I like Him. Not as much as you, but He comes close.'

3

As usual I was paying my respects to Sadhu Vaswani when I realized that Sister Shanti's marble statue, a small one doing a Namaste to Sadhu Vaswani, was at the right-hand corner of the room. I find the Samadhi so peaceful. Pune is bustling outside, but inside the Mission, there is a strange, joyful silence. I would always first go to the Samadhi every time I went to either interview Dada or His disciples.

Naresh would meet me here. He was always happy, but was often stressed out. Naresh was a humble man who I would tease and he would smile as the others laughed. If it was hot in the Kutiya, it was because of the energy and vibrations that Naresh emitted. If the tea was too sweet it was because Naresh must have made it and his sweetness must have seeped into the liquid. If there was no network in the ashram, obviously it was because Naresh's over powering aura left no space for other vibrations to enter. I have driven him crazy. This, of course, was not a patch on his ability to drive me nuts! The Mission is fortunate to have him.

Every day, I arrived to interview Dada, and Piya would look me up and down. Most often, she rolled her eyes as I looked like a thug—uncombed hair, jeans, shirts of various colours with my beard varying in length. Dada would arrive by then and bow to Sadhu Vaswani's frame, the lamp and the bed on which Sadhu spent the last six years of His physical journey. Dada always looked in a beautiful, sharp contrast to me. He was always in white, with His face shinning with love. He was clean-shaven with His shawl neatly wrapped around Him. He would first fold His hands in the direction of Sadhu Vaswani's frame kept on the bed and then the wheel chair would be turned and He would fold His hands to all those present in the Samadhi. He would first look at Jyotish and Umakant, who were in charge of the three cameras, and then He would see me and His eyes would light up with a smile. I would bow and touch His feet, and He would try to touch mine. Then I would kneel down to talk to Him and He would always make me laugh. We both would be given a sweet to have and during the interviews, we both usually spoke with the sweet in our mouth. I doubt if anybody ever noticed this. Then, Piya and Krishna would adjust the mic and make sure there is not a crease out of place, and I would plonk myself near Dada and look on. Once the light and sound was adjusted, I would tell Dada to speak a few words. If Dada was in the mood of speaking to all those present, the sound check would go on for a few minutes. The fans would be switched off and it would get really hot, but Dada sat there unruffled. Ever so often Piya would tell Dada with love and reverence if He could lean His body to one side or the other, and Dada would oblige. He would look at her and say, 'Are you happy? Am I sitting in the right way?' I would tell Him that it was good that Steven Spielberg didn't have Piya or else the poor director would never ever complete his movie. Dada would giggle and everyone else would wonder why.

Naresh and his wife, Anita, would sit a little distance away and look at Dada with great reverence. If Naresh looked at me, I would pull a face and the poor man would try his best not to smile.

Krishna once told me that the secret of Dada's youth is 'His philosophy that one stops growing old when one is constantly learning.' Dada has often said that, 'every day, I learn something new. I perform new experiments in the laboratory of life.'

According to Krishna, once an interviewer from a newspaper asked Dada a number of questions and was impressed by Dada's fiery answers. As he got ready to leave, he asked Dada, 'I hope to come back next year and take your photograph.' Dada smiled at him and said, 'You look pretty healthy, I am sure you will make it.'

I was graced with Dada's presence, interviewing Him eighteen times. Each time I realized that at ninety-seven, going on ninety-eight,

Dada was racing against time and the thought of this planet without Dada in flesh and blood, makes my heart sink. He reminded me so much of my maternal grandmother. A perfect disciple, a reluctant master, a loving and caring grandparent, a dear friend—this is what Dada means to me. If it is karma that brought me to Him, then I must have done some really heavy-duty good karma in my past lives.

The cameras and sound systems were ready.

'Dada, has Sadhu Vaswani ever materialized in front of you after He took Maha Samadhi?'

Dada thought for a long time. Then He looked at me.

'I may not have seen His form, but Sadhu Vaswani was never the form. Even when Sadhu Vaswani was in the body, He was not the body. He was awareness. He was that awareness and awareness does not die. The body dies, the form is gone, all these things that you see . . . the Samadhi and the Darshan Hall and all of it . . . the form is destroyed; the real thing is not there. He was always beyond form.'

'So how does a devotee or disciple connect with his Master's true essence?'

'One way is through silent meditation.'

'What would be the simplest thing for a householder to do? Meditation does not come naturally to one and all, Dada.'

'Surrender yourself at the feet of the Lord. Let us all surrender, surrender, surrender unto the Lord! This is what Lord Krishna tells Arjuna in the Gita. "Oh Arjuna, renouncing all rites and writ duties, come unto Me for single refuge! Do not despair, for I shall release you from all bondage of sin and suffering!" This is the final and most inspiring message of the Gita. It is also the quintessence of spiritual discipline. This is not escapism; this is not shifting our responsibility on to God. In fact, the Lord has insisted that we should never shirk our duties; rather, we must free our mind from egoism and desire. Divine grace is obtained through unconditional surrender to the Lord. The Lord should be made the single goal of our life, the sole object of our worldly endeavours.'

I realized that meditation sounded like a piece of cake when compared to surrender. Surrender is letting go of one's ego. That takes true, mad love for The One. I decided to go back to silent meditation.

'But I asked about a simpler thing. For most people, surrender is not that simple. When you said silent meditation, would it be to sit down and try and be aware of your breath, and just be calm . . . would that be the first step?'

'Yes. The first step, for the age in which we live, would be to sit in a silent corner, forget everything and repeat the name silently of the One who you have faith in.'

'For how long should this be done?'

'It depends on the disciple, but at least for fifteen minutes.'

'Should it be only at one particular time of the day?'

'Yes, it should be at one particular time in the day. And then we could also have periods for fifteen minutes scattered through the day.'

'So we should sit and be in silent meditation at one particular time of the day. Is the time important or can one sit when time permits?'

'It is what, in my simplicity, I call the "appointment with God". Our daily appointment with God. When you fix an appointment with God, then you have to ensure you are there at that particular time of the appointment.'

'Why is meditation so important? Why does every Prophet, Master, religious text, insist on meditation?'

'The word meditation is derived from the Latin root, which means 'to heal'. The healing, calming, de-stressing technique of meditation is essential to the seeker on the path of sadhana. Some scholars say that the root of the word 'meditation' is similar to the roots of medicine and medicate—which means paying attention to something. When we meditate, we pay attention to those depths in our being which are not known to the people outside, which are, perhaps, not familiar even to ourselves! Thus meditation has been described as a process of inner attention. While many regard meditation as a difficult art, it is actually quite simple. Meditation is directing our attention to the Eternal and keeping it there for a while. Within every one of us is a realm of peace, power and perfection.

Through practice, we can enter this realm at will and contact God. When we do this, we become conscious of an infinite power, a wondrous peace, and realize that everything is perfect and in its own place. Like all spiritual experiences, meditation is something that cannot come to us from without. It enables us to be receptive to God's voice, which can only be heard in inner stillness. In His voice is true wisdom; in His message to us is true peace.'

'So is meditation the same as reflection or contemplation or introspection?'

'No, though all of these may be useful aids in preparing for meditation. Some people spend hours with their eyes closed, fantasizing, or stare vacantly with open eyes, daydreaming. These are certainly not to be confused with meditation. Some people describe meditation as an art, others call it a science. It would be truer to say that it is a process or technique by which we link ourselves with the highest state of "awareness" or "consciousness" that we can reach. To grow in the inner life, the life of the spirit, we need to withdraw from the outer world of noise and excitement. Therefore, we stress on the practice of silence every day. Each day, we must spend some time—at least an hour—in silence. At the very start, it can be difficult to sit in silence for an hour at a stretch. So it would be well if we practice silence for about a quarter of an hour, four times a day. In due course, the mind will become as calm and clear as the surface of a lake on a windless day. Such a mind will become a source of indescribable joy and peace. Significant are the words in the Upanishads: 'The mind alone is the cause of man's bondage; the mind is also an instrument of man's liberation.'"

Okay, so first one begins by being silent. Good luck with that, I concluded to myself.

'Meditation is about sinking deeper and deeper within yourself. We know so many things outside of us. Man has been able to set foot on the moon, his rockets go flying past distant planets, his brain power has been developed, science is marching on, technological progress has been made . . . Man has been able to control the forces of nature so much so that he says, "I have mastered nature." He goes and puts a flag on Mount Everest, and he says, "I have conquered the

Himalayas." Yes, you may have conquered the Himalayas, but have you conquered yourself? Man's anger flares easily, he yields easily to the temptations of greed or lust. He has not been able to control himself because he does not know what he is. He regards himself only as the body that he wears.

'I say to my friends time and again, to not identify themselves with the body alone. You are not the physical body you wear. You are the immortal spirit within! "What are you?" Philosophers consider this as the ultimate knowledge that a man can aspire for—self-knowledge. How do you attain this knowledge? You have to dive deep within yourself to find out what you are. And that is the purpose of meditation. Only meditation tells you what you are. In meditation, you keep sinking deeper and deeper within yourself until you forget the outer self, you forget the body. You have no sense of the body.

'In very simple terms, meditation is turning inwards, meditation is focusing the mind on the self, meditation is the healing of the self from within. It is a process of giving your inner self attention. Therefore, I call this the inner journey, a pilgrimage to our interiors. And may I tell you, there may be many pilgrimages; but if I have not gone on an interior pilgrimage, I have wasted a golden opportunity in your human birth. I am reminded of a young man who came to me and proudly said that he had visited sixty-seven pilgrim spots and was now planning to go for the last one, the sixty-eighth one, to Pandharpur. He requested me to accompany him to this last pilgrimage on his map. He implored, "Pandharpur is in close proximity to Pune. I will be thrilled if you can join me." I smiled and said, "Brother, please go ahead to Pandharpur. But if, at any point in time, you wish to go on a pilgrimage within yourself, a pilgrimage to *andarpur*, please come to me and we will take the journey together." Ruzbeh, meditation leads to Divine Peace. You know this very well.' 'Dada knowing and realizing are two completely different animals. Anyway, how do you reach such a state?'

'Okay, so here are a few practical suggestions for beginners. The first step is to sit in silence, in an easy and comfortable posture where the spinal cord, the neck and the head are in a straight line. Practice meditation preferably at the same place and the same time every day. Sit facing the east or north. Go to God as you are—with all your sins and imperfections. Think of an object or a symbol, or an incident from the life of a Great One. As you sit in silence, wear a soft smile on your face. Let your daily life be one of sacrifice. Persevere towards this daily, at the same time, at the same place. This is absolutely necessary. Regularity is the law of meditation.'

'I can understand regularity being the law of meditation, but why is the same place and same time so important?'

'This will help form a habit that will automatically ensure you are in a meditative mood when the hour approaches. But also remember, meditation should be practiced when the body is not tired and at least two hours after having a meal. At the time of meditation, it is advisable to wear loose, comfortable clothes. This will help you to relax fully. The clothes should be clean and, if possible, set apart for this purpose. No particular posture is prescribed for meditation. Adopt any seated posture that you find natural and in which you can sit for some length of time without having to move the body unnecessarily. You may sit on the floor (not on the bare ground, but on a mat, a carpet, or a piece of cloth) in a cross-legged position or be seated in a straight chair with your feet gently resting on the floor. What is important is that the spinal column and the head should be held erect. This helps the *prana* (vital energy) to move freely in the body. Do not strain yourself. Be comfortable, relaxed and attentive. But above all, make it a regular habit.'

'So it really makes a big difference—meditating at the same time and place?'

'It does. If you miss it even for a day you really feel like you have missed out on something. You don't feel happy.

'I remember an incident from my college days. There was one boy who sat next to me and kept writing as the professor talked. I admired his sincerity and diligence, but I wondered why he failed every exam despite taking notes down so assiduously. One day, I peered into his notebook in the classroom and was amazed to read "Maina, Maina" written all over it. Apparently Maina was his girlfriend whom he loved dearly. In an instant it struck me that this is what true love is. One's thoughts dwell constantly on the Beloved and the "I" is completely effaced. The formula for true love is "Main Na!". There shouldn't be me, just you.'

'So what is the real meaning of the word meditation?'

'Meditation, the word, is derived from the Latin word *meditare* which means to heal. From the point of view of the inner self, we are sick; if not all of us, at least most of us are. We need to be healed. For one thing, the unbearable stress and strain of contemporary life needs to be countered with conscious stress-reduction techniques. Meditation is the most effective among them. I truly believe that the curative powers and healing energies within us can be harnessed through meditation practices, and used effectively to fight mental and physical ailments.'

'Meditation does that?'

'Meditation heals. You come to a stage, when you have to jump into it—you have to lose yourself to know yourself. Two thousand five hundred years ago, Socrates said, "Know thyself. O man, you are trying to know so many things, but what do you know of yourself?"'

'Meditation teaches you about yourself?'

'I think it was Emerson who said, "What lies behind us and what lies before us are tiny matters compared to what lies within us." Within us is shakti, the power of the *Atman*, the power of the Divine spark. Psychiatrists as well as spiritual teachers now agree that there are three states of consciousness in all of us—the conscious mind with which all of us are familiar; the subconscious, which is the hidden but powerful part of our psyche, with which we connect only during sleep; the super conscious, which represents the highest degree of awareness that we are capable of. It is the source of the brightest light, the highest power we are capable of achieving. Meditation is the process in which we establish contact with our super consciousness. Yes, meditation teaches you about yourself. All we need to do is to forgive our self. We are under the impression that we are only our body. That body has a name and we identify ourselves by that name. But we are not that name. We all are one. You and I are one, not different. When we rise up to that level, we find that we are not different at all.'

Intellectually, all this makes sense, but realizing this can take lifetimes, if not more, I mused to myself. Dada had lapsed into His meditative silence. I looked around. Something was moving on my scalp; I scratched it. Lo and behold, whatever was moving became very still, as though in silent meditation. I looked at Naresh. I winked at him when I caught his eye. He quickly looked down at his phone, avoiding a smile. Did I have lunch today? I felt Dada look at me. I gave Him my most serene look of concentration.

'With meditation, there is a lot of insistence on proper breathing—Prana . . . Why is that, Dada?'

'You can meditate on the breath. The idea is that you should forget that you are a body. Prana must be purified, for it is our "life breath"—our respiration because of which we live. Many of us control our speech, but are unable to control prana. When breath is properly controlled, drawn in and let out, it helps keep the body and mind healthy, relaxed and pure. Prana is also the vital force that animates the universe, a primary energy with an enriching, invigorating quality. Thus, there is an indelible link between man and the universe, for the same life-force is manifest in both.

'Most important of all, it is prana which links the body and the mind. Hence, its importance for mental, physical and spiritual well-being cannot be underestimated.'

'So the word *Pranayama* . . . comes forth from the word prana . . . vital life force?'

'Yes. Pranayama is a unique, systematic, deep breathing exercise, associated with yoga. Pranayama, when practiced properly, enables the lungs to absorb optimum levels of oxygen so as to purify the blood and thus, ease the strain on the heart. Deep breathing can bring us immense benefits, including a stable mind, steady thinking, inner peace and a healthy life. Pranayama is also a vital accompaniment of *dhyana* or meditation. As wise men from the East and West have repeatedly told us, the mind is the root cause of many diseases and ailments. With the purification of prana, we can attain the blessed gift of a healthy mind in a healthy body.

'When prana is not controlled and purified, we have bad dreams. When we practice pranayama, even our dream-state, our subconscious life becomes good and pure.'

'Thus, a simple thing like breathing properly could be a vehicle to reach that stage? Is there a particular way to breathe, Dada, which can help one not only relax and heal the body via breathing, but also help one receive the maximum benefit—physical, emotional, mental and spiritual? I mean some rhythm to the breathing . . . you know what I mean?'

I could make out Dada had to make an effort to speak. The heart attack He had suffered had taken a toll on His body, movements and speech. Of course, it did not affect His mind, His very being and His humour.

'Yes, there are various techniques of breathing or, should I say, different types of meditation. Start by reminding yourself that every minute, every second comes to us as a gift from God. Every breath, every inhalation and exhalation is an offering of love from God. Then stop doing whatever you are doing, close your eyes, take a slow, deep breath. A slow, deep breath is one in which an inhalation lasts at least five seconds, as does an exhalation. A total breath lasts at least ten seconds. If you breathe in and breathe out like this six times, it will take you not more than a minute. If you do this ten times a day, whenever you can spare one minute at a time, it will take only ten minutes. But let me say this to you, being aware of the breath, being conscious of the prana that sustains your life, can change your life!

'As we take in the breath, let us say inwardly, "I open the door to God, to let Him enter my life". While exhaling say to yourself or aloud, if you like, "Thank you, God, for entering my life". Do this nine times more. Soon, you will realize that God is with you, that He is watching you, that He is watching over you. And this can change your life!'

'Thus, would you say for a common man or woman, who is engrossed in day-to-day activity, focusing on breathing would be the simplest and yet the most effective form of meditation?'

'Yes, focus on breath is the simplest form of meditation.'

'So observe your breath and as and when do the five-second breathing you affirm your faith?'

'Yes, Ruzbeh. Even if you have one minute to spare, even if you have five minutes to spare, just sit on a chair, sit in a relaxed position and concentrate on your breath going in and coming out. And all you have to do is to tell yourself, "You are breathing in, you are breathing out." The word "breathing" could also be dropped. In, out! In, out! But you will get more benefit if you repeat the name of your deity. Then you will, as you keep repeating the name of the deity, become more and more like the deity.'

'And what about silence?'

'Ah, silence is another effective gateway to meditation. In silence, we understand the secrets of true freedom. In silence, we make the discovery that we are not creatures bound by space and time. We are children of Eternity: and Eternity is here and now. We are not the isolated creatures we think we are; we are waves of the unbound deep. We are one with all of life, all of creation. He is in all, all are in Him!'

Hmm. We both lapsed into silence. I took in a breath, counted till five and then held my breath. What had Dada told me to affirm? I had cleanly forgotten. I continued to hold my breath. Damn. Think man, think. Nope. I exhaled. I forgot to count till five. Dada looked at me. It was a look that said, 'After you have finished playing with your breath, we can get back to the interview.'

'Ah, yes. Dada, Masters and scriptures have talked about how while meditating you reach a particular level where it starts working on your astral body and your ethereal body. What is that?'

'Today, it has become fashionable to talk very lightly of the astral, ethereal and causal body. To the beginner who wishes to pursue meditation as a healing, cleansing exercise, all that is not necessary. But people like complications. They don't really want to practice meditation. But they expect to know what it will do for them at the physical level, ethereal level and so on. If you tell them a simple thing, they wish to complicate it.'

'Oh that is for sure, Dada. But still, there is a lot of talk about various bodies, etc., thus is there an astral body and a casual body?'

'There is an astral body. Right now, you and I and every one of us is clothed in three bodies. It is very much like wearing a shirt, over it a coat and over it an overcoat—the physical, the astral and the casual. What happens in death is that man continues to be the same—he has the same habits, he has the same attitudes. All that has happened is that instead of wearing the shirt of the physical body, he wears the coat of the astral body.'

So once a person leaves his or her mortal coil or kicks the darn bucket, the shirt is off, but the coat and overcoat are still present.

'So then what is the etheric double you talk so fondly of in your books?'

'Encasing the physical body is what we call the etheric double. The etheric double as a term, I believe, was used by the theosophists first. It is a mechanism which draws the energy to be used by the body. The eyes are able to see because of the energy that they get from the etheric double. The etheric double takes the *pranic* force and distributes it all over the body. And thus, the hands are able to work and the feet are able to walk.'

'Does meditation strengthen the etheric double? Or does the right breathing do it? Is there any way one can strengthen the etheric double?'

'I think it automatically gets strengthened. It depends on the physical, how much energy it needs. Then, automatically it draws the energy, it does not have to put forth any effort to strengthen the etheric double.'

'Does the body drive it or does the etheric double drive the body?'

'The body in itself can do nothing. It is like the railway engine. For it to move you need the machinery. You need the fuel. That machinery and fuel is the etheric double.'

'Would the diet of an individual, would the thought process of an individual, make any kind of difference to the etheric double?

'It does. Let me put it this way. The harmonious functioning of the human machine depends on the harmonious activity of all the components of the system—the body, the mind and the senses. When the body is abused by self-indulgence, we harm the system. When we exercise restraint and discipline, we put the system to the best possible use. After all, the human soul is a spark of the Universal Spirit, or God, as we prefer to call Him. When we live our daily life in pursuit of the realization of this truth, the body does indeed become a temple that is worthy to be inhabited by the Spirit!

'Therefore, physical discipline, physical well-being is essential to the seeker on that path. Since the beginning of the twentieth century, we have accepted what is known as the psychosomatic unity of the human being. "Psyche" means mind or soul; "soma" means body. Thus, the psychosomatic concept tells us that we are not just bodies—but an entirety that includes the body, mind and spirit, functioning in a symbiotic relationship in which a separation is impossible to make. Therefore, we cannot have a pure mind and an impure body; we cannot have pure thoughts and impure words.

'Self-discipline is perhaps the most underrated and least recognized virtue these days. I always say that self-discipline is the exercise of our spiritual muscles! In lifestyle, as in a diet, moderation must be the key! "Verily, yoga is not for him who eateth too much, nor he who abstaineth to excess, nor who is too much addicted to sleep, nor even to wakefulness, O Arjuna," Lord Krishna tells His dear disciple.

'Alas, we live in a world where old-fashioned virtues like self-denial, self-discipline and self-restraint are no longer valued. Ours is the age of materialism and mass consumption. Everywhere hoardings proclaim, "Buy now, pay later!", "Enjoy yourself, we'll take care of the rest!", "Borrow more money, no questions asked!", "Gratify your appetite here and now!" It works both ways, the etheric double affects the thought and the thought affects the etheric double.'

'So each can affect the other? Now we know, or we assume we know, how to take care of the body. Would there be any way to be able to strengthen the double?'

'The mind must be controlled and disciplined to promote mental well-being. Purity of mind is one of the greatest blessings a man or woman can achieve. Regularity, punctuality, clean habits, *sattvic* food and yoga exercises are all beneficial. Silence is also essential. Silence is the food, the nourishment for the spirit.'

'So we go back to meditation, breathing and silence to help the etheric double?'

'Definitely, yes.'

I have a strong feeling that eventually, for everything else too, we would have to go back to breathing, calm silence and meditation.

'Now, this etheric double is not the astral body?'

'No, it is not that.'

'So what is the astral body then?'

'The astral body is very much like the body of thoughts. When we enter the astral, leaving the physical behind, then thought becomes a tremendous force. You and I are sitting together, you think of rain, I don't think of rain, you will feel that it is raining, I don't feel the rain at all.'

'So whatever you think you will manifest itself?'

'Yes. Imagine the responsibility of each thought then.'

'Wow.'

'Yes, wow.'

'What will the casual body contain then?'

'I really do not know, but I believe that when thought is purified, when it becomes pointed to one direction, when it needs nothing but God, that is the casual body. Concentration, but concentration on that one point. Not concentration on anything else, no. But then, as I said, I am not sure of this, Ruzbeh. I truly haven't given all this too much thought.'

'Dada, there is a school of thought which says that our lifetimes of karma, the entire karmic blueprint of all our lifetimes, is stored in one of the bodies, which they assume is the casual body. And via meditation, the fire that is created starts burning the karma, which is embedded there. So the more one meditates, the divine fire burns away the karma stored in the causal body. What is your view on this?'

'Karma is of three types Ruzbeh. What you are referring to is called *Sanchit* karma. Sanchit karma is the totality of karma—the karma that has not yet been worked out. It lies in a dormant state. So it does not build a body of its own, it is spread in all the bodies. I have not studied the effects of meditation apart from the fact that it connects me with my God and Master. But I am aware that karma is such a thing that in the fulfilment of it, I create new karma. Supposing I want to pay off the karma that I have collected so far; in the process of paying off my old karma I create new karma.'

'So how does one get off this wagon?'

'There is no way of getting off this wagon.'

'Then how do the Masters gain moksha and liberation?'

'There are ways. Now, for instance, one way is through self-realization. I realize what I am, if I realize that I am not this body or this mind, I am part of the Creator and I operate from that spark, then I do not get stained by karma. When I realize that I am not this and I am not that, then karma does not apply. I have gone and touched a dimension where karma cannot reach me. So there are ways. But the easiest way is surrendering to the Master.'

'Because for one to operate from this dimension one's level of awareness has to be very high.'

'Yes, it's difficult, very difficult. So I have taken the most beautiful path. Follow, obey and surrender to my Master. I have left the entire karmic issue at His feet. He knows best.'

'So the safest and the easiest way is to surrender to the Master.'

'Ultimately we have to surrender the ego. Therefore, we have to surrender the sense of "I". "I did it, this is mine, this is what I can do." And the ego has itself to surrender. It is not I who has to surrender; it is the ego that has to surrender. Otherwise the ego can pop up any time. Therefore they say that grace is of three types. There is the grace of God, there is the grace of the Guru, but, most importantly, there is the grace of one's own self, the mind.'

Dada looked tired. I decided to stop the interview for the day. He looked at me with his childlike eyes. I whispered that I would need time to digest everything we had discussed. Dada understood I was lying; He chuckled. I bent down to take His blessings and He tried to touch my feet. I held His hand and I put my forehead on His knee. He smiled and asked if Meher liked the prasad. I said, 'Oh yes, Dada is earning solid brownie points with the delicacies.'

Dada called for more prasad and a bag of delicious cream biscuits were handed over to me. I left the Kutiya and paid my respects to Sadhu Vaswani and Sister Shanti at their Samadhi. It was already dark outside. I closed my eyes in the car and worried for Dada's health.

4

I walked into the Mission and saw Naresh virtually galloping towards me at a few nautical miles an hour.

'Ruzbehji, good news! After your other interviews, Dada has decided to bless you with an exclusive interview. Krishnaji is very keen you do the interview.'

I halted and took a deep breath. I looked at Naresh with disbelief and admiration. Disbelief in the manner with which plans were made, changed and altered; and I would be informed as an afterthought. Admiration that he loved Dada so much that the thought of concurring with me about the last minute meeting had not entered his mind. He was sure that there was nobody in the world who would not want to meet Dada.

'Call me by my name . . . no ji. And have you gone nuts? You keep changing the timings. You drive me up the wall as you change plans. I will be exhausted by the time your band of Sadhu and Dada Vaswani followers tell me their fascinating stories in a room where the temperature, due to the lighting and the fact we have to switch off the fans and keep the windows and doors shut, is at least five degrees above normal. What makes you think I am going to have strength for a session with Dada after that?'

'But, Ruzbehji, you know a Guru has decided to meet you and when a Guru decides to meet . . .'

He paused as he heard me snort like an exasperated bull.

'Go away. Let me sit with Sadhu Vaswani. At least He is constant and consistent. Doesn't keep shifting His resting place on a whim. Go away or I will light a cigarette right here.'

Naresh's face went white. With lightning speed he snatched the packet out of my hand and stood back a few feet, relieved. He then grinned at me.

'I have told them to make lots of chai for you, Ruzbehji.'

I snorted again, but this time I sounded like a bull who is about to undergo a colonoscopy. Make note. Devotees are a different species . . . be wary and be calm.

I entered the Samadhi temple. I put my head on the cool white marble slab and exhaled.

'Dear Sadhu Vaswani, Your people are driving me up the wall and . . . What should I say? I am extremely charged up . . . for the want of a better phrase. I am interviewing a few devotees from out of town. Now Your child, Dada, wants to meet me and continue with the book. You know I love Him, but I haven't come prepared with a questionnaire and, mind You, there was no intimation about this till seven minutes ago. So my humble request would be please come through Dada and me, and let the interview go as per Your plan. Love you.'

I then took Sister Shanti's blessings by holding her folded hands and applying a little of the ash left by the burning of the incense sticks.

The next two and a half hours were spent interviewing Dada's followers. The love and devotion that all felt for Sadhu and Dada Vaswani was clear. Dada's humility is all-pervasive. It is childlike, and has a beautiful and subtle khushboo or aroma. I think Krishna Das, one of the most endearing singers I have ever met, described Dada's humility in the most beautiful manner. He said, 'You know, true and genuine humility doesn't attract any attention to itself. This is Dada.'

I had the good fortune of meeting Krishna Das at the Mission. He had come all the way from Mumbai to spend a few moments with Dada, sing for a short while at the Samadhi and then drive back to Mumbai, before flying off to America that same night. When we met and I gave him a copy of *The Fakir*, he looked at the book, then at me and said he had read the book in 2008, and had found it truly interesting. He even told the folks with him that they should read *The Fakir* as he thought it was surreal.

When I asked what Dada meant to him, he said in his deep, soft voice, 'I was afraid you were going to ask me that. Asking me that is like asking a stone to describe the sun. Only a saint knows a saint. The poor stone can only concede it feels warmer around the sun. You know, when I meet Dada, it's so rare to be in the presence of a being who is nothing but love, and the strength, depth and the power of that love is so strong and so beautiful that you can't resist it. You want to be around it all the time. Of course, the truth is to find this love and strength and power of love within oneself. But without tasting it yourself, you don't know where to go and how to begin looking for it.

'When I meet Dada, I know what it means to beloved and to love. You know, according to me, when a saint gives you something, in reality the saint is truly giving you more of yourself. When a saint like Dada blesses you, He reminds you of your own potential and duty to the world outside, and also your potential and duty to yourself.

'When you have doubts, a saint like Dada washes those doubts away. He gives you more strength to be who you are, to share what you have. And the love you receive from Dada is just so incredible that you become convinced that you don't deserve that kind of love, you are not worthy of it. Except in His eyes, of course we are worthy. It's in our own eyes that we have those doubts and His love just washes those doubts away.

'The first time I sang for Him, He sat quietly with His eyes shut and there was another devotee in the room. After I finished singing the other devotee said, "Oh Dada, when Krishna Das sings, it makes me want to dance." Dada slowly opened His eyes, and He looked at the guy and said, "When Krishna Das sings, it brings peace to my mind." This is Dada.'

Around sunset, Dada entered the Kutiya. He first bowed down to Sadhu Vaswani's beautiful portrait. Then to Sister Shanti's statue.

I was tired, but the moment Dada saw me, and His eyes and face lit up, I felt loved and the exhaustion vanished. A singularly beautiful quality about Dada is that He makes everybody feel special. He treats everybody with such warmth that each one feels that Dada has singled them out with love especially reserved for them alone. In our interviews, a number of devotees close to Dada have informed me that Dada truly enjoys the conversations He and I have, and that He looks forward to these meetings. If this is true, then I truly feel blessed.

I walked up to Him and quickly held His hand, while touching His feet for blessings. He smiled and first apologized for the sudden meeting.

'I came to know you were coming here to interview many people. I didn't want to let go of the opportunity of spending time with you.'

It's this quality, this warmth and tenderness that leaves you with no choice but to love this grand, old, childlike, wise, mischievous being, who is a grandfather, friend, mystic, sage and Master all in one.

Gulshan and Krishna helped Dada on to a chair, with cushion placed on it for Him to sit on. I cannot imagine what this feeling of being dependent must do to a giant like Dada.

Destiny, karma, cleansing, transference of pain and suffering to oneself . . . you can call it what you want, but the fact is that very often life is strange.

Once again, Piya set Dada's mic, adjusted His shawl, His feet, made sure flowers were kept in the right frame—while Dada sat like a good child, barely breathing in case He disturbed the shot. Piya looked me up and down. I grinned at her. She would need a truck filled with radiant flowers to make me look civilized. She knew that. I knew that. Santa Claus knew that.

'Dada, please say something,' Piya requested.

Dada looked at me and smiled.

'Today, it doesn't feel we are in a Hollywood set. It's far more informal, though I feel we can make it even more informal.'

'I know, Dada, but the fact is we need three cameras. I have placed one facing both of us. A wide shot of both of us in the frame.

Then one camera zoomed on to You and one on to me. All this requires lighting and manpower. There is no other room here that can accommodate so many people and equipment except the Kutiya.'

'I know. If only I was mobile, we could have sat in the garden . . .'

'Or just walked about . . .'

'Oh yes, walked and talked . . . that would have been . . . nice.'

He smiled at me. He knew that we both would have had a jolly time talking and walking about, and just being. Anyway there is no sense going into the if's and but's here. After a few seconds, we began once again.

'Dada, the last time You were talking about how it is only through surrender one can get off the karmic bandwagon. Surrendering to the Master, a higher force and surrendering one's ego.'

'Yes.'

'How does one surrender? Can it be learnt, worked upon, strengthened? Or is it inherent?'

'"Oh Arjuna, renouncing all rites and writ duties, come unto Me for single refuge! Do not despair, for I shall release you from all bondage to sin and suffering!" Thus spoke Lord Krishna. This is the final, and for me, the most inspiring message of the Gita. It is also the quintessence of spiritual discipline. This is not escapism; this is not us shifting our responsibility on to God. In fact, the Lord has insisted that we should never shirk our duties. Divine grace is obtained through the unconditional surrender to the Lord. The Lord should be made the only goal in our life, the sole object of our worldly endeavours.

'Surrender is not servitude; surrender is not abject slavery. If there is anything we "give up" in surrender to the Guru, it is our lower nature, our almighty ego, our selfish interests and desires, our negative ideas, prejudices, preconceived notions and biases. All of these constitute a terrible burden that we carry and for which there is no place when we undertake our spiritual journey. They constitute an 'excess baggage' which we cannot carry on to a higher plane.

'Surrender has become such a big issue because the mind and the ego feel insecure. If the ego goes, the feeling of insecurity goes. Then you have faith in the Lord—that He is taking care of me, why should I feel insecure? The problem is that most people think that by surrendering one becomes weak. It's actually the other way around.

'Mahatma Gandhi was the most courageous man. They used to bring pistols to Gandhiji and tell him that they wanted to shoot him. Gandhiji would say, "Your bullets will kill me, only if it is the will of the Lord." But, as a child aged seven years, he was afraid of the dark. To the extent that he would not like to move from one room to another at night. One day, his maid servant told him, "Why are you afraid? There is one who is always with you. He is taking care of you and is all powerful." With sheer wonder, little Gandhi asked, "Who is He, what is His name?" The maid servant replied, "His name is Rama, take His name and enter the room, and nothing will happen to you." Gandhiji says that from that night onwards he kept repeating "Rama, Rama, Rama" and has seen miracles happen in his life.

'So it was through surrender that not only did Gandhiji become fearless, but he walked with the faith that no matter what happened, it would happen with the will of God. That is the power of true surrender. You seek nothing but to work for the Lord.'

'And what about surrendering the ego? How does one work on the ego?'

'Many distinguished scientists have said that when man realizes the vastness, the grandeur and the immensity of the universe we live in, and our own insignificance in the general scheme of things, it is impossible for us to feel egotistical and proud. Just think—at one time, the universe existed, time existed, creation existed; but planet earth did not exist, the solar system did not exist, man did not exist. In course of time, a day will come when this earth will cease to exist and the solar system would have disintegrated. Mankind will no longer exist. And yet, time will live on.

'Of what are we so proud? I often ask myself this—is it power, wealth, fame, youth, beauty? Everything in transient. As Great Ones have continually demonstrated, even world conquerors leave this earth empty-handed. Sant Dadu Dayal tells us, "When one lost what was one's own and abandoned all pride of birth, when the glory we are so vain of has dropped away, then, only then, is one face to face with the Creator."

'It was the great Sufi saint Rumi, who said, "O wise man, try to lose thyself and feel humility . . . Egoism and self-will are opposed to the Holy Name; the two cannot dwell in the same house. None can serve the Lord without humility; the self-willed mind is worthless."

'Also remember, there are two egos really—there is the good ego there is the bad ego. It is freedom from the bad ego that we must aspire for. If you have no ego at all, you cannot live. Remember a person who has completely thrown out ego, where he has no ego at all, will not be able to live for more than fourteen days. He is signing his own death warrant. We have to be under the influence of the good ego—the one Hanuman had. Hanuman had an ego; he said, "I am a servant of Sri Rama," That is ego, but it's a good ego. Therefore He is *Chirangeev*, He lives forever. But if you say, "I am a big wealthy man, all other people are not good." Then that is not the right ego, not a good ego.'

'But then, Dada, what is humility? Is the absence of pride, humility, or is it the absence of the "I me myself"?'

'Humility does not consist in hiding our talents and virtues, or in thinking of ourselves as being worse than we really are. It lies in realizing that all that we are, and all that we have, are freely given to us by God. Therefore, as Thomas Kempis tells us, one of the best ways to acquire humility is to fix the following maxim in our mind: "One is worth what he is worth in the eyes of God."

'I remember an incident which occurred when I was a child. I was doing my geography homework one evening when a family friend walked into our house. He always talked loudly. That day he began to boast about the row of buildings he owned in Karachi. "They occupy almost the whole street!" he said with pride. Now I was a child. In my innocence, I went up to him with my atlas and said, "Uncle, will you be kind enough to point out your row of buildings on this map of India?" I still remember the look on his face. Karachi was indicated on the map by just a dot. How on earth could he mark out his row of buildings on that dot?'

Dada lapsed into silence. I remembered what Krishna had told me the other day.

'Everything Dada does is to glorify his Master. His humility is not put on, nor is it for show. It is natural, an intrinsic part of his being. In fact, in His presence, we too feel humbled, for we begin to wonder what is there to be proud of. The examples of His humility are innumerable. Because of His equal vision, He treats a peon and a prince the same way. In the midst of his work, if He happens to see a maid pass by, He will pick up a fruit from the bowl beside Him and give it to her.

'Once a programme had been organized at Akola, for which Dada had been invited. But, on reaching Akola, He found out that a grand reception had been organized in his honour. Without anyone's knowledge, Dada slipped away quietly and went to the venue. Unobtrusively, He went and stood in the welcoming line, and began warmly greeting all the attendees.

'Every conference and meeting Dada was invited to, there was always a chair reserved for Him on the stage. But, invariably, Dada would go and sit with the audience.

'When awards and titles are bestowed on Dada, He refuses to accept them as He believes they are not meant for pilgrims. He is a pilgrim, so awards and titles cannot be presented to Him, nor accepted by Him.'

I looked at Dada and mused that the planet Earth is less than a dot when compared to the sun. If one were to take all of creation, planet Earth could be mistaken as a printing error. I feel ego is not the absence of pride. I think in reality it is the absence of "I". Maybe I am wrong. Or maybe I am completely wrong. Make a note. Stop your incessant rambling! Dada looked at me and began speaking.

'Surely, our ancient rishis were right when they said, "I and mine are the greatest obstacles on the God-ward path."'

'Which word path?' I enquired.

'God-ward . . .'

'Is that a word?'

'Only God would know.'

We began to laugh. Tears filled our eyes. All those present stared at us, finding nothing funny in the proceedings. Dada and I took in a deep breath and adjusted our faces to a more sombre expression.

'Yes, Dada, you were talking about obstacles on the God-ward path?'

'Yes. My Master, Sadhu Vaswani, described the way of love, the way of devotion, as "the little way". To tread "the little way", He said, that one had to be as humble as dust, realize one's nothingness, to "lose" oneself, so that one could find God. *Ahamkara* . . . the ego . . . is an abyss; it is the pit of pride, the pit of darkness, where Satan dwells. These are His beautiful words from the *Nuri Granth*, a compilation of His immortal songs of devotion:

What art thou?
A mere nothing!
Casting aside vestures of vanity,
Live as a lowly one!
In this speck of a universe,
Thou art but a tiny speck
Why, then, art thou puffed up with pride?
Thou art but an insect
Yet is thy head
Inflated with arrogance!

'A very interesting story is related in the Mahabharata. The Kurukshetra war was over and Sri Krishna had left His body. Arjuna was travelling across a strange country when he was attacked by robbers. Now Arjuna was a fearless warrior and had the Pandava forces to victory in the war. Further, his weapons were all divine gifts. He fought his attackers valiantly, but to no avail. He was beaten and robbed. Miserable and despondent, he sought out Sage Veda Vyasa and begged Him to explain the inexplicable. How was it that he, the invincible Arjuna with his incomparable valour and weapons, faced defeat at the hands of a few ruffians?

'Veda Vyasa then explained to Arjuna that neither he, nor his weapons had possessed any intrinsic power. "Your invincibility came from the presence of the Lord who was your Divine Charioteer. It was His power infused your weapons with their might. Now that He is no longer with you, these weapons are useless. And you fight now with your own feeble strength." Arjuna then realized the ancient truth. Man achieves all that he does only through the sanction and grace of the Divine Will!'

For a long time, Dada kept silent. I waited for more than a few minutes for him to speak again.

'As my Gurudev always said, the best way to kill ego and false pride, and bring forth humility is to always seek the lowest place. We usually push ourselves and come to the front. Rejoice in being in the back seat. If someone comes and says, "This is my seat", give the seat to that person. Don't be afraid to do things which are regarded as menial. Sri Ramakrishna Paramahansa used to pick up the betel leaf in which food was served. He even used to eat the leftovers on the betel leaves. He used to say to His ego, "This is what you deserve." Mary Henderson, a great musician, would never use the personal pronoun "I" in her conversations. She said, "Whatever we do, we do as a team. Therefore, the credit which one can claim for oneself is so small." She did not use the word "I".

'If you are wise and intelligent, it is God-given. If your hard work and effort are commendable, it is due to the grace of God. If you are truly conscious of this and acknowledge His grace in all humility . . . why, this humility too is a manifestation of His mercy upon you.

'Let me share something with you. When I took leave of my near and dear ones, and sought refuge at Gurudev Sadhu Vaswani's feet, the very first lesson He taught me was the lesson of humility. "Be humble as ashes and dust!" My Master said to me that His lonely heart was not in search of money, power or knowledge, for the world was full of such people. He sought the company of the humble ones, the simple ones, of those who had reduced themselves to nothing, who had emptied themselves of all self, so that they could be used by the Lord to do with them whatever He wanted. "We are proud of our power and inventions," Gurudev Sadhu Vaswani said, "and yet, what are we? Grass that floats on a stream!"

'Once I asked Him, "What is the mark of him who has attained?" In His hand was a pencil. With it, He drew the figure of a zero . . . 0 . . . and He said, "This is the mark of him who has attained . . . He becomes a zero." And, on a green card, He wrote a brief message for those who had gathered for His darshan that day. The words were so penetrating that they have stayed in my heart to this day. "Blessed be thou, if thou bend until thou break, becoming nothing, a zero! In the yoga (union) of two zeros is the One Infinite!"'

'For one to be able to go beyond the ego, and the ego is a state of mind, the question to ask is what in reality is the mind?'

'The simple answer would be that the mind is an apparatus that thinks. But let us go to the Gita for the answer. The body is strong; the senses (*indriyas*) are powerful. But the mind (*manas*) is above them. Beyond and higher than the mind is the discriminatory faculty (*buddhi*) that helps us know right from wrong and beyond it all is the Atman—the spirit.

'Brother Laurence, a sixteenth century mystic tells us, "Forget the mind, leave behind all rationality. Go to God with devotion and love. God listens to the voice of the heart and not of the mind. The mind is useful for worldly affairs, but God responds to the emotions of the heart."

'Let me quote a translation of one of the songs of Saint Kanakadasa? It is truly beautiful. He says,

Are you a creature of illusion? Or is illusion your creation?
Are you a part of the body? Or is the body a part of you?
Is space within the house? Or the house within space?
Or are both space and the house within the seeing eye?
Is the eye within the mind? Or the mind within the eye?
Or are both the eye and the mind within you?
Does sweetness lie in sugar, or sugar in sweetness?
Or do both sweetness and sugar lie in the tongue?
Is the tongue within the mind? Or the mind within the tongue?
Or are both the tongue and the mind within you?
Does fragrance lie in the flower? Or the flower in fragrance?
Or do both the flower and fragrance lie in the nostrils?
I cannot say, O Lord Adikeshava of Kaginele,
O, Peerless One, are all things within you alone?

'According to me, the mind is that which separates me from you. The focus on individuality is what keeps us separate, losing touch with the unity of all being.'

'Dada, one can't do much about individuality. The issue is about surrender and moving beyond ego. But one needs a still mind to move down that path and, to keep the mind still, wouldn't one need to be in a state of gratitude and positive acceptance? So how important is gratitude on one's path of spirituality?'

'Gratitude is number one; so much so that sixteenth century mystic Meister Eckhart said, that "If only you offered this one prayer in all your life it was enough. That prayer is, Thank you, God! Thank you, God! Thank you, God!" He said that for everything, we must thank God.'

'True, Dada. Thus, gratitude and positive acceptance are entwined. Gratitude can come about when one lives a life of calm, positive and peaceful acceptance. But to live a life of peaceful acceptance, one needs to be in a state of gratitude always.'

'Two sides of the same coin. Alexander Whyte, the Scottish minister, was known for his uplifting prayers. Even in the worst of circumstances, he found something to be grateful for. One Sunday morning, the weather was so gloomy that one member of the church thought that on that day Whyte would have nothing to thank God for. It was such a wretched day. Much to his surprise, Whyte began his sermon by saying, "We thank thee God that it is not always like this!"'

I couldn't help but laugh out loud and Dada joined in.

'But can you teach somebody positive acceptance of one's lot or to live in a state of gratitude, as only then would peace enter the individual's very being? Can being in a state of gratitude be taught?'

'Ruzbeh, may I reveal a mantra, which is sure to bring peace to whoever chants this prayer? It is a prayer which a saint, a holy man of God, used to offer again and again. Inscribe it in the tablet of your heart. Repeat it again and again, remember it day and night, for it is really simple—Yes Father, yes Father . . . Yes and always yes! Yes Father, yes Father . . . Yes and always yes!

'There are people who are upset with me because I advocate the philosophy of acceptance. They tell me that this will make people lazy and lethargic; they will give up all their drive and ambition, and will simply sink into passive resignation. I beg to differ! People who believe in the supremacy of the Almighty, people who learn to accept His Divine Will, never ever give in to lethargy and pessimism.

'They do as the Lord bids them to do. In fact, they put in their best efforts; they do not slacken, they do their best to achieve what they want. But if they do not achieve the desired results, they do not give in to despair and frustration; they do not give in to disappointment. Acceptance in the spirit of gratitude unlocks the fullness in our lives. It can turn despair into faith, strife into harmony, chaos into order and confusion into clear understanding. It restores peace in our hearts and helps us to look forward to tomorrow with the faith that God is always with us!

'It is not enough to just speak of gratitude or enact deeds of gratitude—we must live gratitude by practicing acceptance of God's will in all conditions, in all incidents and accidents of life. Wisdom consists in accepting God's will, not with despair or resignation, but in peace and faith, knowing that our journey through life has been perfectly planned by Infinite love and Infinite wisdom. There can be no mistake in God's plan for us!

'To seek refuge is to trust the Lord fully, completely and entirely. It is to know that He is the one light we need in the darkest hours of our life. He is the all-loving One whose ears are ever attentive to the prayers of His wayward children. He is the all-knowing. So it is this—he who has taken refuge in the Lord is ever at peace. "Not my will, but *thy* will be done."'

Krishna, while discussing Dada's fall which affected the right side of His body and then the subsequent stroke which affected the left side of His body, divulged that all Dada lovers were praying day and night that He be healed. That He get back on His physical feet. That He be rid of His suffering. When Dada came to know of this, He said, 'If I truly believe in God and the wisdom of His actions, I must accept whatever comes from Him, without any complaint. If I tell Him to remove my pain or heal me, then it shows that I don't trust His judgment, and hence I am suggesting to Him, through my prayers, what He should do. Always trust that whatever He does is for the best. Even my so-called suffering and pain is for the best, even though at this moment it may not appear so.'

This, I guess, is Dada's state of acceptance.

'Were You always the one who willingly accepted the will of God?'

'Oh, God! No. I was one of the most infuriating "questioners". I can say from my experience that I learnt to accept. I was not an accepter; I used to resist, but slowly, I have learnt to accept. But isn't it strange that acceptance is a lesson that life tries to teaches us since the very first day we are born. Now once I am born, maybe I am too short or I am tall, or I am one-eyed. I have to accept it. I cannot take your body and give you my body. So we are taught this lesson of acceptance right from the very beginning. But some of us take time to learn it.'

'How did you learn it?'

'The easiest way is by interacting with the right kind of people. We learn fastest through real-life examples. Books and stories inspire us, but real-life examples open a whole new window for learning and accepting. I learnt, of course, by associating with people of acceptance. The first holy man I came in contact with was a man of acceptance. At every step, in every round of life, come what may, he accepted what was given to him. I was with him when one of his disciples came running to him. We used to call him Baba. This was in Sind. Then Meher Baba was not known to us. Except we knew that there was a holy man who had not spoken for years together. His disciple came and told him, "Baba! Baba! Your son has been caught stealing. The police have taken him to the chowki and the FIR is going to be filed. And I have some influence over the police; if you will permit me, I will see that he is let off." And Baba said, "Whose son? Whose son?" The man said, "Baba, your son." Baba said, "Let him go to jail, perhaps in jail he will understand; he will learn something, so that he comes out of jail a transformed man. Why should you or I be a hindrance in his transformation?" And it actually happened. The son was sentenced to six months of imprisonment and when he came out, he was a changed person. I came in contact with such people when I was very young.'

'But, Dada, having such people around you may have been part of your karmic blueprint. How does a normal human being, whose *sangat* or association may not have the opportunity of meeting Masters or wise people, inculcate the wisdom of gratitude and positive acceptance?'

'Ruzbeh, then it becomes a very difficult lesson to learn. It is not easy because there are so many things that happen to us, and it appears as though injustice is being done to us. But we have to accept it, because this is going over a record of many births. A very good man gets punished, and I am close to him, so I question justice. I question God's Providence. It is difficult to accept a good man or woman suffering for no palpable cause.'

'Dada, we are all chained to the laws of cause and effect, but then even a human being's inherent nature is decided by one's action or inaction in the past life. Then one's state of mind too is conditioned due to one's karma. That would mean whether a human being is going to be surrounded by noble chaps or be in a state of gratitude is also karmic. Thus, do You think the state of awareness is also karmic?'

'I have not thought about it, but it should be. Otherwise, whose fault is it? The workings of creation cannot be flawed. It thus has to be a past life issue for the individual not to be blessed with the state of awareness and gratitude, which will allow him or her to live in a state of surrender.'

'Okay, let us assume a person truly wants to quieten the mind to reach that state of surrender? How does one do it?'

'Significant are the words of the Upanishads, "The mind alone is the cause of man's bondage; the mind is also an instrument of man's liberation." Hence, the need for a Guru, because the mind will not surrender itself to anyone except the Guru. The mind may tell you that it is surrendering, but it will never, never surrender. I remember in my early days, must have easily been eighty years ago, I had a dream. I could not understand it. When I awoke up, I remembered it clearly, but I still could not make sense of it. Then I went to the Master and placed my dream before him. In the dream,

I saw that there was a lizard-like creature and though I believe in non-violence and in compassion to all of creation, I wanted to kill this creature. And I picked up my shoe and beat it. It appeared as though it had died, but after a few minutes it came to life again. This went on a number of times. I thought that it was dead, but it came alive immediately thereafter. What was this about? Then My Master explained it to me. He said the lizard-like creature is the mind. The mind appears to have died, but you cannot kill the mind. The mind has to be surrendered. And that surrender is to be taken by the mind itself, it's only when the mind surrenders, that the true surrender takes place.

'In the Bhagavadgita, Arjuna asks of Sri Krishna, "O Lord, thou hast said that the wandering of the mind is the cause of all human sorrow. Pray, tell me then, how can we stop the mind from wandering?" Lord Krishna tells him, "It is difficult, but not impossible to control the mind."'

'What do you think, Dada? Is it possible for a common person, caught up with the family and the world, to be able to control the mind?'

'Indeed it is possible for each one of us to conquer the mind, but for this, two things are mandatory: *abhyasa* (discipline) and *vairagya* (true detachment). It is only with a Guru's grace that we can attain these two qualities. As we cultivate reverence for the Guru, the impulse arises within us to follow the path of self-discipline. Many people make this effort, but only those blessed with the Guru's grace succeed in their efforts. Such blessed souls follow the path of self-discipline successfully and gradually attain the state of true detachment. It then becomes possible for them to control the mind and inner peace soon follows. He who is blessed with inner peace is happy in every state, every condition of life.'

'Dada, if there was self-discipline and detachment then there would be no need to quieten the mind. There would be no need for the mind to be in a state of noise. But these are virtually alien concepts for common folk like me.'

'The mind, as they say, is a monkey; its power must be curtailed and kept under control. Otherwise, it can lead us to moral ruin. Even *tapasvis* and *yogis*, after years of penance and *sadhana*, fall prey to its desires. As Guru Nanak Dev has said, "The mind runs in ten different directions." The mind roams far and wide. The mind is like a galloping horse, wild and volatile. The mind needs to be integrated. The integration of the mind will create a new spiritual energy, which will take you on the right path.'

'So the mind is nothing but one's individuality?'

'One's individuality . . . that itself is the expression of the mind. The mind refuses to accept that it is not the supreme power in us. The mind insists on itself and its convictions. Why then do so many of us get caught in the chains of human bondage? Why do we allow ourselves to get entangled in the web of *maya*? Why do we wallow in misery and suffering, unmindful of the fact that we are of the divine essence? I would say that it is due to the limitations of the human mind that we are unable to grasp and retain our essential identity as spirits.

'How much greater, how significant you will feel when you consider yourself part of the universal spirit that sustains and moves through the earth, sky, water, air and fire? What will be your feeling when you realize that you are deathless—and that you belong to the Infinite? This, the rational mind cannot grasp when it reigns supreme.

'In the wise words of the Chinese sage, Lao Tsu, "It is only when I let go of what I am, that I can become what I might be."'

'And when one surrenders to the Master, God, Goddess, one has surrendered to one's individuality too?'

'Yes. That is perhaps the secret of spiritual life.'

'Complete surrender. But then I guess You will say that achieving complete surrender can only take place by the Master's grace?'

'The final leap can only take place with the Master's grace, but there are miles and miles to walk. And each one of us has to tread the path. To reach home, that is the grace of the Master. But one can reach home only when one begins the journey, one keeps walking the path and comes somewhere close to one's home. Then, leave all to the Master. Let me give you an example. I was very fond of arguing because, perhaps, I was a good student or they said I was a good student—I had four double promotions. I completed my graduation at the age of seventeen. So I thought that I held the totality of knowledge in the palm of my hand. I used to argue a lot. I used to argue with my Master in this very room that we are sitting in today. The Master gave me a long rope. Sadhu Vaswani had worked as the principal of various colleges. People from far and wide would come to hear His lectures. One of His students rose to become the DPI (director of public instructions) in some state. In Bihar, I think. I could be wrong. Anyway, he happened to visit Poona and he called upon Sadhu Vaswani. But Sadhu Vaswani spent much of His time with Himself in silence. So I told the gentleman to wait and we started talking to each other. Some argument began and I would not let it go. And he was also the DPI. After about an hour, Sadhu Vaswani opened His door, and I went and told him that so and so has come to meet you. He called him in. The very first thing that this man said to Sadhu Vaswani was, "Who is this boy whom you have kept with yourself? He keeps on arguing over nothing." My Master called me and put His hand of blessing on my head, and told me "You have argued many years, have you received anything?" That is all He asked of me. And from that day, till today, till now, like magic, I have stopped arguing. Now if anybody tells me anything I say "yes".'

'Dada, these miracles and the path and the Guru, and this beautiful palate of spiritual colours may not be the destiny of one and all.'

'It is not easy. The path of surrender is very, very, very difficult. But it becomes easy if the Master wants it to happen. Then it becomes possible, otherwise it is impossible.'

'But then why would the Master shower his grace only on some and not on the others?'

'Our scriptures distinguish four aspects of divine grace: Ishwara Kripa, Guru Kripa, Shastra Kripa and Atman Kripa.'

Even grace is complicated, I realized. In ancient times they had an explanation for every single thing. Make a note. Shut up.

'Ishwara Kripa is divine grace or assistance that comes to our aid when all else fails us. Consider the plight of Draupadi, as she was about to be disgraced, dishonoured and de-robed by the Kauravas. King Dhritarashtra did nothing to stop the dastardly deed of his sons; the kuru elders, Bhishma, Drona and Kripa were powerless in the face of such evil. As for her five husbands, they bowed their heads in utter humiliation and shame. All earthly sources of help failed Draupadi utterly, in her hour of desperate, piteous need. However, Draupadi knew that there was One whose grace is unfailing. One whose support is perennial. Therefore, she called upon Sri Krishna. He came to her aid promptly. We have all benefited from Ishwara Kripa in our lives, though circumstances might not have been so dramatic. Think of such occasions—for instance, when you narrowly escaped a fall or a motor accident, when you miss a train or a flight and learn later that it met with a major accident. It is God's grace that has saved you, though we acknowledge this only on rare occasions and during momentous events.

'Guru Kripa or the grace of the Guru, is the amazing protection that the Guru offers to His disciples. When we surrender ourselves to His will utterly and completely, the Guru's guidance is made available to us at every step of the way.

'Shastra Kripa, the grace of the scriptures is not obtained merely by reading the words or the pages of sacred texts. It is when you approach the scriptures with the right frame of mind, with the right attitude, when you are eager to assimilate Their truth, that Their essential meaning is revealed to you. When you internalize the truth of the texts you read—and not merely quote or recite from Them—you have reached a crucial stage in your spiritual development.

'Atman Kripa or Swa Kripa is the grace of your own soul. It enables you to take a deep interest in spiritual matters. You are not distracted by materialistic goals; worldly affairs do not take you away from the chosen path to God. You are not tempted by the passing shadows of life. The grace of the soul enables you to pursue the pilgrim path with patience and perseverance.

'We have to be receptive to grace. The grace of God is all abounding; it is everywhere. All we have to do is to be receptive to it. Take the example of a room which has doors and windows, but all of them are shut. Even when the sun shines bright, the room remains in darkness. On the other hand, the room which keeps its doors and windows open is flooded with sunshine. We too should keep the windows of our hearts and souls open, and allow the sunshine of grace to flow in.'

'Often the Master can make the journey exceedingly difficult for a while,' I added my two bit.

'Oh yes. Because the Masters, they do it on their own. They sometimes behave in such a way that doubt creeps into you. Those are the periods when the disciple is tested. They don't need to but they will do it.'

'Have you been put through such tests by Sadhu Vaswani?'

'More than once, yes. Once I actually ran away from the Master. I spent the whole night outside in the park, lying down on a bench. But then I found that I could not stay away from Him. And very often, profound lessons can be taught in the simplest ways. In the journey of life, always be a disciple, always be a seeker—ready to learn from all those who have been sent to teach you.

'When I was young, I studied in a Sindhi-medium school. Once, during that time, I had to travel from Karachi to Hyderabad. It was arranged that I should travel in the company of one of the schoolmasters. When the train began pulling out of the station, the master began talking to me and kept me entertained. We stopped at station, where the halt was a very long one, making it very boring. Then that the master asked me, "What is the purpose of life?" In the midst of that long and tiring halt, the master explained to me that attaining God is life's purpose and goal.

'The master had brought with him puris and potato *bhaji*. We fell upon it with gusto. I don't think I have ever eaten such delicious puris since then. He continued, "If one does not attain God, then no matter what good deeds we do—open institutions, construct rest houses, dig wells, perform pujas, fast, etc.—is all in vain. Till then, we are at the stage of an animal in our lives."

'We are born first from our mother's womb. We are born again through the Guru. Till we don't attain God, we are trapped in the lower self, being smashed and ground in this world. We have to bear a lot due to the law of karma. What you sow, so shall you reap. If something bitter is sown, one cannot expect to reap a sweet mango from it! And only one's Guru can save us from this cycle of birth and death.'

'What if you don't have the proximity of your master? Does it make attaining God or being saved from the cycle of birth and death impossible?'

'It doesn't, but you are put in a situation in which you feel that you cannot do without the proximity of the master. Man is made an independent creature. He should be able to do everything on his own. Buddha found the way Himself.'

'That is one in a billion, but for the normal people . . .'

'But it is open to all. I feel everything is possible. You can, like Buddha, find your own salvation. It is a difficult path, but not an impossible one. But a Master's presence makes your life so much simpler and can protect you from innumerable pitfalls.

'But in this era, which is called the Kali Yuga (Kalyug), if I say I have a Master and He truly is my Master, I must not hide anything from Him. This is very, very necessary. But more often than not, I will hide things from my Master. Very few disciples will bare their very souls to the Master. Often, the disciple makes it difficult for himself. It does not affect the Master.

'Let me repeat, the inextinguishable light dwells within each one of us, but we cannot see it, for it is hidden behind veils of our ignorance, veils of our mind and matter. The great wall of the ego stands between us and the Param Atman, and we cannot see the light. It is the Guru who can destroy this great wall of the ego and lead us from darkness to light.

'The "third eye", the inner eye of the spirit remains closed for most of us, its vision impaired by our bad karma. The cataract of the ego, the veils of arrogance and pride, have all covered this inner eye completely. The Guru is the "eye specialist" who can restore our inner vision.'

'Dada, but these Gurus You talk about are virtually non-existent in today's time and age.'

'Ruzbeh, when the disciple is ready the Guru will come. That is a certainty. Anyway, the Guru reaches out to all of us and with

His grace, annihilates the ego; He tears away the veils which shield us from self-realization. He reveals our true identity to us—*Tat Twamasi*! The Guru's gift of grace has devolved from God Himself, for God knows that the world is in dire need of Grace. His presence is of course universal—He gives us the Guru, for our individual benefit, for our personal liberation.'

Dada kept quiet for a long time. From whatever little I knew of life and mankind, I was quite certain that most of mankind was not queuing up for personal liberation. Standing in line for money, power, sex—oh yes, the list doesn't end. But personal liberation . . . I don't think so. No wonder God has virtually stopped giving us true Gurus.

'This is why our ancient scriptures enjoin us to venerate the Guru as God—Gurur Brahma, Guru Vishnu, Guru Devo Maheshwara . . . Guru is Lord Brahma, Lord Vishnu, Lord Shiv . . . in fact, the Guru is beyond Them.'

'Once, a very old man came to see me. He could hardly walk. He said to me, "I have come to seek your blessings. I am going to Haridwar, to see the Laxman Jhoola." I was concerned for him; I asked him why he was so intent on taking up such an arduous journey at his advanced age. He replied, "It is my intense desire to see the Laxman Jhoola. It is my dearest wish to have a dip in the sacred Ganga at the point where Laxman crossed the holy river. I believe I will have a vision of God when I behold that sacred spot."

'Now, in vain, I told him of the radiance within; that Ram, Sita and Laxman were seated within him. Instead of taking an arduous journey to Haridwar it would be better if he sat at home and undertook the sadhana to get a glimpse of light within, for then he would not only have Their darshan, but he could be with Ram, Sita and Laxman, who were all seated on the jhoola of his heart. But to no avail.'

Dada went silent for a long while.

'"Ye are gods," Jesus said to the Jews. "Your substance is that of God Himself," said a Sufi teacher. "Whoso knows himself, has light," said Lao Tse, the Chinese seer.

'"I too am a disciple like any one of you," the great Sufi Nizamuddin Auliya, often said. He used to add, "It is a privilege of a disciple's to decide who will be his Guru. It is not the privilege of the Guru to decide who will be his disciple.'"

'Dada, but let us say one does not have a Master. Then what would you advise?'

'Sometimes your Guru can teach you through a photograph, a word, a hoarding. Let me narrate to you a childhood experience. In our house, my father had hung pictures of sages and saints on the walls. There were no worldly pictures. I could not reach any of them, except for one. There was a picture of Sri Dayaram, the smallest of all, which was hung so low that even my small hands could reach it. In our house there was a cot, which used to be kept under the bed during the day. I had told my family that I wished to sleep on my own at night. They said that I could sleep on the cot. I did not mind; I liked being on my own, even if it meant sleeping on the cot. Being on one's own makes you feel like royalty. When all my family members would go out of the house, I would go under the bed and lie down on the cot. I would take this picture down and take it with me. No one would even know or was aware of this.

'I talked to this picture several times. Hence, I feel that this rishi is the closest to me. As I lay on the cot, He taught me three things. Simplicity: His life shone with simplicity. His photograph bore witness to that. Silence: Lord Krishna's face must have been looked upon by Him innumerable times. He passed His life in silence. He was totally engrossed in it. He would meet His son just once a year. His son would sit in a train, and come and meet Him. Humility: He was extremely humble. Considering His status and stature, which was so elevated, He still had no arrogance in Him. This rishi was highly educated and intelligent. But the tremendous mercy poured on Him converted Him to one who was poor and humble. No other work was important any more. His three teachings, which I obtained as I lay the cot, have been seared into my mind. Thus, though I never had the good fortune to meet this Guru, He, via His photograph, conveyed to me the most valuable lessons of life. Thus, be open and the Guru will guide you.'

The problem is that there are so many thoughts going on in one's head that how would one be able to ascertain whether the

Guru was guiding him or if he was merrily deluding himself by being notoriously self-destructive, all in the name of the Guru within.

'Let me tell you another story and from that if an individual follows a few precepts of life, then maybe, just maybe, an individual can chart his or her own spiritual course with the help of the eternal Guru within.

'I was blessed to meet a sage whom I called Baba. Shanti used to prepare prasad and Baba loved mithai or anything sweet. He also loved malai, fresh cream and curds. There was a time when Baba lived in solitude, many miles away, in a forest. It was during summer time, when it was boiling hot, and He would tell me, "Jashan, bring some curds for me." He added, "As you bring this yogurt to me, go on repeating the Lord's Name at every step. If you forget the name at one step, then go back one step. Repeat the Name of the Lord with every step; not a single step should be taken without it. If you do not do so, I will not eat the curd."

'Sometimes, at some of the steps, I would forget the Name and I would retrace those steps, in spite of the scorching heat. Then, once more, I would take the Name and move forward with the encouraging thought that now Baba would eat the curds. Baba emphasised on *naamjapa*.

'In those days, I lived in Karachi. I came to beloved Sadhu Vaswani afterwards. Baba would say to me, "My dear, prepare, get ready and then go to Dada (Sadhu Vaswani)."

'On a very dark night, Baba said, "Come to me tonight." In those days Baba lived near Artillery Maidan. The area was deserted and it was frightening to go out there at night. He told me to come to Him at 11.00 p.m. It required courage to cross that dark and lonely maidan. Baba was making me brave.

'It was a dark night and there were mounds of dirt on the road. I asked Baba, "As the night is very dark and the area is deserted, may I bring a torch with me?" Baba replied, "Son, light the torch of the naam and come." Though I was petrified, I went in the dark, repeating the name of the Lord.

'Baba greeted me with a lot of love. Making me stand before Him, He said, "My dear, today I am teaching you a lesson, beyond which no other lesson is required. Till now, I have taught you a lot. But today is the crux of all my teachings." I could not see Baba's face, so I focused on His voice. Baba's way of passing on His teachings was strange. It was like being pierced by an arrow. He said these words so forcefully that they reverberated within me.

'Baba said, "Dear Jashan, primarily remember, what is the goal of life? What is the use if you read scriptures and do not become one with God? The wealth of the world is nothing if there is no union with God. If you don't have God, you have nothing. Till you are not one with Him, you are nothing." These words were said with such conviction that they got buried deep within me. Baba's face could not be seen, but nature helped. There was a flash of lightning and in that moment I could see Baba clearly. His eyes were shining like bright lights.

'Baba said, "The first thing, the goal of life, is to attain God." I asked, "Baba, tell me, how do we attain God?" Baba explained, "When someone has the desire to earn money, then he will work day and night for that money. He may even cheat. He will not even hesitate to lie. Day and night, all his effort will go towards earning money. When your desire is to become one with God then you will do all to become one with God. There are two roads to become one with God.

'"One is to go within. This body is the nine-gated city within which is His dwelling. But we have forgotten Him. There are different ways of becoming one with that Beloved. There is the way of dhyaan or meditation. When God's grace falls on you, you become the receiver of that grace and that enables you to grow. God is present within you, outside of you, in everything, in every dwelling, in every creation of Nature. You will get His fragrance in everything. He is present everywhere. You have to become one with Him.

'"The second road to become one with Him can be external. For that, you have to bestow love on each and every one. You have to regard every aspect of nature with love. But, if you want to meet God within, then go within and attain His love."

'One day I was sitting beside Baba. He looked at me with love and what did He say? He said, "Son, always look to God's door for mercy.

Never be filled with pride or arrogance. Day and night, call out for His love and mercy. Call for mercy, beg for grace. Only that can wash away your unpleasant karma. It will cleanse you. God will forgive you when you forgive others. Not only must you forgive, but you must also forget all the mistakes and release the love in your heart. Then, all your mistakes will be forgiven by Him." Christians always pray for this: "Forgive us our trespasses, as we forgive those who trespass against us." Dear Baba continued, "Son, do not see the faults of others. Give everyone your love." Beloved Baba's blessings on me were abundant. I remember Him so often.'

Dada lapsed into silence again. I guess what He was trying to tell me so it could enter my thick head was a simple truth of life. The Gurus have told us what to do on the path of spirituality and on the path, homeward bound. Take the Name. Be humble. Be truthful. Be filled with love and compassion. Seek the Lord's mercy. Forgive and forget. Do not judge. Do not slander. Do not covet what does not belong to you. Do not resort to violence and hate and anger. If an individual does not have a physical Guru, the internal and eternal Guru, residing within each one of us, teaches us. The real issue is even if we have a Guru, do we surrender and obey, and do as told without getting the ego involved, without the mental mathematics? I doubt it. I made a note to myself to stop giving my two paisa gyaan and focus on Dada.

'Dada, in the Kalyug, let us assume one finds a Master. What is the first thing needed on the path of spirituality?'

'My concern is that you can get hundreds of thousands of Masters, but where do you get a true disciple. Sadhu Vaswani tells us, "He who loses himself in his teacher is the true disciple. He who follows his own will and his own desires is not a true disciple. He who has doubts in his heart and is dominated by personal ambition, may be intellectually strong; he who argues endlessly and emphasizes the rightness of his own point of view, may be an able debater, but a disciple he cannot be, for he is a worshipper of himself."

'Before I came to Sadhu Vaswani, I had met a holy man. He poured His grace on me in abundance. "Dear one," He would repeatedly say to me. "If you wish to walk the spiritual path, your only sadhana should be obedience. But remember, obedience has to be total and unconditional." Now being strongheaded, I used to find it very difficult to obey. I had my own mind and ideas. One day, I went to visit this holy man, bowing down, I sat before Him. He lovingly blessed me. In my conversation with Him, I confessed that I wished to follow the path of obedience.

'Though I was prepared to follow the path of obedience, I was not ready for the ensuing hardships. But something in me made me pledge to walk this path. The sage gave me a meaningful smile.

'One day, He called me and asked me to go to visit a certain person and blurt out the following words to his face. On hearing the words, I felt as if a mountain had collapsed on me. I pleaded with Him, "I will not be able to talk rudely to this person. I have so much respect for him. How I can be discourteous to him?"

'My mind was in turmoil. But since I had given him the pledge of obedience, with trembling legs I began to walk to the person I had to meet. My feet refused to budge. I would take one step forward and then two backwards. Finally, I reached that person's house and knocked on the door with great trepidation. The door was opened by someone else. I enquired if the particular person was in. I was told that he had gone to Shikarpur the previous day. I heaved a sigh of relief. Within me, I felt grateful to God for saving me from an embarrassing situation.

'I went back to the sage and informed Him that the person was not there. I wanted to find out if there was any need for me to visit him after he returned from Shikarpur. Very casually, He said, "There is no need to go again." I thanked God profusely for having saved me from this dilemma. Initially, the thought of going had sent shivers down my spine and I was pondering on how I would say such harsh words to the person's face. But it was only a test the sage wanted me to pass.

'On another occasion, the dervish bade me, "Jashan, today go to the printing press. There is a certain book which is being printed. Tell them not to print the book in the way they have planned to. Instead, they should print it the other way." Again I was perplexed. I wondered how it concerned me. Why did I have to interfere in the working of a printing press? But I did not show any dissent. I had to obey the sage.

'With an uncertain mind, I went to the printing press. Within me was a voice chiding me, "You are quite stupid to have agreed to this errand. Why should you intrude in the affairs of others?" Despite these negative thoughts, I went to the press. On reaching there I enquired who the person in charge was. I was directed to the cabin of the boss. I struck up a conversation with him. I said, "I have heard that you are printing such a book?" With a grin, he shook his head and said, "It has already been printed, as well as distributed. There are only a few copies left. I am very pleased with the way the book has been received by the public."

'Phew! I was so relieved. God had once again come to my rescue. I bade the man good-bye and returned to the sage. I narrated the whole incident to Him. He made me sit beside Him and affectionately said, "Son, I was aware of it!" It seems like He just wanted my ego to be destroyed. Whenever there was anything that I did not want to do, He would make me do it in order to subdue my ego.

'On yet another occasion He asked me to go to a mosque in a nearby village. "I would like you to go right now and put some oil in the lamp there," He commanded. "There is a train which will take you there."

'It was almost midnight and my mind started churning up arguments to dissuade me from taking this nocturnal journey. But I paid no need to the mischief in my mind. I proceeded to fulfil the task entrusted to me. I arrived at the station at night. It was eerie and isolated. When I reached the platform I was informed that the train would not depart now as there was some problem on the line. Once again, I realized that He was testing me. Preparing me.'

Dada lapsed into silence. I have heard of innumerable stories of Gurus testing their disciples with outrageous demands, which leave the strong-hearted light in the head and weak in the knees. Nobody, just nobody, can drive you up the wall like a Guru can.

'If you want to walk the spiritual path, you must find a Guru and then surrender to him implicitly. We are told that once Guru Nanak asked His devotee to come to Him immediately. The devotee, at that time, was getting married; the wedding ceremony was being performed. The minute he heard that the Guru was calling him, he left the ceremony and the bride, and went to the Guru. What this devotee did was very difficult and courageous. All his family members were upset with him. Most of us would have said, "How can I walk out of my wedding ceremony? My father will be furious. My mother will be heartbroken." But this devotee ignored such worldly considerations and went to his Guru. The spiritual path is long and endless. The only shortcut is surrender.'

'Dada, apart from complete faith and surrender, Sufis and yogis keep insisting that one should eat less, sleep less and talk less. Why?'

'That is a way to reach God. When Sadhu Vaswani was asked which way do You follow to reach God? The Gita speaks of Karma Yoga, Bhakti Yoga, Gyana Yoga and Raja Yoga, and other yogas. There are so many other paths, what is the path that You follow? He said, "My yoga, the path that I follow is Alpa Marga." And they asked Him, "What is Alpa Marga, we have not heard of it?" He said, "Alpa means small. My way is the little way." What are the sadhnas on this path? Alpa Bolan, Alpa Ahar, Alpa Nidra—these are the three sadhnas. Alpa Bolan means speak less. Alpa Ahar is eat less and alpa Nidra means sleep less.'

'Does this make a difference if one is on the path?'

'Oh yes, Ruzbeh. Yes, it does. If you are sincere and you follow this path, you find it an easy path. I have tried to follow the Karma Yoga path, but I find it is very difficult. Because the mind is made such that without your knowing it, somehow or the other, at some point in time or the other, the thought comes up . . . "What a good deed I have done by this thought, action, word, karma." You did not do it, it was done through you.

'Bhakti Yoga is allied to Alpa Yoga, the two go together. Gyana Yoga is very difficult. All the time to be aware that I am not the body, that I am the energy within, dwelling in the body. That the body is only a cover, it is only a mask that I have worn, it is the most difficult thing. I have tried that but I found that this Alpa Yoga is the easy way.'

'You have spoken a lot about Sahaj Yoga . . .'

'Alpa Yoga, the small way, is Sahaj Yoga.'

'What is Sahaj Yoga?'

'Sahaj Yoga, Alpa Yoga—they are all same. Sahaj Yoga is the yoga of surrender; you surrender yourself to the Master. My Master is there, I leave it all to the Master. And every Master teaches that we must speak little. Our difficulty is that we speak too much. There is a saying which is ascribed to Jesus, though it is not given in the Gospel. There are so many accounts of Jesus that are not given in the Gospel. And according to one such account, Jesus says to His disciples, "A time will come when you will be asked to render account for every idle word that you have spoken." Every idle word! We speak so many words, we say it was a joke. I have no right to make a joke if I am on the path.'

I nearly fell off my chair. I have mastered the art of putting my foot into my mouth or somebody else's mouth. If Lord Jesus is going to ask me to render an account of every idle word spoken by me . . . Oh boy, He better pack well It's going to be a long Lent.

I think Dada realized that I was tired. He smiled and began to remove the mic. After a while, I took His blessings. He, as usual, tried to touch my feet. I beat Him to it and held His hand. In seconds, He held my hand and caressed it. He asked me if I had been given tea and snacks. I told Him I was being well taken care of. He smiled. He called for prasad. He handed me a box of cake.

I told Him I would see Him soon. He smiled, looked at me for a few seconds and then nodded. When leaving, I saw Him busy reading a note. He didn't wear reading glasses. The camera team consisting of Jyotish and Umakant were present in the room, along with Krishna and Piya. Dada was to record something more. He was engrossed in His work. He was a ninety-seven-year-old rock star!

I went to the Samadhi temple and paid my respects to both Sadhu Vaswani and Sister Shanti. I thanked Them.

I then walked to the car. I got a call from a friend and I told him no more idle chatter. He asked me if I had fasted while doing the interviews. I replied in the affirmative. Ah, he said, the lack of oxygen to the brain makes one think in this fashion.

I sighed. Made a mental note to try not to have only wise-assed friends.

5

Two days later, I walked into the Mission along with my friend, Samir Maniar. I wasn't too well, and he insisted on driving me to the Mission and bringing me back home. When you interact with devotees, it is clear that their entire existence depends on the Guru and the moment I saw Naresh pacing up and down, I knew there was likely to be a change in plans. I sighed and introduced Naresh to Samir.

'Ruzbehji, before Dada's interview, would you want to interview a family from America?'

'No.'

'They will go away tomorrow.'

'I am heartbroken, but I will survive their absence.'

'They will go away to America. Even Krishnaji is very keen you interview them.'

'Okay, tell them to pack properly and leave for the airport twelve hours before their departure. And as terrorists are wreaking havoc, tell them to carry knives and chilli powder with them, in their main luggage and in their handbags. Go away now.'

'Ruzbehji they are very good . . .'

'Naresh, when we leave our body, we will have to sit across Lord Jesus and talk about every bit of idle chatter we have participated in. I will not let you exasperate Jesus the Christ. Silence is the key. Humility is the electric guitar. Go perform a quiet gig someplace else.'

But this is a normal occurrence when one works with devotees and disciples. It is not just with Dada's followers. Go anywhere. Their entire life revolves round the Master. They function on another time zone. The time zone being that of the Master. Nothing else matters. I have seen it while interviewing the inner circle. Be it Krishna, Piya, Gulshan, Priya . . . their entire life centred on Dada. Their schedule, their priority, even their needs revolved around their Master. Often the Master would be willing to accommodate them and be flexible, but for the inner circle, it was not only them but the entire world that had to function according to the timings of the Master. I found that devotion beautiful, but very infuriating as an author.

I entered the Samadhi temple and prayed to Sadhu Vaswani for peace and calmness. I took Sister Shanti's blessings too. I had made up my mind. No more unplanned interviews. Hard love. One needed to instil discipline and at the heart of every successful venture is immaculate planning.

Ten minutes later, I found myself in front of the family talking about their experiences with Dada. An hour later, Dada entered the room. Krishna was behind the wheelchair. She looked worried. Piya looked me up and down. She nodded in appreciation. I had sort of trimmed my beard, and thus I looked less like an anthropoid ape and more like a disgruntled chimpanzee.

Dada, after His prayers, turned around with His palms folded. He saw me and smiled. His smile always reached His eyes. I introduced Samir to Dada. Dada couldn't touch Samir's feet as he had prostrated himself on the ground. I chuckled.

'Today, I felt the presence of Sadhu Vaswani while being wheeled in here. It was as though He is with us. It was a warm presence. As though He was blessing us.'

'Humbled, Dada. I need all the blessings.'

'So do I, so do I,' Dada sighed. He looked tired. He wasn't well. Naresh had told me that Dada wasn't keeping too well, but He had insisted on meeting me and doing the interview. 'He likes meeting you, Ruzbeh, for some reason.' Naresh had said this with a straight face.

Krishna sat in front of Dada. She seemed worried too.

'We can do this interview some other day, Dada.' She spoke as though she were speaking to a child.

Dada looked at her with surprise in His eyes.

'Why? I am fine.'

'You are not fine. You need to rest. This will tire You.'

'I enjoy talking to Ruzbeh. This does not tire me. It is like two friends talking. Am I not right, Ruzbeh?'

'I love talking to You, Dada. But You do know I can talk to You any other time too . . .'

'No, no. I look forward to our talks. It invigorates me.' Then, turning around to face Krishna, He said softly, 'I am fine, don't worry.'

Krishna sighed. I guess she too understood that once Dada had made up His mind, nothing much could stand in His way. While Piya was adjusting the mic and Dada's shawl, Krishna quickly signed to me, suggesting we conclude the interview fast. I nodded. I wanted to tell her that even my eight-year-old daughter doesn't listen to me, what made her think Dada would?

I began the interview immediately.

'Do You miss Sadhu Vaswani's physical presence?'

'I believe He is with me. I believe, even from the physical point of view, that He, and it is only He, who is doing everything for me. I believe I am just an instrument carrying out His work and His mission. I may not be doing it very well, but I am trying to with the best of my ability and with all of His grace.'

'I understand that, but once in a while it is nice to be able to be loved by Your Master. Held by Him. Just be in His physical presence.'

'I know with the passage of time that need for physical proximity grows dimmer and dimmer.'

'Dada, why would Sadhu Vaswani prick Himself with a pin every time he had a thought He was not proud of?'

'Yes. When He was a student in college himself, then when He went to Berlin . . . yes, He would carry a pin and pierce Himself if He was not happy with a thought.' Dada then went silent.

Make note: Avoid all pins.

'There must be an easier way to work on one's thoughts, Dada?'

'I believe it was more to set an example. There is an easier way . . . I am sure too.' Then He smiled and we both began to chuckle.

'A wrong thought can come in various forms. Fear, anger, jealousy, hate, lust, pride, temptation. Prophet Mohammed said, "Temptation comes as a passer-by, it comes and knocks at the door of your heart, it asks to be let in as a guest. But once you open the door of the heart and let it in, it becomes the master of the house." When you find a negative feeling trying to enter your heart or mind, kick it out. Slap yourself or take a pin and prick your flesh. The negative feeling will go away.'

I know it sounds hard core, but the fact is that when one is assured that pain is going to ensue the moment you have allowed yourself to indulge in a wrong thought by physically hurting yourself, the survival instinct and self-preservation will kick in.

'How do we, as common people, reach a point where we can have some kind of control over one's thoughts?'

'The moment an undesirable thought is about to enter your head, just slap yourself. Once it enters, then it becomes the master of the house. So don't let it enter at all.'

Great. All we would be doing is thrashing ourselves black and blue then.

'The mind can make or break you. Through the mind thoughts originate. You told me the other day, Ruzbeh, that Prophet Zarathustra based your entire spiritual religion on the tenets of Good Thoughts, Good Words, Good Deeds. It all starts with thoughts.

'There is that great American teacher, William Phelps. He says, "That man is the happiest who thinks the happiest thoughts. That man is the most prosperous who thinks the most prosperous thoughts. That man is the most spiritual, who thinks the most spiritual thoughts." Decide what you want to be! This is the miracle of the mind. With the mind you can change your life.

'It was Benjamin Franklin who said, "The greatest discovery of my generation is that by altering your pattern of thinking, you can alter your life."

'There is a doctor in America, Sarah Jones, and in her prescription she writes: 'Give your mind a good shampoo every day!' A patient may go to her with common cold, a patient may go to her with pain in the ear, a patient may go to her with headache, with stomach ache, but she writes this in every prescription. That is get down into the very depths of your consciousness and cleanse it of all the old rotten, miserable thoughts that bind it today. Liberate your mind, un-clutter your mind, cleanse your mind. Our minds are full of dirt. Think of the thoughts we are thinking day after day. We pay scant attention to our thoughts. We say how does it matter, it is only a thought! No! The thought is the beginning of everything. Therefore, think thoughts of joy, of love and peace! Think thoughts of service, of sympathy and sacrifice. Think thoughts of health, happiness and harmony. Think thoughts of peace, of prosperity, of success! Cleanse your mind of all dirty thoughts. Thoughts of lust, hatred, greed, selfishness, miserliness, envy, jealously, ill-will and resentment. Whenever you hold a thought of hatred within, you can never be happy! Happiness and hatred can never go together, just as light and darkness can never go together. Either you have light or you have darkness. You can't have both together.

'There was a man, and I remember this happened several years ago, who said to me, "There is a fire burning within my heart, and the flames of this fire will not be quenched till I have shot down the man who was indirectly responsible for the death of my father." There is a fire he said, burning, yes; hatred is like a fire. Jealousy, anger, lust, envy, revenge, these are all fires, and they will keep burning in your heart. And eventually they will burn away all your happiness, all your joy, all your zest for life, the enthusiasm for living . . . all is burnt away.

'On the other hand I recall an incident in the life of our Beloved and Revered Master, Sadhu Vaswani. There was a man who had given into evil ways—he gambled, he drank, he ran after women. Just to derive a little solace, his wife used to come to the evening satsang every day. The husband did not approve of it, and one day he came in, waved his fist at Sadhu Vaswani and said to Him, "If only you knew how much I hate you!" Sadhu Vaswani was one of the most loving, one of the most humble men that ever trod this earth, one of the gentlest of human beings. And Sadhu Vaswani looked most lovingly into the eyes of this man and said to him, "My brother, if only you knew how much I love you . . ." Just those few simple words transformed this man. This man, who only a minute or two ago had said how much I hate you to Him, fell down at the feet of Sadhu Vaswani, with tears in his eyes. He begged for pardon, "Forgive me, O Holy one of God; I have greatly sinned." And this man's life was transformed. There is one force, one power that can transform the life of another, and that is the power of love. Nothing else. You think you can scold a person and set things right? No. By scolding, you are only suppressing his desires, his tendencies, his attitude and his thoughts. Suppression can never transform a person. It is only love that can transform an individual, and this man's life was transformed. From that day onwards, he used to accompany his wife and his children every day to the evening satsang. It was Gautama Buddha who said, "Hatred ceaseth not by hatred, hatred ceaseth by love." Go on giving love to everyone, not erotic love, not love as you understand it, but that pure love, that chaste love. And that love will transform your thoughts, which eventually will transform your mind.'

'What happens when hatred enters one's heart? How does one get it out?'

'Prayer. The thief has entered and we need prayer to stop him. And prayer . . . one word of prayer is more powerful than two words of prayer. In prayer we go on and on. It is a mile-long prayer. Just one word! Just chant, "Save! Save! Save! Save me Lord!"'

'Is that why *Naam Simran* is so important?'

'Yes. Naam Simran, *mantra japa*, prayer and *dhyana* are at the very foundation of *abhyasa* or spiritual discipline. Together, they quieten the agitated mind, cleanse the mind of all its impurities, leaving us calm and serene to enter into meditation. Naam Simran is the way for the age in which we live. If Naam Simran were not there, there would be no holy man in this age of allurements and entanglements.

'All these holy men that you see are the product of Naam Simran. Our saints and sages tell us that chanting the Name of one's God, Goddess, Guru can absolve us of all sins and lead us to salvation. But this is possible only when it is uttered with perfect faith and reverence; and the Name that is heard in the heart within is far more efficacious than one that is uttered aloud.

'The mind keeps wandering; it has acquired the habit of wandering, birth after birth. This wandering must stop, because if the mind wanders we wander with the mind. We have become wanderers. What is the way to stop this wandering? One of the ways is to keep on repeating a mantra. "Man", "tra". "Man" is the mind, "tra" is that which stops its wandering.'

'That is the meaning of Mantra?'

'That is how I look at it. It may not be literary or true, but that is how I look at it.'

'I think your meaning is simple and beautiful. Is mantra, Naam Simran, Japa, prayer, the same thing?'

'There are thousand and one mantras; I could choose any one of them and keep on repeating and re-repeating them. Naam Simran is the repetition of one of the many names by which our Ishtadeva, the chosen one, is called upon. Japa, real Japa, I think has to do with the breath; the breath that we take in, the breath that we let out. As we take in the breath, we repeat part of the mantra and the remaining part we repeat when we breathe out.'

'Now Japa will be mainly silent? Would it be silent because then you got to concentrate on the breath also?'

'It is more efficacious if it is silent.'

'Now a Japa could also mean that one is repeating either a Mantra or the Naam . . . It could be either of them?'

'He is the Nameless One, though the sages have called Him by many Names. Do not quarrel over Forms or Names. You stick to the One that draws you; let the others stick to the One that draws them. Choose any Name that appeals to you, repeat it again and again. Repeat the Name, yes, but not merely with the tongue. Repeat it with tears in the eyes. Repeat it until you can repeat it no longer, until you disappear from yourself, your 'ego' is dissolved and you sit in the presence of the Eternal Beloved. The Name of God is like the waters of the Ganga. The River Ganga is like a mother . . . Ganga Maa! It purifies those that bathe in it. As you come out of the waters of the Name Divine you will feel cleansed, washed and purified. Chant the name of God not in a mechanical way, but with deep feeling and emotion of the heart. Pour into the unclean mind, the purifying

Ganga water of the Name Divine. Purity is needed: Whenever an unclean thought comes to you, immediately, in that very instant, say to yourself, "I was made for greater, nobler, loftier things. I shall not be a bundle of unclean, impure desires", and start repeating the pure Name of God, on and on and on.'

Oh, boy! I would have to spend most of my day chanting this affirmation, I concluded.

'We may, also, meditate on some form of God as we utter the Name Divine—Krishna or Christ, Buddha or Nanak, a saint or a Holy One. There should, however, be no attachment to the Form. All Forms, ultimately, have to be left behind. Significant are the words of Meister Eckhart: "He who seeks God under a settled Form, lays hold of the Form, while missing the God concealed in it." Meditate on the Form to which you feel drawn and then go beyond it. Enter into the Form to meet the Formless One!

'May I suggest to you a simple exercise? Every morning, as you sit in silence, close your eyes and imagine the Life of God coursing through every part of your body, filling it through and through. The Life of God is in us already; we have to be conscious of it. Say to yourself, "Every moment, the Life of God—call Him by what Name you will; Krishna, Buddha, Christ, Guru Nanak, they are all so many names of Him who is Nameless—is filling every nerve and cell and fibre of my being!" So Naam Simran is chanting the name of God, Goddess, Guru. While Japa is also Naam Simran, but according to me when done with the help of breathing. Take half Name or mantra while inhaling and exhale the other half of the Name or mantra. But very often for many Naam Simran and Japa are one and the same.'

Dada paused. So my understanding is that when Naam Simran is done with the help of breathing—breaking half the Name or mantra while inhaling and the other half while exhaling—it qualifies to become japa.

'The Sanskrit word "japa" is derived from the root word "jap", which means "to utter in a low voice or repeat mentally". It is said that after intense and continuous practice, the repetition goes on in one's mind without conscious effort, even during work and sleep, as a sort of constant spiritual awareness. Ultimately, this may result in the state of Samadhi or oneness with the Divine Self. Like the purifying power of fire, japa also has the capacity to burn all the karmic residues of our past sins and negative karmas, leaving us in a state of higher consciousness that is close to true bliss or *sat chit ananda*. Japa is also of three types: chanted aloud, whispered in a low voice or uttered in the silence of the heart within. Whichever form of japa we practice, the benefits we reap will be many—peace of mind, tranquillity, increased concentration, positive energy levels and freedom from fear and anxiety.'

'And what is a mantra?'

'A mantra is a sacred utterance; it is especially associated with India's great ancient scriptures, the Vedas, which are a collection of hymns and sacred utterances that have survived several millennia through oral transmission. Thus, a mantra is linked with oral utterance; its special powers are in the depth of its meaning as much as in the sound vibrations it produces during oral recital. Thus, many people believe that there is a transformative power associated with the mantra, which can bring about a spiritual change. In Hinduism, it is a sacred verbal formula repeated in prayer, meditation or incantation, such as an invocation of a God, a verse from the ancient Spiritual scriptures, or even a syllable or portion of a scriptural utterance containing mystical potentialities.'

'What is the significance of a Mantra?'

'Every word has power. Some words have less, some have more. A mantra is a word or a combination of words which have great power. If you recite a mantra, again and again, you release tremendous spiritual energy, which, among other things, helps you still your wandering mind. If the mind is still or focused, our peace of mind grows, which is the secret of true happiness. Normally, the rays of the sun do not have the power to burn. But if a number of rays are focussed at a point, fire can be produced. Likewise with the mind—if it can be concentrated on one word, one idea or one set of powerful words, tremendous power is released. And the mind, in addition to what is happening outside, can know many things that are happening inside. Naam is individual, mantra is universal. Usually

Naam remains a secret and has to be repeated in a particular way. The mantra can be repeated by anyone in the way that he chooses.

'Any mantra or Holy Name or word or syllable that draws you, may be taken up. God is the Nameless One; the sages have called Him by many Names. All Names will lead you to the Nameless One. There are the ancient mantras, 'Om' and 'Rama'. There is the maha-mantra, "Hare Rama, Hare Rama, Rama, Rama, Hare, Hare; Hare Krishna, Hare Krishna, Krishna, Krishna, Hare, Hare."

'There are other mantras: "Om Namoh Bhagavate Vaasudevaaya", "Om Namah Shivaaya", "Om Sri Rama, Jaya Rama, Jaya, Jaya, Rama", "Rama Krishna Hari", "Satnaam Waheguru", "Om Mani Padme Hum", "Jesus", "Lord Jesus Christ, have mercy on me", "Jehovaah", "Allah", "Ahura Mazda". The list is endless. Choose your favourite mantra, choose one that has a special appeal to you, choose one that suits your need; having chosen it, make it your own; internalize its energy, its positive vibrations and its life-giving pulse. Repeat it constantly until it becomes part of your consciousness.'

'And what is prayer?'

'At its simplest, prayer is turning to God. At its most mystic, prayer is stopping the current of your worldly life to give a few moments to God exclusively! Prayer is reposing all your faith in God; not helplessly, in passive submission, but with active, dynamic faith that your life is safe in His hands. We know what it is to pray. Whenever we are in trouble, whenever we are hard-pressed, when we are surrounded by adverse circumstances, when we are passing through a dark night when not a single star doth shine, when we suffer from a disease that the doctors declare as incurable, when we face a financial crisis and are on the verge of bankruptcy, when we are involved in the problems of personal relationships—what do we do? We call upon friends, we run to our relatives, we turn to our lawyers, doctors, to the government and police officers, but we don't go to God.

'If you pray in the morning, as you take up your position in the battlefield of life, and your actions do not bear witness to the prayer that you have offered, you are no better than a hypocrite. Therefore, let your actions bear witness!

'A holy man, whom I used often visit once, showed me his old safe. The safe was empty. But there was a time when it had been full of gold coins. He worked as a railway contractor and received hordes of gold coins as bribes. Seth Vishindas Harchandrai would handle the railway contracts.

'Suddenly He heard a voice say to him, "These gold coins are not yours. If you spend one of them on yourself, you will suffer." This is what he told me: "One night, while I sat the voice again said to me, 'Wake up, my child, and fill a bag with gold coins. I will lead you to a house across the railway tracks, where you will hand the bag over to an old man who will open the door.' I did as the voice bade me to. When I knocked at the door, an old Muslim man opened it. I handed the bag over to him. The old man was amazed to see the bag when he opened it, his eyes became moist and he called out 'Ya Allah, you are so merciful!' Then he turned towards me and said, 'This is an orphanage and we have practically run out of food to feed these abandoned children here. By Allah's grace, at least with these coins we will be able to eat well for some time.' This saint concluded His story by reminding me, 'Learn to listen to the soft, still voice of God!' I also remember another sage telling me, 'Prayer is the key of miracles. With this key unlock the miracles.'"

'And what is the most effective prayer, Dada? The words, the intentions, the focus, the love, all of them?'

'Let me tell you a story. There was a labourer, who every day at 4.00 in the afternoon, when his hours at the factory finished, would go to a temple nearby. That was just the time when they used to have the aarti in the temple. He went and joined in the aarti and he felt so happy. One day, some accident had taken place in the factory, so they detained this man. This man had to give a statement with regard to the accident, but his mind was there in the temple. He asked them to let him go so reach in time for the aarti. As soon as he was set free, he went running to the temple. The moment he reached, he found that the priest coming out of the temple. He asked him, 'Is the aarti over?' And the temple priest said, 'Yes, the aarti is just over and I am coming out.' This poor labourer, he was so grief stricken he could not say a single word, all that he could say was, 'Ahh! Ahh!' This cry came out of his heart. The temple priest said to him, 'Suppose I were to give you the merit of the aarti that I did today and in exchange you gave me the merit of your anguish, this moan this ahh! Would you accept this bargain?' The man said 'Yes! Gladly!' That night he had a dream. In the dream, the Deity the man used to worship in the Temple came to him and told him, 'You have struck a bad bargain. What have you done? This anguish, this moan is more acceptable to the Lord then all the aartis performed.' Whatever you say to the Lord, let it come out of the heart.'

I guess true prayer starts with love and ends with surrender. Hmm.

'The great Newton . . . you must have heard of him?'

'The chap who made a big fuss about a falling apple?'

'Yes, the very same Newton once fell in love with a girl, but his mind was always occupied with science. One day, he was sitting by the side of this girl whom he loved. He had his pipe with him. So, what he did was while he was sitting with the girl, he caught hold of her little finger and inserted it in the pipe, and kept turning it as she shrieked in pain. And Newton said, "I thought I was cleaning the pipe with the iron sticks that they have." Then he mused to himself, "I found that marriage was not the thing for me. If I got married, I would not be able to give to my wife what she would expect of me." So there are people whose minds are elsewhere, but they keep talking to you. You would surely not like to listen to such a man. How can God listen to us when our minds are wandering all the time and when our lips are mechanically repeating certain words that we have read from the scriptures? Let your prayers come out of your hearts. Spontaneous utterances are the best prayers that you can offer to God, but, until you arrive at that stage, it is necessary to offer some prayer or the other, rather than not offering a prayer at all. You must pick up a prayer, keep repeating it until the stage comes when you can spontaneously speak to God.'

'But there are so many times where the most spontaneous of prayers go unanswered? Why is that then?'

'On the cover of your book, *The Fakir*, you have written, "The One who makes the thunder roar also hears a butterfly sigh". That is God. The tiniest whisper of a human heart, the slightest stirring of the human soul is audible to His ears, but God has His own ways of answering. There are three ways in which He answers our prayers. The first way is where He says, "Yes! Yes, my child, whatever you ask for is for your good and I'm going to grant it to you." The second is, "No! What are you asking for is not for your ultimate good. Therefore, I will not give you what you're asking for, because you don't know that it will do you harm."

'That man, the great man Dean Anglo, he wrote at the age of seventy-five, "I feel grateful to God for not having answered all my prayers. If he had answered everything that I had asked him for, my condition would have been most miserable." There are so many prayers where we go to God and pray to Him for certain things which are not for our good. It's like a little child, a child of three years, going to the mother and asking for a matchbox. The mother will not give him the matchbox. Now, the child, from his point of view, thinks how cruel the mother is. You understand from the point of view of the child. We are like children in the presence of God. We don't understand what is good for us. So the second way He answers our prayers is by saying no.

'And the third way in which He answers our prayers is to say, "Wait, now is not the time. At the proper time, I shall give it to you." A boy went to his multimillionaire father and asked for a Maruti car. He was only fifteen-years-old and the father told him that when he could get him a fleet of cars, he's asking only for one. "I can get you a fleet of cars with drivers if you want, but you will have to wait for three years. When you turn eighteen, I shall get you a license and I shall get you a car," he added. So these are the three ways in which God answers our prayers. God always answers our prayers, but whatever be His answer is, remember it is for our ultimate good. This is the faith that you must have in Him. Therefore, to every prayer you must add these words: "But Lord, not my will, but Thy will be done." God, I want this, I want that . . . a whole list can be placed before God, but finally tell Him, "Lord, not my will but *Thy* will be done."'

'Dada, do you mean those prayers said with love and surrender, and most importantly with the right intention, left at the feet of the Lord is the ideal prayer?'

'Yes. And once you begin to pray for a selfless thing, you never stop. You keep at it. You should not get tired of praying. St Augustine is regarded as the chief of Catholic saints. His mother who is also considered a saint, St Monica. But Augustine became a profligate, so much so He kept a prostitute in His house. The mother knew that telling Him would be to no effect. He was an intellectual so she started praying for Him. She prayed not for one day or one week or one year or one decade, she went on praying. Eventually, the profligate became a saint. If you start praying, you don't have to give up. You have to keep on praying, keep on praying.

'I often tell those who care to listen that when we were in Sind, we went to a place called Thata. In Thata, there is a hill called Makli. We wanted to see that Makli Hill. So we started early in the morning, we walked and walked and walked, but we didn't reach Makli Hill. So whenever we saw somebody coming in the opposite direction, we asked the person, "How far to Makli Hill?" In Sindhi, in our language, they would reply, "*Saduh pandh*." Saduh pandh means only a little distance. Just there, right there, as if it's just there by the door. So it went on and on, and we kept walking, and every one would keep saying, "Just there! Just there!" In prayer too, our attitude should be such: just there, we have reached, just there!'

'Why is it said that in the Kalyug the most effective sadhna is chanting or Naam Simran?'

'Because people find it difficult to have yagnas or religious ceremonies, to do tapas or penance, to give in daan or charity . . . also, it is easy to say give daan, but when it comes to giving, I have seen people hesitate. Once, there was a man who came to our Mission; it was past midnight, he knocked on the door. I opened it and he gave me a bundle of notes. He said, "This is for the poor." I asked him, where was the hurry? He could have done this tomorrow. He said, "No, I was lying down when the thought occurred to me that I must give this amount for the service of the poor. It is probable that when I get up in the morning, my mind would have changed. And I would have thought to myself, why give you this amount, why not give a little less?"'

'Have you been doing chanting or Naam Simran since You were a child?'

'The first experience where I remember chanting was when my beloved father passed away. I was only eleven-years-old and it had affected me greatly. So my mother said, "If you want your father back, you should chant the mantra. Stay awake the whole night and chant. If you succeed in staying awake the whole night, without a break, and chant the mantra, your father will come back." That was the beginning, but I could not do it. I would wake up for an hour, two, three, once even for four hours, but sleep would overpower me. I never succeeded in staying awake all night.

'Let me tell you a story. I was young when I found company in a devotee of God. I had not yet come to live with beloved Dada. I became close to this holy person. A bond of love had formed between us. He had bound me with his love. He could say anything at all and I would never find it strange. I was crazy in His love. The days I did not meet Him, I felt I had lost something.

'One day He said, "Dear child, will you do something for me?" I replied, "Anything you say. I will even pluck the stars for you." He said, "Dear one, I don't need anything. But for my sake repeat the Name of the Lord so many times."

'Thus, He forced me into the habit of reciting His Name. Since then, I learnt to regularly do japa. This was the grace through which I learnt naam japa.

'Then there was another Holy person whom I saw every day. Often, I would go visit Him in the daytime. The secret of His life was the divine Name. Once, I went to spend the night with Him. All night, He stayed awake and recited the Holy Name. Through the Name He helped so many. He would say, "Jesus Christ comes to me, Sri Krishna comes to me, Guru Nanak comes to visit me." Guru Nanak Dev was His Ishtadevata. He would say, "God has books of accounts sitting open. Some of the sorrow Ram will remove. Some of the pain Krishna will remove, and some of the difficulties Guru Nanak will destroy."

'He would stay awake and repeat God's Name. The Name holds within it unusual glory and power. That is why repeating the holy Name is so important. Connect your heart to it. There are sages, who by encouraging people to do japa, have removed all their sorrow.

There is a unique power in it. The Name removes any type of sorrow and pain.

'I try not to eliminate my sorrow. But I do take refuge in the Name. I believe that the pain will automatically go. Just as I take this support, I hear a voice, "O foolish one! God has sent this parcel to you. But you are returning it." Thus, perceiving the pain as a gift from the Beloved, I accept it. I look upon sorrow as a gift from the fountain of the Lord. My Gurudev Sadhu Vaswani has blessed me with this gift.

'He would always say accept pain as a sweet, there can be nothing bitter in it. This suffering should be accepted as something from the Beloved. The pain then appears as a river of joy. Take dips in that river. The glory of Naam is great. Bind your heart to it. Unfortunately, our hearts are attached to the world. Instead it should be connected to Naam.

'If one commits any sin, one repents. But sin also has its own value. When we fall in its trap, we take the support of the Name. Sin is God's weapon. Through it, He first strikes the individual and then He lifts him up. Hence, do not laugh at the sinner, don't hate him. "One does not know how Krishna comes and makes him His own. Sing His Name, meditate on His Name. Lose yourself in His Name."'

There was such a faraway, sad look in Dada's eyes that I wanted to end the interview.

'Coming back to mantra, there are certain mantras that are more like seed sounds . . . they don't make any sense.'

'A mantra is sound. A mantra is not something with a name, meaning. That is not a mantra then.'

'So you mean words like *Shrim, Hrim, Krim, Kleem,* they are mantras?'

'Yes.'

'Now those can only be chanted aloud, right?'

'Any name can be chanted aloud.'

'No, these wise folk keep saying that the mantra has the sound and the sound creates vibrations, and blah blah blah. So does one have to chant it loudly or if it is chanted within, would it be as efficient?'

'Even if it is chanted within, it creates vibrations. Vibrations are created wherever a mantra is uttered. It could be inside, it could be outside. It is more efficacious when chanted inside than uttered outside.'

'Why do you think it is more effective if chanted within? First of all, the word has no meaning. I guess it's like sound engineering. Each sound has its corresponding vibrations and impact. What You are saying is that even if that meaningless word, which has tremendous energy in its vibrations, will be effective even though the sound is not verbalized?'

'If it is chanted within, it is chanted with a greater degree of concentration. And the resonance lasts longer. It is resonance that helps concentration grow. The magic is in the resonance.'

'If the mantra is chanted loudly, even if the person isn't truly concentrating, logically, the vibration of the sound of the mantra has to yield some positive effect. The vibration in the sound of the mantra, I doubt, cares about too much attention or focus. It is all about the sound and impact. But while chanting within, one would need to be truly focused and involved as there is no sound created outside. Is that why most people say their prayers and mantras should be audible as it's safer for the one chanting? There will be some impact or the other due to sound engineering and vibration?'

'Yes. If you are not certain of your focus, then at least let the sound vibrations help you. About mantras, it is said, "Pavitra, Pavitra, Pavitra Puneet". Pavitra is pure, it is pure in itself. The Mantra is pure. Puneet is the one who utters the mantra, who also becomes pure. So it has a double effect.'

'So, the one reciting becomes pure. Is this why Kabir said, "I used to chant the Lord's name and by repeated chanting, now the Lord chants my name." You have written this; I found it beautiful.'

'Yes. And He says at another place, Kabir *maan nirmal bhaya jaise Ganga neer, pache lago Har firah kaha* Kabir, Kabir! Meaning, "My mind became so pure, that the Lord came after me running asking me, Kabir, Kabir please stop. I want to meet you."'

'Who was Kabir?'

'There are many who believe Kabir was the Lord Himself. Therefore, they never say that Kabir was born in the year so and so, they always say, Kabir manifested Himself in the year so and so.'

'When Sai Baba was questioned, and they asked Him what his religion was, He had said, "Kabir". There is a strange similarity between Sai Baba of Shirdi and Kabir, because nobody knows about Baba's birth or religion too.'

'Yes, and both Kabir and Sai Baba spoke in parables, and led the simplest of lives and preached Oneness.'

'Dada, nowadays you get CD's of mantras, which are played at homes or pretty much anywhere actually. Does that also help?'

'This raises another question of who is benefited. The one who utters the mantra or the one who hears it? If it is the one who utters it, then no. But if it is the one who hears it, then yes. Therefore, whenever we hear that one of the members of our own circle is about to pass away, then they tell the family members either to do a kirtan in the presence of the individual or if that be not possible, because nowadays it is difficult to get people to come together and sing or pray together, then to play a CD of a kirtan, because the music from the CD will create those vibrations, which will help the individual.'

'So if it can help the dying individual, it can also help those who are still up and about?'

'We have not scientifically studied this. But it at least purifies the environment. There is one of our dear ones, he is in Jakarta. He was in coma for a long period of time. Then I sent them a CD with a mantra in it. And I told them to keep it next to his ears and play it. And let it keep playing night and day. After a number of days, he awoke. They thought it was a miracle, but it would have been a miracle if he had become a normal being. He is still alive, but has no sense of recognition, nor can he think. So I would like to believe that even hearing a mantra or Naam, via the CD, will help. How much will it help . . . This I have not really studied.'

'Why are we told to chant a mantra a particular number of times . . . You know, they say it should be chanted nine times, eighteen times, twenty-one, twenty-seven, 108 times or Zoroastrians who pray 101 times?'

'I think it is more pragmatic because when you leave anything open to individuals, they don't take that thing seriously. The moment you create some system, some mystery, people take it seriously. Though they say usually a mantra or Name, should be repeated 1,25,000 times.'

Hmm . . . And I thought 108 times was a bit much.

'Why, so that you get into the habit of chanting?'

'Yes, but even if it is repeated once, it has an effect. It creates that vibration.'

'I like this sentence that you had written where you tell somebody "If you can think of your work while praying, why can't you pray while you work?" I think it really makes a lot of sense.'

'Yes, it happens through practice.'

'So basically the whole purpose is to create oneness between the individual and the Naam?'

'But the two are not different. It is something that we have forgotten. It is stored in our ancient memory. Let me tell you a story. There was a man who was going to meet his Guru, who had an ashram some miles away. There were no buses, there no way to get there, but walk. As the disciple walked the distance, darkness fell swiftly. He saw another ashram on the way. So he went into that ashram and said to them, "Will you let me spend the night here?" The leader of the ashram said, "You are most welcome, but where are you going?" And this pilgrim said, "I am going to see my Guru whose is ashram is some distance away from here." "You are going to see your Guru? Your Guru has died, He just died. And you are talking of going to see your Guru." This came as a shock to the pilgrim. He decided to go see Him before they cremate Him. So, the next morning he did not walk, he ran to the ashram. He found his Guru sitting there. Surprised, he asked, "How is this? The leader of the ashram where I spent the night said that You died, but You are very much alive." So he told the Guru all that had happened at the ashram where he slept. And his Guru asked, "What was the time you had this conversation with the leader of the ashram?" The disciple said, "The time was around twenty minutes past nine." "That leader was right," said the Guru. "At twenty minutes past nine, I forgot God just for a minute." Forgetting God even for a minute is tantamount to death. We are not alive because we have forgotten God. He is the breath of our breaths, He is the life of our life. Let Him be in the background of your consciousness, do your work but remember Him. "You are there, aren't you?" Just this little thing will keep you on the path. When you get up in the morning take up a line from any scripture that may be dear to you, or take up a line from a great one, a thought of a great one. "*Sad ke sang mukh ujal hote*!" This one line is enough. "*Sad ke sang mukh ujal hote*!" Is my face *ujal* or not? How may it be *ujal*? It will be *ujal* when I will see drawbacks of others, I will not think of drawbacks of others. There are good points in each one, there is some good in the worst of us as there is some evil in the best of us. Therefore, I will only see good in others. Keep repeating that line again and again; this will keep you in recollection. It will let God be in the background of your consciousness, all the time. It will almost be as if you are having a date with God.'

'Dada, do you give Naam to your followers?'

'I have no followers, only friends . . .'

'Ya, ya, right. Okay, do you give Naam to your so-called friends?'

Dada grinned.

'There was a time when the Guru gave Naam to the disciple; the disciples' heart would come to life. Our hearts are dead; they have to be brought to life. And they can come to life if the Guru gives the real Naam. But real Naam is given after years of testing by the Guru. There was a man who went and became the disciple of a Guru. For twenty years he served the Guru. The wife of the Guru said to Him, "This disciple has served you for twenty years. Why don't you give him Naam?" The Guru said, "You will have the answer tomorrow morning." The disciple would come at 4.00 in the morning to ask if there was anything that he could do for the Guru. The Guru told His wife, "Tomorrow morning, as he comes at 4.00, you go and stand on the terrace, and whatever you have in the wastepaper basket, just throw it on him." So the next morning, when the disciple came, the wife of the Guru threw whatever there was in the wastepaper basket. And it all fell on the disciple. He was a rich man, this disciple, and he was not used to such behaviour. He looked at his Guru's wife and was seething with anger. He still managed to control himself and told her firmly, "You do not know what I can do, but I am not going to do it as you are the wife of my esteemed Guru." The wife came and reported it to the Guru. The Guru said, "You see, there is still so much ego in him. It has not yet gone and unless the ego goes, you cannot do anything for the disciple."

'Ten more years pass, thirty years in all, and the Guru then told His wife, "Now, he is ready to receive the Naam. You go and stand on the terrace when he comes, and you throw all that has collected in the makeshift lavatory outside on to him." The wife said, "I threw only paper on him the last time and he reacted in such a strange way. I am afraid he might truly lose his temper and do something he might regret this time." The Guru said, "No, just see what the result is." The next day, she went and stood on the terrace at 4.00 a.m. and threw all the contents of the lavatory on the disciple as he entered the house. And this man looked at the wife of the Guru and said, "Mother, I am no better than this that you have thrown on me." The Guru then said, "Now he is ready to receive the Naam." That was true Naam given and earned.'

I guess what Dada was trying to say is that nowadays most don't have the power to give, but, most importantly, very rarely does a disciple have the right and the qualities to accept something as potent as the Naam. No wonder Baba Sai rarely ever gave Naam to any of His disciples.

I ended the interview as I could hear the call for sangat on the ground floor. A bhajan had begun; a woman was singing. The devotion was palpable. There was true love in the voice. Even sitting this far away, I knew the woman was completely out of tune. But she was belting out the number oblivious to the world. Dada sat quietly while the mic and wire were removed. I knelt and told Him that I loved Him. He smiled. "I love you too," He said, His eyes twinkling. Even though He was unwell, He never showed any signs of strain. He was always smiling. He called for prasad for Meher. He blessed Samir with prasad too.

We went downstairs to the Samadhi temple. I thanked Sadhu Vaswani and Sister Shanti; I told Them I loved Them.

I got a call from Meher.

'Dadda, please tell Dada to give me more cheese chips as prasad. I didn't enjoy those cakes.'

'It's prasad, holy offering. One doesn't ask for specific prasad. One eats what one gets.'

'One can't help it if one didn't enjoy the cakes a rude man brought home the last time. Just tell Dada. He will understand. He is a Guru. Gurus understand everything. Unlike fathers.'

'I can't hear you Meher. Hello . . . Hello . . .'

6

Dada has written over hundred and thirty books. If you go through His works, you will find they are mind-boggling. I wish I could reproduce the things He has written about. The engaging stories narrated. The simple philosophy. His extraordinary memory. His simplicity, humility and wit. There are biographies written on Him; I knew I didn't have it in me to do justice to Dada through a biography. I was more interested in knowing the philosophy, the wisdom and the spirituality that throbs in Him. Thus, from the start I was clear—this had to be conversations with Dada. In case anybody in the world wanted to ask a question about spirituality, I wanted Dada, through the book, to be able to help the person. The more I met Him, the more I realized that there is truly nobody like Him. He will never talk ill of anybody. I doubt if He has ever felt ill will to anybody. There is not an iota of pride in Him. He is like a spiritual Santa Claus—only giving, never seeking. All He does seek is to make His Master and all the Masters who have blessed Him with their Presence, happy and proud of Him. You won't find marketing aggression here. He won't advertise His book or try to be in the news. He isn't that person. He goes about life silently serving with all humility and you won't even know the kind of seva done by Him and through Him. The organization goes about its work quietly. Every day, a few hundred people are fed. The KK Eye Institute performs forty-five operations free of cost every day, which totals to around 15,000 free eye surgeries every year. The F&B Heart Institute performs innumerable free, and subsidized, heart surgeries every year. There are no major promotions done about this philanthropy. You won't know about it if you don't bother inquiring. They keep a very low profile on social media. It's just simple, old-fashioned, hard core seva.

I have met a number of Dada devotees or as Dada says, His friends. What everyone mentions without fail is Dada's humility, love, soft presence, practical guidance, humour and everybody either treats Him as their Master or God in human form. Many of them told to me that they had not seen God, but they had witnessed God's presence and divinity through Dada. Most people I interviewed are professionals, people of the world, age and sex no bar. In fact, often they would shyly confess their love for Dada and reveal that His presence is all-pervasive in their lives.

'Dada was always very prompt with his correspondence. He would immediately send a reply to those who wrote to him. They would share their problems, or the different events in their lives with him. His letters, whether in the form of condolences, or congratulations and advice on a marriage, etc. were all masterpieces. He would end each letter with a positive thought. Those who received these replies wondered at how Dada knew the problem that they were going through and provide them assurances for the same.

A few days later, after praying to Sadhu Vaswani and seeking Sister Shanti's blessings, I went and sat in the Kutiya. Dada was yet to arrive for our interview. I had this one place where I would sit and just be. It was to the left, as soon as you entered the Kutiya. I would sit with my back against the wall, shut my eyes and sort of zone out. That day, a little later, I realized that Dada had already entered and was sitting facing me.

He smiled that twenty-thousand watt smile of His and, after our song and dance of taking and receiving blessings, He looked at me and said, 'You seem tired. I hope I am not the reason for your tiredness?'

'No, Dada, You make me feel good about planet Earth. I am fine.'

He smiled and shut His eyes. By the time I began the interview, I felt as though somebody had injected me with energy and bathed me with some spiritual stuff that made me feel rested and whole. I knew Dada must have prayed for me or done some healing as there was no way that in five minutes I could feel so different. Dada sat like a good boy while Piya went through the rituals of getting Him ready for the shoot. If somebody looked at Him, He projected all the presence, naughtiness and humaneness of a grandparent. This suited Dada just fine as it was a good guise to hide His true Essence, that of a Master.

The other day Piya had spoken to me about Dada's silent healing.

'He will never talk about miracles or powers. Though He will tell you everything. He will do everything for you. There are several people who have seen Him when they are ill, although in reality they were in another city or country. They call me and say, "Dada came to me. He gave me a cup of water. After that I became well." So many people have seen Him. They say, "I was going to the operation theatre and I saw Dada coming to me and blessing me, and then I was sure that I would be fine." I will narrate an incident to you. So we were in Puerto Rico and a lady called Shweta called us from Pune and said, "My husband has been taken to the hospital. Please tell Dada to bless him." It was an emergency. And then she called after a couple of days and said, "I rang up another Reiki master and told him to pray for my husband. That master told me that there is a person in white already taking care of your husband and you don't need anybody else." Imagine, now we were in Puerto Rico, she was in Pune and that Reiki healer was in Hong Kong. He wasn't aware of Dada, but had described Dada. Her husband became better soon after that. There are several similar cases which we hear about and see.'

'But then He refuses to have anything to do with all of this?'

'Yes, He refuses to have anything to do with healing or miracles. All of them. The other day, He became very still. He became very quiet. Very silent. And we were just wondering what had happened. Then we came to know that a lady in Delhi, who was very dedicated to Sadhu Vaswani, had become very sick and she was about to pass away. And she told people, "I am seeing Dada. Dada is with me." She passed away around the same time He had withdrawn into Himself and became silent. So that is who He is. He went to ease her passage to the other side. She was really suffering. But He helped her pass away peacefully. I have seen Him take upon Himself the illness of others so often.'

'You have been with Him for so long, you must know when He has taken on some illness or some problem of others?'

'Oh yes! He is completely alright one minute and then suddenly He becomes very ill. After a while, He returns to normalcy.'

I looked at Dada and smiled. He smiled back like a shy child. Dada can speak in front of thousands of devotees, but, in reality, I have a strong feeling that He is truly shy by nature.

'Dada, is there a difference between the spirit and soul?'

'Yes. The spirit is free, but when the spirit is joined to the intellect and the mind, and through the mind the senses, it becomes a soul. The soul is to be freed, that is why you have the *Gurbani*: *Tritapan ka tap*, that is, the ills of the soul. Because the soul is in conjunction with the intellect and with the mind, and the mind is influenced by the senses. In the order of priority, it should be the other way round. Above the senses is the mind, above the mind is the intellect, above the intellect is the spirit. But the senses somehow or the other mislead the mind. The mind permits itself to be misled and this mind again misleads the intellect. And the intellect has an influence on the soul. So it has gone in the opposite direction.'

'So the spirit and the soul belong to the individual?'

'No. The spirit is One, it does not belong to the individual. It is One. It becomes differentiated when it joins hands with the mind and the senses.'

'So when the spirit in each individual is influenced by the mind and the senses, that gives rise to the soul. Thus, the soul is the individual consciousness within each one of us, while the spirit is the Oneness component, from which we have come. Would the intellect and wisdom be the discriminatory power of oneself?'

'Yes. The intellect says no because it has learnt to say no; the mind has not learnt to say no. The mind easily gives in. But the intellect, through experiences over various lifetimes, tries its best to prevent one from moving away from the Source. Ideally, the intellect or wisdom should govern the mind. But, in most cases, the mind governs the intellect, which leads to the fall of each of us.'

Basically what little I can understand is this: We all come forth from God. Sparks from the Great Flame. In our original form, we are still the spirit. In fact, we are still the Param Atman, as we are not corrupted by thoughts, desires and the mind. The moment the Param Atman in each individual gets influenced by thoughts and desires, it gives rise to individuality—it gives birth to individual souls. From Param Atman, we become just Atman. The soul is personal consciousness, which is encased in divine consciousness. This is my two-bit philosophy.

'The soul, due to thoughts and desires, covers the spirit. The soul, part of the One, passes from body to body. The spirit is unaffected by external things. The individual consciousness gets affected by things. The self abides, the bodies are transient.

'You may well ask: Why does the soul pass from body to body? My answer is that it does so to gather experiences and to evolve towards its abode in the Eternal. Just as the diverse bodies of our childhood, youth and age do not cause a doubt in our minds about the continuity of the self, so too the diverse bodies of different incarnations, especially the new body after death, should not cause us to doubt the continuity of the Atman.

'The spirit is the ocean, the soul is the wave, intellect is the drop of water and the mind is a collection of those drops of water. But the spirit is one . . . one ocean.'

'And our journey is to get the soul back into the state of the spirit.'

'When the ocean is calm, there are no waves. Then the soul and the spirit are one. But most of the time there are waves.'

'Thus one of the ways to make the ocean calm is through the practice of calm silence and peaceful acceptance. Is there any other way to bring about a state of centeredness or as they say "peace of mind"?'

'Either to practice silence or to engage oneself in some noble work. There was a case of an African American singer, Tom somebody. He used to sing songs which inspired thousands and he loved to sing. He was on a surgical table once and the mistake was that he was not given sufficient anaesthesia. He woke up during the operation and the surgeon feared he would die because of the shock and the pain. Tom was half asleep, half awake. So the surgeon said, "Tom, Tom, sing that song." And Tom sang the song, and the surgeon completed the operation in that time. So the mind can be silenced even without meditation. If he had told him "Tom, meditate . . ."'

We both began to chuckle.

'The mind is a wonderful instrument, which has been given to each one of us by the Lord. It is through the mind that we are able to think. It is with the help of the mind that we are able to do our daily work and this mind has tremendous powers. This mind can perform miracles, many of which are unbelievable.

'The capacity of the mind is unlimited. The potentiality is there, the mind needs to be trained. This mind and this brain, which God has given us . . . They are wonderful instruments! They have great potential, but we must be careful and think only the right type of thoughts. Remember our minds are linked, because each of our mind is only a fragment of the universal mind.

'You must have heard many cases of thought transference. A person thinks here, sends out a thought and somebody in a distant country receives that thought and writes to him. You must have heard of cases of telepathy. People they fix a time, they say at 6.00 in the evening, we shall sit in silence and we shall speak to each other across the spaces. Space is of no concern; space is not a limitation to the mind. I know of at least one case where there were two people who loved each other intensely. But one of them had to go to a distant place. Before going, he said to the other that every evening at 6.00, he would sit in silence; the other person too was to do the same and they would talk to each other. And they would note down these "conversations" they had. They found that about 80 per cent of what they had written down matched. Our minds are inter-linked; our minds are not isolated. Therefore, our mind can influence every other mind. This is the great responsibility that each one of us has. The thoughts that I think can influence the whole world.

'The great Rishis of ancient India said, "As a man thinketh, so he becomes." We are only shaping our future life with our own thoughts. As you think, so you become. Therefore, be very careful of your thoughts. So many of us, we lay blame on what we call our destiny, our stars. It all begins with the mind and through the mind, our thoughts. If you hold a thought consistently in the mind over a long period of time, it will drive you to action. A thought of impurity will take you down the road of impurity! The thought of service, of love, of compassion will lead you to an act of love, compassion, service. And actions, when repeated, form habits that determine our character. It is our character that determines our destiny. We are the masters of our own fate! We are the builders of our own fate. We are the builders of our own destiny. Therefore, be very careful about the thoughts you think.

'Take care of your mind, as it is through the mind we think and feel. The brain is a great instrument. It was a computer engineer, I forget his name at the moment, who said that the brain is by far the greatest computer. And he went on to tell us that the brain is capable of registering about 800 memories per second.'

'Eight hundred memories per second?'

'Yes, and it can go on doing so for seventy-five years without being tired. The brain is capable of storing anywhere between 10 billion and 100 billion pieces of information, whereas the biggest computer that we have is capable of storing only some millions of pieces of information that are fed to it. He also said that if you were to build a computer which could match the capability of the human brain, you would need space equal to the tallest building in the world. You would need all that space just to match the potential of the human brain. And he said you will need 1 billion watts of electrical energy to run it. The expenses would run to astronomical figures.

'Each one of us has received such a brain. Einstein, the great scientist, said, "We are able to use only a tenth of the power of the human brain." Perhaps he could use a greater part of the brain, but most men use only 1/10th of the potential of the human brain. That is fine. But whatever power we can use the brain in, let us begin to use it the right way. Therefore, think pure thoughts. Think thoughts of love, joy, peace, health, happiness, harmony, success, prosperity, service, sacrifice, simplicity and sympathy. Think those thoughts and only those thoughts that are going to influence the whole world. This is the miracle of the human mind.'

'Thus, when you are involved in something noble or for the larger good, or you connect your consciousness to the Divine, then that is a state of meditation too. Dada, You have talked about Lord Buddha's five ways of meditating . . .'

'The Buddha speaks of five types of meditation. The first is the meditation of love in which we adjust our heart so that we wish for the happiness for all living things, including the happiness of our enemies.

'The second is the meditation of compassion, in which we think of all beings in distress, vividly representing in our imagination their sorrows and anxieties, so as to arouse a deep compassion for them within us.

'The third is the meditation of joy, in which we think of the prosperity of others and rejoice with their rejoicings.

'The fourth is the meditation on impurity, in which we think of the evil consequences of immorality and corruption. In this meditation, we realize how trivial the pleasure of the moment is and how fatal are its consequences.

'The fifth is the meditation on serenity, in which we rise above love and hate, tyranny and oppression, wealth and want, and regard our own fate with impartial calm and perfect tranquillity.'

'Did Sadhu Vaswani ever teach different kinds of meditations?'

'No. His method was different. He let us free. But He must have kept a watch on us, of which we were not aware.'

'What was His main philosophy? I know, to serve people. But for His disciples, what were His main teachings?'

'His main philosophy was that while you serve people, you should not feel that you are serving them. He used to say, "Clasp God to your heart, then let your hands be busy helping others." So His emphasis was always on this thought: that you can, in no time, become anything more than mere instruments in the hands of the Lord, but, slowly and surely, when you selflessly serve as the instrument of the Lord, the Lord, in all His glory, makes you Himself. He spoke of various stages each individual can be on the journey of the eternal life. He said, "First one is a wanderer, then the wanderer becomes a seeker. Then the seeker becomes a pilgrim. The pilgrim becomes a disciple. The disciple (shishya) becomes a son (shishu). The son becomes the father himself."'

Wow. What a beautiful explanation. The pilgrim becomes a disciple. I guess by pilgrim Sadhu Vaswani truly meant devotee. The devotee becomes a disciple. Dada Vaswani, I am certain, has made sure that He has, on purpose, remained a disciple and a son. He shall always remain a disciple and a son of Sadhu Vaswani.

'Sadhu Vaswani once wrote a poem:

What am I?
A tiny candle; The flame is Thine!
What am I?
A singing bird; The song is Thine!
What am I?
A little flute; The music is Thine!
What am I?
A little flower; The fragrance is Thine!
What am I?
An earthen lamp; The light is Thine!

'Sadhu Vaswani often said, "I am not even a speck of dust. I am not an English zero, but a Sindhi zero, which is just a dot." Such was the humility of this great man. Would we ever think that we are nothing? Our mind would never ever let us consider ourselves the dot . . . which is almost invisible. Our mind makes us egoistic and thus, it is this ego which makes a few of us even deny God. A renowned philosopher from Germany, writes in one of his books, "Have you not heard that God is dead? Hasn't this news reached you yet?" I have also noticed that those men who deny God think very highly of themselves. They consider themselves above God. Kerala was the first state in India to elect a communist government to power. Communism denies the existence of God. Once, an assembly of people was called in a small village in Kerala. A stage was erected and a communist leader went up on to the stage and holding his watch in the air, he gave a call to the audience to deny the existence of God. He tried to mislead the gullible villagers by challenging God and said, "If there is God, then within three minutes He should kill me. If God is all-powerful, if He is omnipresent, then He should accept my challenge. He must kill me within three minutes, to prove that He does exist." Having made this declaration, he began the countdown to the three-minute deadline he had set for the Almighty! Hearing this, the villagers were appalled. Being humble folk, they were God-fearing by nature; they were believers. But they were taken aback at the speaker's audacity, challenging God to prove His existence. Surely, God would have to rise to the challenge! They waited anxiously for those never-ending three minutes to finish. The suspense kept mounting. Time ticked slowly, one minute, two minutes, three minutes passed. But God did not strike the atheist down! The communist leader did not fall to the ground. He stood there, erect. And he crowed in triumph, "Where is your God? Show me your God! If there was a God, He would have accepted my challenge and struck me down. But, there is no God and you had better believe it is so." In that provincial gathering was a devotee of the Lord. The devotee was a wanderer, who travelled from place to place, from village to village. During his pilgrimage, he happened to pass through this village. When he saw the gathering of people and the communist leader challenging the existence of God, he went up to the stage and said, "What is it that you are trying to prove by challenging God? Why do you think He has not accepted your challenge? If, standing on this stage you would deny your father and say, 'I have no father and I am born of my own accord', would it be true? Would you dare utter this kind of challenge to your father? Which father would accept your challenge and kill you within three minutes?" There was pin-drop silence. The devotee of the Lord continued, "The Father in Heaven loves you much more than your father on earth. God is smiling at your childish ignorance. God is smiling at your pride and ego. He permits you to do what you like, because you are his foolish child. For heaven's sake, do not deny God. God is, God was, God will be forever and ever more!"

'The account of this incident does not tell us about the discomfiture of the foolish speaker. But it does add that the simple villagers cheered the man of God heartily and thanked him for protecting their faith.'

I guess this is what the mind can make us do. It can makes us deny our very existence, for, in reality, have we not come forth from The One; the sparks of the Great Flame. By denying the Great Flame, are we not denying the spark, which is but our individual selves?

I made a note to myself: Stop adding your two-bit.

'Sadhu Vaswani would always say, "Can a drop of sea water deny the sea? Can a flower deny the root? Can a ray of light deny the sun? How can I deny Thee, O Lord?" These words still echo in my ears, whenever I have a chance to hear an atheist speak. All of life is a gift from God. In fact, neither you nor I, nor any of the millions of species on this planet, can exist without God. We are bound to God, just as a child in the womb of the mother is connected to her life-blood by the umbilical cord. If we are separated from Him even for a brief moment, we would simply drop dead. Why is it that we are sometimes prone to think that God is not with us? Why? Why do we feel lonely and helpless? If God is an ocean of love and He is always with us, why does He allow us to doubt His Love and His Divine Power? Why do we experience this feeling of being abandoned and orphaned? The reason is that there is an invisible veil between God and us. It is the veil of the self, the veil of the ego, the veil the mind creates. Gurudev Sadhu Vaswani often said, "When the ego goes, God glows."

'If only you erase the ego, slowly, and direct the mind to good thoughts, good words and good deeds, you will see God. Once, a question was put to Sadhu Vaswani, "What is true knowledge, the absolute knowledge, the greatest wisdom?" Gurudev Sadhu Vaswani replied, "True knowledge is the realization that I am nothing, He is everything. This realization makes man humble and gentle. And there is no wisdom greater than this."'

I guess when you begin to think in this manner, the mind automatically begins to turn inward. Slowly, the mind shuts its constant cribbing, neediness, wallowing and nonsense, and slowly the individual self drops the veil. And, one day, with His and Her Grace, realizes its true self. I could be wrong. I could be right. Make note, you are nuts. Let Dada speak.

'Once upon a time, a man sent his two sons to an ashram. His dearest wish was to give them true education. The sons came back home after spending some years in the ashram. The father embraced them affectionately and said to them, "My dear sons, welcome back to your family. Go and rest for a while; refresh yourselves. When you are rested and relaxed, come and meet me. I would like to have a dialogue with you."

'The sons did as they were told. After a comfortable rest and a good meal, they sat down to talk to their father. The father asked them eagerly, "My dear sons, tell me what have you learnt from the Guru in the ashram?" The elder son was very proud and egoistic. He mockingly said, "Father, it is impossible to tell you all that I have learnt. I have delved deep into the ocean of knowledge. I feel that my third eye is opened. I do not know from where to start and where to end. For the knowledge I have gathered is immense and the experiences I have had are infinite. I doubt very much if you can even begin to grasp the extent of my learning."

'The father then turned to the younger son and asked him, "What have you learnt during your stay in the ashram?" The young man remained silent, his head bowed down in deep thought. After much cajoling he said, "Father, it is true that my Gurudev has taught me many valuable lessons. But, sitting at His lotus feet, I came to *realize* that all the knowledge I gained from Him was not enough and that I had to learn much more from Him. On hindsight, I feel that I haven't learnt much. What I have learnt is only a small drop in the vast ocean of knowledge." Hearing this, the father was very happy. He said, "My dear son, the years you spent at the lotus feet of your Guru were selfless. I think you have acquired true knowledge."'

I guess why all Masters insist on meditation is that it is through this and calmness, the sand settles and when the sand settles, one can truly see how clear the water is and one can begin to think straight. As Dada had said earlier, the mind influences the soul, but true intelligence influences the mind. And if the mind is influenced the right way, the soul gets influenced the right way and if the soul is influenced in the right manner, it takes its first step towards self-realization.

'Though intelligence is very important, humility and devotion are the signs of true knowledge. Gurudev Sadhu Vaswani has said that at the highest stage, man is without self. Today, any man with a smattering of knowledge thinks he is something extraordinary. Many intellectuals and scholars came to Sadhu Vaswani to discuss truth, knowledge and wisdom. Sadhu Vaswani heard their views silently, without interrupting them to put forth His own point of view. Some of them would try to provoke Him into an argument. Smiling, He would say, "It takes two to have a discussion." He often advised us to stay away from discussions. If one person speaks, the other should keep quiet. Those who walk the spiritual path should not indulge in unnecessary debates. We waste our energy in unnecessary discussions and debates. In such discussions, there is always a person with an egoistic bend of mind, whose sole purpose is to challenge and debate to win an argument. Such futile activities take us away from the truth and absolute knowledge. A man of true knowledge knows that he is nothing and all that he has—intelligence, knowledge, intellect, even the ability to express himself forcefully—are all given to him by the Almighty God. This realization is true knowledge. He is linked with God. He becomes an instrument of God. Such a man is a beacon of light for others. That is one of the reasons that Gurudev urged us to be humble.'

'Does everything noble start with humility, Dada? Does it mean that in reality if the mind is influenced by intelligence, intelligence is influenced by wisdom and wisdom is influenced by devotion, which is influenced by humility, then what you are implying is that the mind in reality is influenced by humility. True humility.'

'Yes, true humility, which means being absolutely aware that one is but an instrument of our Lord. Once, a young man asked Sadhu Vaswani, "Why should we be humble?" It was night-time and the sky glittered with stars. Gurudev Sadhu Vaswani gazed at the sky and said, "My dear one, look at the sky and the millions of stars shining above you. Each star has its own universe. In such a vast galaxy of universes, this planet Earth is merely a speck of dust. And you are a tiny speck upon that speck of dust. Then, why are you proud?"

'During His European tour, Sadhu Vaswani visited Paris. There He was taken to see Napoleon's Memorial. Napoleon was a great general, who became the de facto emperor of France and he conquered many nations. Gurudev Sadhu Vaswani said later, 'When I stood by the grave of this great soldier, my eyes shed tears. The ruler of the great empire was just a fistful of dust."'

'Dada, if humility is virtually the foundation for self-realization as it guides the mind, which in turn guides the soul on the true path, how does one reach that state of humility?'

'Ruzbeh, all I can tell you is what my Gurudev often said to us, "The hum of humility is humiliation." If anyone criticizes you, if anyone degrades you, if anyone hurts you, then consider yourself lucky. Accept the harsh words of criticism and humiliation, because he lightens the burden of your ego.

'Although Sadhu Vaswani was revered by people and venerated as a saint, there were a few men who felt it fit to criticize Him. One day, a man came to Him and said unpleasant things about Him. Sadhu Vaswani listened to him carefully and smiled. He was the very personification of humility. His soft, gentle voice was like a soothing balm on the wounds of life. Devotees yearned to have His glance of kindness and hear words of blessings from Him. In response to the man's harsh words of criticism, Sadhu Vaswani bowed His head and said, "My dear one, you have taken great pains to come here to meet me. I am indeed grateful to you! I have learnt an important lesson from you!" The man felt ashamed of himself. He had expected fury from the saint. Instead, he received unmitigated kindness. That became his moment of transformation. He fell down at the feet of the Master, repenting and seeking forgiveness. "I have been a mindless critic of Yours for a long time. I have said words about You which are nothing short of blasphemy. I have humiliated You! I have spoken against I have written articles in newspapers denigrating You. Please pardon me!" Sadhu Vaswani embraced him, and said, "My dear one, I am on a path where humiliation is welcome. All the unpleasant words you have said and written against me are welcome. I have been taught to accept criticism and humiliation as welcome gifts!"

'This is the lesson that we too have to learn from the Master. Remain calm in the face of humiliation. Do not be disturbed by criticism. Do not be ruffled by people's adverse reaction to you. If you want to grow in the beauty of Higher Life, then accept criticism and praise in the same spirit, and you will be richly blessed!'

Krishna once narrated a similar occurrence from Dada's life to me.

'One day, an ambitious young man who had undertaken the arduous task of traversing the country on a bicycle, came to meet Sadhu Vaswani to get His blessings before embarking on the journey. Dada Jashan greeted him at the door and told him that he could not meet Sadhu Vaswani at that time since the Master was in His room and His door was closed. He would have to wait until the door opens.

'The man became very angry and said, "Who do you think you are? How dare you come in the way of my meeting Sadhu Vaswani? I am on a cycle tour. I don't have the time to wait."

'Dada calmly said, "But, my friend, Sadhu Vaswani's door is closed and we cannot disturb Him now." The man was furious and slapped Dada hard across the face.

'Dada remained unperturbed and remembered what His Gurudev had said in the morning satsang, "We must not retaliate." Sadhu Vaswani had quoted Jesus Christ saying, "If someone strikes thee on the on the right cheek, offer him the left." So Dada offered the man His other cheek. The man was furious and felt Dada was being impudent. Therefore, he slapped Him harder than before.

'A few moments later, the door opened and Dada guided the man to Sadhu Vaswani's presence. Sadhu Vaswani was His cordial self and greeted the man with great warmth and generosity, and loaded him with prasad.

'A bystander, who had watched all this happen, reported the events exactly as they had happened to Sadhu Vaswani. Sadhu Vaswani was moved to tears and embraced Dada Jashan very warmly, "My child, you have borne witness to a great truth and I am confident you will attain great heights." The great truth of humility.'

I remembered this story and looked at Dada. Tears welled up in my eyes. Dada, who had spoken about Sadhu Vaswani, also had tears in His eyes. When one sits in the presence of such humility, one can only bow down. This is what I did. I knelt down and put my head on Dada's knee. He, for the first time, caressed my head. I could have wept loudly.

The next day, I spent a bit of time at the Samadhi temple. Sadhu Vaswani's statue seemed different that day. It looked as though it were alive. Meher had instructed me to ask Sadhu Vaswani why He always stood with His right hand raised and one finger pointed skyward.

'In every photograph of His, He stands with a finger pointed to the sky. And you always tell me never to point a finger at anybody.'

'He is not pointing a finger at anybody . . .'

'He is. At God. God lives in the sky. He has a very big house there.'

'Ya, right.'

'He does. He lives in heaven and He has to live in a house. How would it look if God didn't live in a house?'

'He lives in our heart.'

'How can He live in our heart. He is not that tiny and if He lives in our heart, who takes care of heaven?'

'My head is hurting . . .'

'Tomorrow, you will tell me He lives in our head. Either He lives in heaven or in the heart or in the head. I think He lives in heaven. Please ask Dada Vaswani's Guru, why is His finger pointing to the sky?'

'Maybe He is telling all of us that God is One and to focus on Him.'

'You are very funny, daddy. You say anything sometimes.'

So I sat in front of Sadhu Vaswani and sort of put forward Meher's question to Him. Then I told Him that I was not in any hurry and not to get distracted, as I would need Him to come through Dada—we had begun to discuss about Him and His philosophy. I bowed down to Sister Shanti and put a little incense ash on my forehead and left.

I remembered Piya telling me about Sadhu Vaswani. Piya's mother used to frequent the Mission when Piya was in her mother's womb. She grew up seeing and being part of the satsang and, even as a child, she was certain that this is where she would spend the rest of her life.

'I always remember the memories of Sadhu Vaswani walking in front of our house. We lived across the Mission, and He used to come to our house and have a cup of coffee with my grandfather.

'He used to come to our compound; it was called Cannaught House at that time. He used to come walking with Dada on one side and one of the brothers on the other side. He would go to a couple of houses and then He would come to my house. I remember very, very clearly how He used to come and have coffee. Small cups of coffee. We have still kept those cups because Sadhu Vaswani drank from it. I still have those tiny cups.'

'How old were you then?'

'Two or three years old. I don't remember.'

'Yet you have a faint memory of Him coming and sharing coffee with your grandfather?'

'Those days were different. Sadhu Vaswani would visit a few homes and my house was the last one. We used to live in one of the houses that made up a row. He could be seen just outside my window and there would always be a huge crowd. People from other houses would drop in and there would be seventy or eighty people gathered. We kids would surround Him and it was so beautiful. Bada Dada would come and sit, and He would talk to us or He would just sit, say a little or may be write something. We used to give him green pieces of paper on which He used to write and Dada Jashan would read out what Sadhu Vaswani had written. And then He used to explain to us the meaning of what was written. Sometimes, Sadhu Vaswani would talk but often He would let Dada explain. Sometimes a spontaneous satsang would break out.

'Because the Cannaught House was so close to this Mission, Sati dadi would sometimes bring a cup of tea for Sadhu Vaswani, with the saucer over the lid. She would bring it all the way from this place to that without spilling a drop and then He would have the tea in front of us. He used to dip a biscuit in the tea and have it. It was so homely; we used to feel like an extended family.'

'My fondest memory is the way He used to look at me and the way He used to bless me. I used to be so small and He used to hold us by the shoulder or something . . . that's how I remember. I remember His touch. His hands were so soft. His skin was so translucent. I remember putting a rakhi on His hand and I would tell my mother, "I don't want to put the rakhi on him, as the string of the rakhi might tear His hand." I used to be so scared of hurting Him. That was the impression in my head. He used to be so soft. His eyes, His look were so tender and loving. You couldn't move away from His gaze.

'I remember my mother and I were going out somewhere, and Sadhu Vaswani was passing Cannaught House to go to the Council Hall. In front of the Council Hall, there was a lot of space and there were a lot of banyan trees. We used to sit under the banyan trees. My mother said,

"Let's go to Sadhu Vaswani" and behind him there were another fifteen or twenty people following him to Council Hall. He was distributing one rupee notes.'

'Those days one rupee was a decent sum of money.'

'Oh yes, and everybody took a note from him. I very clearly remember He gave me about twenty notes. One after another, He just kept giving me the notes. Kept looking at my face and kept putting one rupee notes in my small hand. I can't forget that day ever. I have kept all those notes in a silver box. I have everything He gave me. I have the garlands that He used to put around my neck when I used to give speeches in front of Him. I have everything. They are so old now, but I have got them all. These are my true treasures. I remember how He used to kindle the havan, light the fire. It used to be so nice and my grandfather also was always there.'

'The way you're describing Sadhu Vaswani, He must have been a very gentle person.'

'The most gentle of souls.'

Anyway, twenty minutes later, after chai, I sat by Dada's side. When Piya wanted to test the sound, Dada looked at me. As though He needed my permission to speak as I hadn't asked any question. It is these little things that make you realize the supreme level of humility He has.

'Bhakti, or devotion, and gyan, or wisdom, have to walk hand-in-hand for a seeker or a pilgrim to not only help them walk the path, but also move closer to the Destination. You cannot have gyana without bhakti, you cannot have bhakti without gyana. You can't get gyana without bhakti and you cannot get gyana until you have that deep love, and longing, yearning, deep yearning of the heart for gyana. What is longing and yearning? It is bhakti. There are people who have bhakti directly for gyana, then they achieve God. But bhakti is very necessary. All the three are very necessary: karma, bhakti, and gyana. They are not separate from each other; it is these three that have to be integrated into life.

'Our beloved Gurudev always said that life begins when the child is born. Now this child wants to do things, he is happy doing things, he does something and says, "Mama, I've done this." His emphasis is on doing things, but when he grows up, he wants to know the what, why, where, who of life, of the universe, of the creation in which he lives. That is the stage of gyana. After passing through that stage, he arrives at a stage where he realizes that nothing counts except love. Love is the be all and end all of life. He becomes the bhakta.'

Dada looked at me and smiled. I cleared my thought.

'Dada, what was the one thing Sadhu Vaswani emphasized on?'

'Oh, without doubt it was purity of life. He was of the firm belief that there can be no growth in perfection without purity. The senses must be pure; whether they are overfed or starved, the result is weakness. Maharishi Patanjali, too, asserts that yoga is not to be taught to those whose bodies are unsound. Therefore, the prayer is, "May my senses grow in perfection!"

'Sadhu Vaswani spoke of various aspects of our life that needed purification. The very first is *vaak*, voice or talk or speech. Voice is the outer expression of thought. Vaak must be purified if you wish to grow in the perfect life. Utter what you believe to be true. Speak out the truth, but not in bitterness. Purify your utterance by means of love. Do not wound or hurt the feelings of others.

'Next to vaak is prana. Prana too must be purified, for it is our "life breath". Many of us control speech, but are unable to control prana. When breath is properly controlled, drawn in and let out, it helps to keep body and mind healthy.

'Next to prana is chakshu which is interpreted as sight. If only we realized how many sins are committed due to untrained, uncontrolled sight! A volume could be written on the modern degradation through sight, degradation brought about by watching impure, unhealthy, unwholesome entertainment and reading sensational novels.'

Yes, that is true. I couldn't agree more. And with the Internet and the mobile phone, the propensity of young minds being lured into the sinking sands of degradation through sight is frightening. Ask any parent this.

'Remember within pleasure, there is a seed of pain. That's the law of life. That seed is going to sprout, it is going to germinate. You will get a tree and the fruit will have to be eaten by you. The fruit may be sour, the fruit may be bitter, the fruit may be sweet. The fruit will depend upon the seed you are sowing. If it is a seed of pleasure, the fruit is going to be bitter. That bitter fruit will have to be eaten by you. The world in which I lived was different. This world is so full of temptations; it is very easy for me to preach things which the present generation will not understand. I am not sure what would come of me if I was born at this time and age. I never saw any movie which was not shown to us by either our elders or our school. The greater the temptation, the greater is the strength that one will draw by resisting it. Within us is that strength. There is the fount of strength within us all and you have to draw on it.' 'So Dada how does one gather that strength?'

'For purification and strength, one needs true discipline and Sadhu Vaswani said that discipline should come from within and it cannot be imposed from the outside. It is self-discipline. You must decide for yourself, what do you want in life? If you want to be a wreck, if you want to ruin your life, follow the path of pleasure.

'There are two ways indicated by the great Rishi in the Upanishads. He says that at every step the option is before you to either walk the way of *preya* or to walk the way of *shreya*. Preya is the pleasant, shreya is the good. Preya is a slippery path. It is very easy, very smooth. Shreya is the rugged path. It is the upward path. It is like moving on a slope. But if you move on the path of shreya, you reach the high ground and who knows, you may even reach the highest peak. If you move on the path of preya, you ruin your life. You have to make your choice. The option is before you at every step.

'You can purify your actions by offering it to the Lord. It is true that in the Gita the Lord speaking to His dear, devoted disciple, Arjuna, says to him, "Arjuna, whatever you eat, whatever austerity you practice, whatever you give to charity, whatever you do, do it as an offering unto me. If you do everything as an offering unto the Lord, Lord this be my offering unto Thee, pray accept it, it gets purified and it becomes bhakti."'

'But what is true bhakti?'

'Bhakti is another word for love. Love, bhakti—they are the same thing. But this love is unconditional love; you love without any condition. The love that one gives to God is bhakti. Do everything with that emotion of love and it becomes bhakti, and that bhakti will purify one and all.'

'Is that the path to true purification?'

'Yes, but Ruzbeh, purity comes with truth; otherwise, you cannot be pure or shudh. You can be shudh only if you are true. Blessed are the pure in heart for they shall see God. The first is purity and then there is illumination, and with that comes unification.'

'What is illumination?'

'In every heart, there is a point of light shining. It is the Light Divine. You can see it only when you turn within yourself. My beloved Master Gurudev Sadhu Vaswani has written a beautiful, small book titled *In the Veil of Dawn*. This book is a gold mine of wisdom. It describes the light glowing in the interior of the heart. Rishis of ancient India have described the human heart as a cave; deep inside is this light which shines bright. It is a point of light within. This light is beautiful to behold.

'Man is ever in search of inner peace. It is only when man turns within that he begins to find peace. Enter the cave, the dark deep cave of your heart, and behold! The bright point of light, magical, eternal, and overwhelming, fills you with its radiance. You may commit many sins; you may live a life which is evil and dehumanizing. All that is outside the range of light. The dark, evil doings are on the surface of life. All this evil can never, ever extinguish this light within as it is eternal. The day this light pierces the darkness of the heart and glows with its unique inner radiance, you will receive answers to your many questions. Once you have its vision, you will know your true identity. You will know the reason why you are here. You will know the purpose of your life. You will clearly see the goal and the path you must walk to attain it.

'This physical body should be a temple of worship. For it enshrines the Light. That is why it is said, *Shariram Brahma Mandiram*: the body is the temple of God. We should enter this temple and have His darshan, rather than roam/wander far away in search of Him. Unless we witness this light within, we will not be able to experience God. The vision of this inner light is God realization.

'True, the light of the Param Atman shines within each one of us; but, alas, we live in the outer darkness, unaware of the Light within. Like the aristocrats of the medieval ages, we are absorbed in hunting—hunting for pleasure in the forests of the senses. What do we know of the Light within us?

'Let me repeat, the Light inextinguishable dwells within each one of us, but we cannot see it, for it is hidden behind veils of ignorance, veils of mind and matter. The great wall of the ego stands between us and the Param Atman, and we cannot see the Light Divine. It is the Guru who can destroy the great wall of the ego and lead us from darkness to light.

'The Guru reaches out to us and, with His grace, annihilates the ego; He tears away the veils of ignorance, which shield us from self-realization. He reveals our true identity to us—*Tat Twamasi!* That thou art! It is His grace that liberates us from bondage to the circle of life and death. This gift of grace has devolved on the Guru from God Himself, for God knows that the world is in dire need of grace.

His presence is of course universal; He gives us the Guru, for our individual benefit, for our personal liberation.

'This is why our ancient scriptures enjoin us to venerate the Guru as God. This is the greatest blessing that the Guru can bestow on us. He leads us out of the darkness of *moha* and maya into the light of detachment and peace. After this realization, we enter the Realm of Light; we will reach our eternal home illuminated by the radiance of that Light.

'It was Swami Vivekananda who said, a century ago, that the man who has taken up five ideals and makes them a part of his life, is far more learned than a man who has consumed a whole library of books. A whole library of books, just imagine! What is needed in life is to be a witness in your daily life. Therefore, the rishis spoke of these three stages in the life of every seeker. The first is *shravana*—listening. Listening with attention. Nobody listens with attention today. Students don't listen with attention, there is no attention. A teacher was trying to teach a lesson to his students when he looked at the boy and found he was not paying attention. So he wanted the boy to look at the board on which the teacher had written important points. He called out to the boy and said to him, "Ramesh, board, board." And Ramesh got up and said, "Yes, sir, very bored." The very first step is shravana.'

Dada's eyes twinkle when He smiles. It is a child-like smile—one of complete honesty.

'The second is *manana*. What you have heard, what you have read, what you have recited, you must go and reflect on it. You must go and sit in silence. And reflect on the teaching. There may be something that you may not have understood properly. Then you must enquire with the right person, or whoever guided you, and in the spirit of reverence, place before the teacher or guide your difficulties.

'Then is *nidhyasan*, you must meditate on this truth so much so that you make it a part of your life. You become a living moving picture of that ideal. Today, there is no integration in our thoughts words and action. We think one way, we speak another, we behave in a third way. This is yoga. Yoga is integration. An integration has to be worked out between thoughts, words and deeds.'

'Are there road maps on the search of self-realization, Dada?'

'The sufi Masters tell us that there are three journeys on the road to self-realization. During the first journey, man wanders endlessly and moves away from Truth. The restless mind pushes man to seek all the pleasures of the world and he gets caught in worldly affairs, forgetting the purpose of his journey. We may easily recognize that this is the journey most of us are currently pursuing! The second journey begins with the awakening of the soul. It begins with the awareness that we have to return home. For long have we floundered. For long have we wandered. It is time to go back. A voice within us urges us to return to home. We realize it is time to return. When this awareness hits us, and I use the word hit deliberately because it is a sharp and painful awakening, we are disturbed and unsettled, even slightly disoriented. We begin to question the worth and value of all that we have achieved in worldly terms. We are seized by a sudden feeling of restlessness, a feeling of discontent, which in turn leads to self-interrogation, introspection, and a review and re-evaluation of our chosen goals and objects. "There must be more to life than this!" is the one thought that impels us at this stage. Then the third journey follows as a logical consequence to the second. We realize that we have wandered from our path; we feel that we have lost our way somewhere in the course of our wandering. We make the crucial U-turn that will take us back to God. God is our source and origin; He is also the destination of our earthly journey. He is the ultimate goal of our life. When we make the U-turn, we have begun our most crucial journey. It is then that we begin the serious, persistent search for God. This is the quest that has taken yogis, rishis, *munis*, *jignasus*, sufis, mystics, to river banks, to *tapobanas*, to mountain tops, to places of worship. Realized souls find Him whom they seek, without too much trouble. But the rest of us are not so fortunate. We wander hither and thither; many places beckon us and we are lost in these wanderings. The first journey may be the result of an unheeding, unaware attitude; the second journey is the dawn of true awareness; and the third and final journey must always be a conscious, deliberate exercise, undertaken of our own free will and the effort to translate that will into reality. In other words, it is a journey towards self-awareness! But it is not the end! For I believe that there is a fourth and final journey, which represents the ultimate—it is the journey within the self, within God. By its nature, this quest, this journey, is indefinable, infinite. Most important of all, it is highly personal and, therefore, exclusive to each one of us.

'At this stage, I wish to state something clearly: spirituality is not a problem to be solved or a puzzle to be unravelled; it is cultivating an awareness, an attitude to life. The following anecdote from Buddhist scriptures is a case in point. An elderly grandmother once approached the Buddha and told Him that she longed to live a spiritual life; but she was too old and frail to withstand the rigors of monastic living. Moreover, her household chores were so tedious and time consuming that she could not set aside enough time to meditate. "What can I do?" she wailed. "Respected grandmother," replied the Buddha, "every time you draw water from the well for your family, remain aware of every movement and motion of your hands and wrists. As you carry the water jug on your head, be aware of every step that your feet take, as you attend to the chores in your kitchen, maintain continuous mindfulness moment after moment. You too will discover the art of meditation." And, thus, through the art of meditation, you will begin the true journey.'

'Dada, according to you, what is spirituality?'

'I think I would like to answer the question in another manner. There is such a thing as definition by negation; you can grasp certain concepts by clearly understanding what they are not. This works especially with abstract and complex concepts. Thus, poverty is the absence of wealth. Sadness or depression is the absence of joy. In this sense, negation becomes what we call a logical complement; defining a thing by what it is not.

'We can safely assume that spirituality is not the same as religion. It is not a rite or ritual or a set of practices. It is not dogma or doctrine, and it is not the prerogative of the evolved seeker. It is not abstract or esoteric to practice, and is not all mysticism and esoteric rites. It has nothing to do with what we call "the supernatural" and is not about theology or philosophy. It is not meant exclusively for the old or the wise or the religiously devout or the super-intelligent or the realized ones. Spirituality is not a set of specific actions or way of doing things and it is not asceticism or renunciation, though some people have chosen them as preferred modes to attain self-knowledge.

'Through this process of negation we arrive at what spirituality is all about, but I must emphasize, it is different for each one of us. According to me and the little experience I have, spirituality is essentially a quest for self-discovery. It is choosing what you would want your true self to be and become. It is an attempt to go beyond the external world of materialism. It is a desire to transcend the ego, its limitations, its fears and insecurities. It is an effort to discover or understand the unity of all creation. It is the knowledge that I and my fellow human beings and my fellow creatures are part of the one whole. It is uniquely personal and yet emphasizes the interconnectedness of all creation. It is an aspiration to discover and fulfil the purpose of human existence. It is discovering the power of love, compassion and respect . . . in fact, reverence for all forms of life. It is the awareness that there is more to one's life than worldly success and achievements. It is discovering the Divine within you and within all of creation. It is discovering true joy, peace and contentment. It means something different to each seeker. At its best, it is yoga, a union with God. But, very importantly, for me as an individual, it is easy to detach spirituality from religion, but not from God! I do believe that atheists and agnostics can also be deeply spiritual in their own way. But for me, spirituality is man's quest for God.'

'And according to Sadhu Vaswani?'

'In Chapter XII of the Bhagavad Gita, the Lord outlines for us the attributes and qualities which make a devotee dear to Him. These are listed in the last eight verses of this chapter, which are described as the Gita Amritashtam, meaning the nectar of the Gita in eight slokas. Before the evening satsang in the Sadhu Vaswani Mission, we hear these eight slokas in the divine, melodious, mellifluous voice of our Gurudev Sadhu Vaswani. What are the qualities of the true bhakta who is dear to the Lord? He is free from ill-will and egoism. He bears no ill-will to any creature; he is forgiving, and is poised in pain and pleasure. He is content and ever in harmony, his mind and understanding dedicated to the Lord. He does not disturb the world, nor is he disturbed by the world. He is without ambition, and free from passion and fear. He does not rejoice, grieve or crave for anything. He is the same to both foe and friend. He is the same in honour and dishonour; he is free from attachment. He takes praise and blame alike. He is satisfied with whatever the Lord has granted him.'

Make note: My God must be hopping mad with me.

'And, Dada, what is this higher and lower self-philosophy? Do we have a higher and lower self?'

'Have you heard the story of the man who had two wives?'

'Oh, yes, many. They all are filled with humour and never ends well for the man.'

'I meant this particular story. Let me narrate it to you. One wife was old, nearer to the man in age, while the second was much younger. The younger one wanted her husband to appear young. So, whenever she saw a grey hair on his head, she would pull it out, day after day.

'The first wife, on the other hand, was anxious that she should not appear to be older than her husband. And so, she took to the habit of pulling out some of his black hair, day after day. She was convinced that this would make him appear mature and respectable.

'The result? The man soon lost all the hair on his head! There are two "selves" within us, the higher and the lower. The higher nature impels us to overcome all that is negative in us, like greed, envy, anger and hatred, but the lower nature is inclined to suppress all that is positive and lead us towards evil. The human soul is torn between these two conflicting forces of good and evil. It is only when we strengthen the positive forces within us, and identify with our higher self, that we can attain God-realization.

'So it is with our lives. It is only when we will live consciously, vigilantly, aware of everything we say and do, that we can achieve good karma. We need to act with wisdom, enlightenment and balance. Sadhu Vaswani believed that there are two selves. And we were under the influence of the lower self. We needed to contact the higher self.'

'How do you contact the higher self?'

'One of the ways is selfless activity. There are other ways, but one of the ways which every one of us could follow is selfless activity, *nishkam* karma.'

'So, basically, selflessness is needed to move from the lower self to the higher chap.'

'Selflessness is very necessary because if man is selfish, it is as he if rooted to the ground. He has to fly, but for that he needs to be selfless; and usually selflessness comes forth from the sense of seva which in turn comes forth with the grace of Guru, God, Goddess. Because without grace, there is always this danger that the disciple may become egoistic and egoism is a deadly poison as then it brings about selfishness. Therefore, at every step, as the disciple moves forward, he has to thank the Lord. He has to feel grateful to God. It is God who has brought him either to a state of selflessness or into the contact with the Guru, who has guided him to such a place of selflessness. And the words "gratitude to Thee O Lord" should be on the lips of the disciple all the time.'

'So selflessness is most important to operate from the higher self, but, Dada, could it be that when an individual is operating from the higher self, it is then he comes forth from the place of gratitude and selflessness?'

'Nothing happens without His grace, Ruzbeh. Without His blessings, without His favour, the seeker is nothing. There have been cases where a person has not been conscious of the blessings of the Lord. It appears as though he has done it all on his own. But, let me tell you, behind all his efforts, without his knowing it, there is the blessing of the Lord. He may know it, he may not know it, but the upliftment that he has received is the grace of the Guru and the Lord. Blessed is the man who knows it. Such a man walks the way of humility.

'When you become aware of all that you have to be grateful for, when you actually begin to count your blessings, you will be overwhelmed with gratitude for all that God has bestowed on you so unstintingly. Your peaceful sleep, your loved ones whose dearest wish is just to see you happy, your friends who add value to your life, your good health which you utterly fail to appreciate until you fall ill, the fresh air and sunlight around you, the marvels of technology which have made your life so easy, the society and community which lets you live in peace and order, where would you be without all this?

'Gratitude is the foundation of a peaceful life, a secure and stable mind; it is also the essence of spirituality. Many people think that if they had a little more of this or that, a little more than what they now have, they would indeed be very happy, satisfied and thankful. They are quite mistaken. If we are not satisfied with what we have, we are not likely to be satisfied even if it were increased many times!'

'But why is it that even spiritual people, those who are selfless and doing good, noble work still harbour intense envy or jealousy? Isn't that a paradox?'

'Envy is closely allied to multiple negative traits; covetousness or craving to possess what is not ours, jealousy or excessive fear of losing what we have, extreme attachment and possessiveness, resentment and bitterness at the good that happens to others.

'Envy leads to ill-will, destructive thinking, constant criticism of others, disliking others for their good qualities, denying and negating their talents, skills and achievements, and rejoicing in the misfortune or downfall of others.

'Envy is often used interchangeably with jealousy; there is a difference between the two in terms of the degree of feeling and the target of the feeling. To put it simply, envy is directed towards objects and material possessions. Thus, I feel a pang of resentment and malice when I see the brand new car my neighbour has bought, and compare it unfavourably with the small, old car that I drive. Jealousy is concerned with people, relationships and attitudes. Thus, I feel sidelined and ignored, when my colleague is praised by the boss, or my wife praises a friend of mine for his qualities, attributes or achievements. At heart, jealousy is fear of losing something which I possess—the love of my wife, the respect of my colleagues or the admiration of my boss. It is said that envy involves two people, while jealousy involves three; but, I think this is an oversimplification!

'There are people like Duryodhana who are envious of everything and everyone in the opposite camp; there are people too like Othello, who is tortured by a purely sexual jealousy of his young, innocent wife. ". . . the green eyed monster that doth mock the meat it feeds on . . ."

'How may we overcome the poisonous, cancerous traits of envy and jealousy? If I may offer a few practical suggestions. First and foremost, we must realize that envy can do us far more harm than it can do to those whom we envy. Envy leaves us miserable and frustrated and bitter. The person against whom it is directed may not even be aware of our meanness towards him and if our envy shows up so openly that he is aware of it, it can only lower his opinion of us!

'In spiritual terms, envy is an offense against God, for it leaves us ungrateful to God for His many gifts, while we pine for all that we do not have. The antidote to this is to thank God all the time, for the countless blessings He has conferred upon us. Where gratitude to God is, there can be no envy of our fellow human beings.

'An effective and constructive way to overcome envy is to send out love and blessings to our rivals, when an envious thought so much as crosses our mind. Thus, if you are envious of X, utter a silent prayer "May God bless dear X! May he/she always be my friend."

'Try and appreciate your rivals for their genuine achievements. Admiration and appreciation are positive emotions, and will draw what you admire into you! As they say, imitation is the best form of flattery! By imitation, I do not mean blind copying, but rather emulating or becoming like the people whom we admire. Emulate the winning traits of your rivals—like punctuality, courtesy, pleasant manners, honesty, efficiency, time management, etc. Not only will this enhance your performance, but it will also add to your self-esteem and make you feel proud of yourself.

'Envy is negative; aspiration is positive. Therefore, visualize yourself succeeding, achieving your goals like those whom you admire. But don't just stop with daydreams; turn your dreams and aspirations to reality by taking concrete action to achieve what you desire.

'An idle mind is always likely to fall prey to negative traits like envy. Therefore, let us engage ourselves in constructive good work, like selfless service and offering help to people who need it. When we focus on constructive tasks, negativities are driven out our minds.

'Nurture a healthy sense of self-esteem by becoming aware and appreciative of your own good qualities. Remember that you are unique and that God created you for a special purpose.

'Avoid comparing yourself, your status, your possessions and your achievements with others. Unfavourable comparisons only lead to frustration. Realize that each one of us has our own role to play in the eternal drama of life.

'Anything that causes the mind to lose its balance is detrimental to our happiness, and the best way to restore the mind to balance and harmony is to practice the virtue of contentment. Prayer and recitation of the Name Divine are quick and easy ways to attain contentment.

'Robinson Crusoe, alone on his deserted island, says, "I do not possess anything I do not want, and I do not want anything I do not possess." Contentment can come from wanting less and feeling more grateful for what we have.'

And last but not the least I mused, everybody eats out of their destiny and karma. If somebody is raking it in good, obviously the chap has done something to bring the windfall of prosperity or success or good looks or qualities or popularity. Like there is a saying in Hindi which goes something like this: Nothing happens before its time and there is nothing more can be provided than what is written in one's destiny.

7

'Dear Sadhu Vaswani, today I will be asking a lot more about You and Sister Shanti. I hope You are ready to come through. Qualities like humility and modesty are very noble but it does not make for very good raw material when someone is trying to collate a book together. So I will need You to come through freely.' I bowed to Him and Sister Shanti and then sent a quick prayer to Sai Baba of Shirdi to convince Sadhu Vaswani, in case the latter was in one of His many silent, meditative moods. I walked up to the Kutiya.

Naresh had one look at me and in a few minutes, a cup of tea was placed in my hand.

'Ruzbehji, our Dada always enquires if you have been given tea. I think He knows how important nicotine in all forms is to you.'

'Go away.'

After a few minutes of just being in the Kutiya, checking the cameras, Jyotish approached wielding a camera and I could make out he wanted to tell me something but wasn't sure how to frame the words.

'Trust me, I am very selective of who I bite. What's it?'

'The sweatshirt you have got on will interfere with the sound.'

'And you decided to tell me five minutes before the interview?'

'You always bring a fresh change of clothes when interviewing Dada.'

'Not today as I came from home directly.'

Krishna joined us. She came up with a solution. There was a play being enacted on the life of Sadhu Vaswani. They had stitched clothes that Sadhu Vaswani used to wear. A white kurta was brought for me. I changed and it fitted me just right. For me, it was like an affirmation that Sadhu Vaswani was with us during the interviews. Such a show of proof could only come forth from my Sai of Shirdi, who never was very subtle about making His Presence felt or His miracles known.

And how different in temperament were both Sai Baba of Shirdi and Sadhu Vaswani. Baba didn't mince words. He swore sometimes like a sailor on shore. He performed miracles at the drop of a hat. He smoked and He cooked even non-vegetarian food for His devotees. Yes, He barely ate and was always in communion with the Lord, but He was like a Royal Lion, who was the mother of all Rages. And then you had Sadhu Vaswani. A pure vegetarian. Soft-spoken. All miracles were performed silently. Never spoke a harsh word and was always in control of His temper. But the differences were all superficial. They both took on the sufferings of their flock. Both were immersed within and throbbed with the flow of Divinity. They served and served and served. Respecting the laws of karma but in their own way safeguarding the innumerable devotees for whom they were God in human form. Eventually it is all about playing different roles to achieve the same outcome . . . to spread radiance, fragrance, love, compassion and bring each and every child back home.

I sat down on my seat on the floor and zoned out. A few minutes later, Dada, Krishna, Piya and Gulshan entered. After some time, Dada looked at me and His eyes lit up. We tried to touch each other's feet and I won hands down.

'Dada, Ruzbeh is wearing the shirt that the actor who will play your part will wear.'

Krishna explained to Dada the chain of events. He smiled. Spoke something in Sindhi. Piya smiled.

'Dada says you look very handsome but you know nobody can look as handsome as Dada.'

'Goes without saying,' I acknowledged the fact.

When things were being arranged, I informed Dada that today I would like to ask a few questions about Sadhu Vaswani. Not only about the Master that he was, but the man too. Dada smiled. He has the most childlike smile. He is, if you ask me, with the angels most of the time. Only a part of Him has remained behind for the mortal world.

'Sadhu Vaswani was simple in His dress and diet and daily living and as the truly great are, He was, in His simplicity, sublime. At one time, He lived in the Hari Mandir, a big hall in which a mattress was spread on one side. Sadhu Vaswani slept on the mattress at night, and during the day, sat on it and did His work. There was a small desk on which He did His writing, as He sat on the floor. And there were many books spread all over.

'One day, a Frenchman visited him. He had learnt of Sadhu Vaswani through the writings of Paul Richard, who had said about Sadhu Vaswani, "I have been blessed, for amidst the deserts of Sind, I have found a true Prophet, a messenger of the new Spirit, a saint, a sage, and a seer, a *Rishi* of new India, a leader to the great Future . . . Sadhu Vaswani."

'The Frenchman had expected to see Sadhu Vaswani living in a beautifully furnished house. He was astonished to see that Sadhu Vaswani's dwelling was a simple hall with a mattress, a desk and books. He asked Him, "Where is your furniture?" Sadhu Vaswani asked him, "Where is yours?" The Frenchman said, "I have no furniture. My furniture is in my home in France. I am only travelling through here." Softly, Sadhu Vaswani answered, "So am I, my friend."

Then Dada faced the camera. While He was talking to me, I motioned to Piya and Jyotish to make sure all this gets recorded. Dada continued.

'Think of Jamshed Nusserwanji. Born into a wealthy family, he spent all his wealth in the service of the poor. He was elected and re-elected as the mayor of Karachi in undivided India for nine terms! The city's cleanliness and sanitation at that time spoke volumes for the quality of his work. Though he had a large, palatial building allotted for his use, he actually lived in a small room, which served as his bedroom, sitting room and office. He slept on a simple wooden board. Born with the proverbial silver spoon, he learnt to renounce luxury, and to live a life of simplicity. What a beautiful example of simplicity this great soul left behind for all of us to emulate!

'Then there was Leela Shah; not only did he renounce wealth and power, he did not crave for name and fame! So much so, when he passed away, this great saint owned practically nothing! Like Sadhu Vaswani, Leela Shah also thought of himself as nothing. "We are but servants of God," he would often remark. There were just two simple log cabins . . . more like huts . . . in his Nainital ashram; one for himself, and the other for his guests. He slept on the floor, and often walked barefoot. His hut had no doors, only an entrance, which was so low that people had to bend down in order to enter. Has it not been said to us? "To enter into the kingdom of God, we must first become humble as ashes and dust."

'I do not expect anybody to live a life of renunciation. I only want you all to remain free from the burden of your own wealth! I do not want you to become like the camel, which, Jesus said, could never enter the eye of the needle. I do not want your wealth or your vanity to become obstacles to your entry into a better life hereafter.

'The human tendency is to accumulate possessions. Great and small needs, perceived needs and felt needs prompt us to acquire more and more wealth, more and more things, more and more comforts and amenities. Possessions take us far, far away from the ideal of simplicity!

'Airlines, as you know, are very strict in restricting passengers to carry only a specific quantity of baggage. Excess baggage is charged heavily.

'Many of our possessions, our luxury cars, designer clothes, diamonds, jewels, rings, bracelets, silks and woollens are also "excess baggage" in the journey of life.

'Sadhu Vaswani reiterated the same clarion call that Thoreau gave us, the same call that Mahatma Gandhi made the mantra of his life: "Simplify! Simplify! Simplify!"

'Simplicity is not self-denial. It is a return to those values that matter the most in life. It emphasizes spontaneity and naturalness; it enables us to escape the empty shows of pomp and artificiality. It helps us to rediscover the crucial fact that the best things in life are not those which we buy with our money!

Then Dada turned towards me and smiled like a shy boy, His eyes inquiring if what He had spoken was enough. I began to laugh. He joined in with me. I doubt if anybody understood why we were both chuckling away. Then I took a deep breath and heard Dada too breathe in deeply.

'Why was He, Sadhu Vaswani, called Dada and why are you also called by the same name?'

'Dada, in our Sindhi language, means elder brother. When they referred to the Master as Sadhu Vaswani, he said, "Don't call me Sadhu, I am not a Sadhu, I am your Dada; just a simple Dada". It was His sense of oneness and closeness with His followers that made Him feel that He was one of us. Dada was the name He chose for Himself.'

'Is this why you have also continued with the tradition?'

'I don't know why they call me Dada. I don't think of myself as Dada. I think of myself as a child.' He smiled.

'Was Sadhu Vaswani's father, Diwan Lilaram, a very ardent follower of Maa Kali?'

'Yes, he was a much devoted worshipper of Maa Kali. He used to recite the "Chandi Paath", sometimes standing on one leg.'

'He had been bestowed with the gift of healing.'

'Oh yes,' he said, like a child full of wonderment and amazement. 'He had the gift. People used to come to him and he had a box where people put in their offerings. He was not rich; he had land but they were not productive, so the income was less. But he would never touch any offering in the box. He said all offerings were meant for Maa Kali and thus were meant for the poor.'

'Do you think that is the way to go about when your own family is going through a very hard period? You are not charging for it but somebody is putting an offering out of his or her goodwill. Isn't that being a little unfair to the family because you are giving your time and energy at a huge price?'

'I think if you move on the spiritual path, you will naturally believe and naturally do things which people will take to be hard on the family. That is what Mahatma Gandhi also did, and his elder son could not understand him. And he asked his father, "Why are you so hard on us?" The seeker on the path does not wish to be caught in the spirit of attachment. So, in every one of his acts, he is careful to see that he takes a detached view of life. I remember reading about a judge in the bygone days, His son had committed a heinous crime and the case had to be decided by him. He said in the open court that he would write the judgment that night and come and deliver it the following day. The wife pleaded with her husband that night, shed tears and told him not to give him capital punishment as he was their only son. The judge did not say a single word in answer. He went to the court the next day and delivered his judgment: it was capital punishment. He got out of the court and embraced his son who was now a prisoner. He went home and just five minutes after he entered his house, dropped down dead. But he did not depart from what he thought was his duty. I forget the name, but I think it is Charuchander Datt who sentenced his son to capital punishment and dropped dead soon after.'

'Dada, I understand the judge who gave a true and honest judgment according to what he thought was right. But I don't get Mahatma Gandhi or even Sadhu Vaswani's father. Even their family is part of the cosmic family. To say that I prefer the cosmic family to the biological family is also not in the right spiritual vein unless you are trying to prove some other point. If you can let your own family starve to feed another, are you not being unfair to somebody or the other. What fault is theirs that they belong to you?'

'This one thought that he is my son will always be lurking at the back of your mind. You can't escape that. Therefore, Gandhi did not give the scholarship to his son though I think he deserved it. But he said, just because he is my son, I will not give it. I will give it to somebody else. Gandhi was the trustee, he had to decide. And this is what broke his son's heart. He asked, "Is this the way to treat me just because I am his son?"

'Thus, though you are spiritual in one aspect, you are not being spiritual in the other. I didn't understand this; I think it would be nice if you were just fair to all concerned . . .'

'I have given this a lot of thought. It would have been fair had he passed on the right to judge whether his son deserved the scholarship or not to somebody else.'

'I think that would have been the right thing as well as a spiritual thing to do.'

'Get out of the picture and let somebody completely unbiased take the call.'

'Did Sadhu Vaswani ever talk about His father and mother?'

'Very rarely. Sadhu Vaswani was more drawn to His mother than to His father because His father passed away while He was still studying in school.'

'Did His mother have a very deep influence on Sadhu Vaswani?

'I wouldn't say a deep influence, but He had great regard for his mother.'

'But He was very close to his brother Shri Pahilajrai, wasn't He?'

'That was my father. He was the elder brother of Sadhu Vaswani. The two were close to each other. On one occasion, I remember Sadhu Vaswani saying to me, "If there was one member of our family who understood me, it was my elder brother."'

'I have read that He had a deep reverence for His brother.'

'Yes, He did have reverence for His brother. Once, He accepted an assignment at St John's College, Delhi; in those days it was regarded as a prestigious event. He had to give an annual address there. He was in Delhi when He got the news that his elder brother had fallen seriously ill and He cancelled all His appointments to come home. But I must say that His elder brother also had great reverence for Sadhu Vaswani. It was mutual love and respect between the brothers. Usually, if there is a younger child in the family who takes to spirituality the family doesn't understand Him. But, His elder brother had deep reverence for Him and understood His spiritual aspirations. Sadhu Vaswani was an exceptional person. He excelled on several fronts. He was not only a Sadhu but also a learned man, a professor, a scholar, a poet, and also a great organizer.

'He was a very good orator, wasn't He?'

'Oh, what an orator He was! In the days of His youth and manhood, whenever He lectured, the very stage on which He stood up and spoke used to shake.' Dada gestured and His face glowed with admiration, love and pride for His Master. He held his breath and His eyes bulged with excitement. If you want to see a genuine love story, you must experience the love Dada feels for His Master.

'And He was a scholar, topping His class almost always. He got the Ellis Scholarship from the Bombay University, standing first-class-first, and it was a great achievement. A great honour in those days. He started as a professor in a Calcutta College, and He was there for around three to four years. Then He came to teach in a college in Karachi. While He was in Karachi, He went to Berlin to attend the Welt Congress of Religions—the World Congress, as it was known—and soon after His return from there, He was appointed the principal of Dayal Singh College, a big college in Lahore. But soon, there was a point of difference between Him and the secretary of the Board and He immediately resigned. The secretary apologized but Sadhu Vaswani said that once a resignation has been submitted, there was no turning back for Him. He then became the principal of the Cooch Bihar College. At that time, Patiala was a bigger state than Cooch Bihar. The ruler of Patiala once heard one of His lectures and told the head of Cooch Bihar that he wants Him to be the principal of his college. And that is how Sadhu Vaswani went to Patiala. He resigned from service as the principal of the Patiala College. He was the head of the college till His mother expired. The day His mother passed away, He gave in His resignation by telegram.'

'Why did He resign the day His mother passed away?'

'Because it was His promise to the mother that so long as she was alive, He would not talk of taking up what he called *fakiri*, i.e. a life of asceticism and renunciation in quest of the spiritual. His mother had made Him promise her that till she was alive, He would be part of the material world and He obeyed her. The day she passed away, He was free of His promise and thus He resigned on that very day.

'In those early days after His resignation, He was an associate of Mahatma Gandhi and Freedom Movement. In 1921, He was interviewed by a press correspondent, who asked Him, "Do you think freedom is coming to India?" He said, "Sure, if the sun rises in the east, freedom is coming to India. But my one anxiety is that when freedom comes, India may be found wanting.'

'He was always concerned that as and when freedom came to India, we would not have the right people to take charge of the administration in running the country. This aspect was a major concern for Him. So He started ashrams for young people, the Shakti Ashram at Rajpur, the Parashakti Ashram at Mangalore and so on. He thought He would work with the youth and prepare them so that they can take charge of the different departments once India got freedom. And His words have come true now . . . we do have freedom, but we are found wanting . . .'

'Oh boy and how wanting! What did He feel in the later days, once India got freedom and then the power circus began? Was He disillusioned by how the country was being governed? Was He disillusioned by the way Indians had taken over their own country? First, the British oppressed our poor. Now our own people oppress their kith and kin?'

'He was not disillusioned, but He was disappointed. He found that parochialism and provincialism was cutting India into bits. That made Him very sad. He said, we are all Indians first and Maharashtrians or Punjabis or Bengalis after that. We are Indians first and then everything else follows. He didn't want to leave Sind after Independence. He said, "If I leave Sind, who is going to take care of the poor people who cannot leave the place?" There were thousands of people still in Sind, and these people of all communities, the leaders of the communities and the people who counted, they were all His friends. They told Him, "We will give you a guarantee that nothing will happen to you. You stay on, we are with you." So we never thought of coming to India but things took an ugly turn; it was the day Jhinna passed away. We had a satsang, as we did every evening, and at the close of the satsang, prasad was distributed as usual. Some of the Mohajirs who had come from outside took offence. They called this karah prasad seera. They said, this Hindu organization is making merry, they are celebrating. So what they did was they caught hold of one satsangi brother, cut him up into bits and put the pieces in a gunny bag and kept it under a public bench. So when the people came to know of this, they told Sadhu Vaswani, "For Your sake, so many people are putting their lives at risk . . . it is Your responsibility to protect those who have not gone to India because they wanted to be near You."

'Eventually, Sadhu Vaswani had to take a call. He had to take a tough decision. It really cost him quite dearly to decide to leave His beloved Sind. He had so many brothers and sisters there. For us, things were not different after the Partition. Instead of serving Hindus, we served Hindus and Muslims. We used to go to their camp, taking with us clothes and food. So, time went on. In our schools, instead of Hindu girls, Muslim girls came. And we kept Hindu teachers, but the work went on. But when this incident happened, Sadhu Vaswani thought it over and eventually decided to leave Sind and come to Bombay. It broke His heart but he had to do it for the well-being and protection of His flock.'

'So when He decided to leave Sind, did a lot of satsangis accompany Him to India?'

'Except one or two, everyone else left Sind just to be near Sadhu Vaswani.'

'How old was Sadhu Vaswani at that time?'

'He must have been seventy years old then. We were in Sind for fifteen months after partition. We came to Bombay on or around 12 November 1948.'

'That means you were there for a reasonably long time.'

'On 15 August 1947, we got independence, and in November 1948, we came here.'

'And how old were you that time?

'I was thirty years old.'

'Did Sadhu Vaswani think about Sind a lot?'

'Oh yes, till his very end. I think a part of Him was left behind in Sind.'

'He never went back even to visit?'

'No. He never went back. His health deteriorated and we didn't think it worthwhile. Some of us went to Sind a few years ago.'

'How did you feel?'

'It was not the Sind I knew. No. It was a disappointment. The whole atmosphere had changed and the topography too had changed.

It had become so dirty. Karachi was otherwise regarded as one of the cleanest cities of India.'

'Do you think about Your early days a lot?'

'I think about it often. It is the land of my birth and thirty formative years were spent there.'

'How was Sadhu Vaswani's relation with Mahatma Gandhi?'

'They were friends. In the earlier phase, when Mahatma Gandhi started his Freedom Movement, they were associates. But then they quietly parted. But whenever Gandhi knew that he had to go to jail because of the Freedom Movement, he would always make sure a book of Sadhu Vaswani was packed along with his meagre belongings. This was told to us by Chaturvedi who was close to Gandhi. Gandhi would say, "Now they will come and call me, but see that you have put Vaswani's latest book in my bag. I will go and read it in jail."'

'Dada, was Sadhu Vaswani in jail once?'

'For four days.'

'You were there with Him that time?'

'Yes, I was very young then. They wanted to jail all the leaders, and there were twelve leaders in Sind. So they had a bus full. All the twelve got inside and I wanted to get inside the bus to be with my Master to serve Him in prison but they would not let me go. It so happened that the policeman who was in charge of that bus was a tall person who was sat with his legs wide open. When something happened, he happened to look in another direction and I slipped through his legs. You see, at that time, Sadhu Vaswani was not well. He had gout and His knee had become swollen. So He needed help; He could not move about freely on His own and needed a wheelchair. That created a sensation in the whole town of Karachi and people said they would propose a no confidence motion in this government. Then the ministers came to the jail and requested Sadhu Vaswani to come out of the jail promising to do whatever He asked for.'

'And what did he He ask for?'

'It was something to do with family life. Families were disintegrating. He said this should not happen, because family is the unit of society and if families break, then society cannot last. The government would not understand. They said they had no laws that they could apply. Sadhu Vaswani said laws are for men, men are not for laws. But we were there for four days.'

'How was the stay?'

'It was a memorable one because it was the first opportunity I received of being alone and serving the Master. It was like being on an excursion.'

'And how old were you then?'

'I was studying for MSc, I was about nineteen years old.'

'How was Sadhu Vaswani's temperament? I understand He, His every cell, expressed love but was He a strict Master, was He a disciplinarian and did He get angry?'

'In all the years that I spent with him, I found him angry only twice. Yes, he was strict. On matters of principle, he was very strict but otherwise, He believed in letting a person grow freely in his own way. Just as no two trees grow in the same way, He, likewise, did not impose a particular method to be followed. He let everyone grow in His own way. So much so that if He saw some of us not going in the right way, it was just a slip, He would not interfere. He was a believer in freedom, freely you must grow.'

'What were the two reasons he got angry for?'

'He had adopted a girl as His daughter, Shanti . . . He wanted her to study. Shanti would not apply her mind to studies. She was so consumed by the thought of God and Men of God that she did not believe the need to study. This made him angry.

'On the second occasion it was with me. So once with Shanti and once with me. Two times I saw His anger, that was it. You see, there were periods when He behaved in such a way that some of us would feel ignored. He wanted to train us, but we didn't understand then. On one such occasion I missed going to the satsang and I went somewhere else. When He came to know, He became a little angry.'

'So obviously what this shows is that Shanti and You were the dearest to Him?'

'He behaved in a manner that everyone felt that she or I was the most loved.'

'How was your relationship with Shanti?'

'She was like a young teacher of mine. Shanti taught me a lot and I learnt much from her. I had the pride of knowledge when I came to Sadhu Vaswani because as I told you, I had received four double promotions. I stood first in college, they made me a Fellow, they kept a post open for me and told me to come and join any time. So that perhaps went to my head and Sadhu Vaswani wanted to take that pride out of me. There was one thing He could not tolerate in us and that was pride. Shanti was humble.'

'What was the age difference between you and Shanti?'

'I was a few months elder to her. I was born on 2 August 1918. She was born on 25 April 1919, but she was wise beyond her age. And I did learn a lot from her. She was a truly spiritual soul and she was in complete love with Sadhu Vaswani. When He passed away, she did not feel it worthwhile to continue to live. She said, "Now, let me go."'

For a long time Dada kept silent. So many memories came flooding back. All those He shared a past with had passed away. Like a wise old sage, He must sometimes feel alone or even abandoned. Make note, Ruzbeh. Shut up.

'The entire period Shanti was alive after Sadhu Vaswani passed away, you did not leave Pune for an overnight stay, right?

'Yes I never left Poona but that was also because of the ashes of the sacred body of beloved Sadhu Vaswani had not been enshrined. We wanted to build a Samadhi and until the Samadhi was built, I always returned to Poona. So it was decided that we will not be away during night. We would be by His ashes at night. So when the Samadhi was ready, the ashes were enshrined and then we started to travel.'

'And Shanti passed away after how long, after Sadhu Vaswani?'

'Shanti passed away on 15 May 1970 and Sadhu Vaswani on 16 January 1966. There is a small booklet on Shanti called the Child of God.'

'How come Sadhu Vaswani adopted her?'

'Shanti, even as a child, was in search of God and a Guru and she learnt that a saint had come to their town and was delivering a sermon or *upadesh* early in the morning at six. So she told her elder sister, "Tomorrow morning, you must take me there". And the moment she saw Sadhu Vaswani, her search for God and Guru came to an end.'

'And how old was Shanti at that time?'

'All of ten years of age.'

'Her elder sister was?'

'Neni.'

'So at the age of ten, Shanti met Sadhu Vaswani but when did Sadhu Vaswani adopt her as His daughter?'

'I guess when Shanti was twelve or thirteen years of age. It is believed that He saved her when she had typhoid, though He never once referred to this incident. Then Shanti said to Him that, "I had entered the Krishna Mahal when You brought me back here so now I belong to you, I don't belong to this house." Since that day, she left everything and lived with Sadhu Vaswani.'

'So Shanti's parents agreed to part with their child?'

'They agreed, they all had great reverence for Sadhu Vaswani. Shanti's father was a doctor who revered Sadhu Vaswani. In Sind, Sadhu Vaswani was known as a saint and a man of God. Humility personified. Simple. Pure. Soft spoken.'

'So you and Shanti have practically grown up together?'

'Yes, mostly, because when she was ten years, I was only a few months older. But she had great intuitive powers. I could not understand the ways of Sadhu Vaswani but she told me that if you want to live with a saint, you have to put up with the workings of a saint. She was all love and devotion and never was there an I in her. It was all Sadhu Vaswani.'

'You had run away once, isn't it? Why?'

'Yes. I had run away once as I couldn't bear Sadhu Vaswani's silent behaviour with me. That night I spent in a public garden and slept on a bench. But in the morning I went back. Sadhu Vaswani knew it. But it was to teach us discipline and a lot of attributes to walk the path.'

'So He was strict with you?'

'Yes quite strict but nothing outward. It was all done silently.'

'I guess He was preparing You for the oncoming responsibility?'

'I don't know. He never said anything.'

'After Sadhu Vaswani left His body, what kind of discussions would you have with Shanti?'

'Not much because when Sadhu Vaswani left His body, they asked me to be the principal of St Mira College. So most of my time used to go there and there were other duties at the Mission too. There was not much time for anything else. There used to be a cot here in this corner which used to be Sadhu Vaswani's bed. She used to lie down here. I would leave for my room on the top floor early in the morning and after meditating in silence, I would come down. The first thing was to come and bow down to Shanti and then of course, if there ever was anything she had to say, she would say it. Several years have elapsed since she left her body, but I don't think we ever disobeyed her. Whatever she said we would do. We saw the spiritual element in her. In the evenings also I used to come and sit here by her cot. We used to sleep on the floor; she was the one who slept on the cot because her knees would not bend. In the evening, we used to keep a teapot and a chair here and I used to attend to correspondence, sitting near her. Then quite a number of our friends used to gather here. This used to happen every day, so now as I recollect, it would be wrong to say that there was no interaction.'

'When You say "friends" would come and sit here, what You really mean is Your disciples and devotees. Any way, You spent as much time here so that she had company and she had people around her?'

'Yes. And she loved children. Children used to come to her.'

'What was her age when she passed over? Around fifty-two or fifty-three. That's beautiful. Thus nearly forty years she spent in the close proximity of Sadhu Vaswani and you.'

'Yes.'

'Did you know that her time to leave her body was approaching?'

'No.'

'Did she leave suddenly or was it a slow process?'

'Suddenly. It was our routine to go for a walk every evening. She used to accompany me, but she would not walk much because that would strain her knees and she would sit and I would walk up and down here in the compound. That evening, she told me, "You go, I am not feeling well today, I will be here." I told her that I have no wish to go if she wasn't feeling well, but she insisted that I go. I walked about for ten minutes or so when someone came running and said, "Shanti has expired." I came back immediately. There she lay and the doctor who lived very close to our Mission had come too and he said, "There is no pulse and there is no breathing." I sat by her side and put her head on my lap and I don't know why but I just told her, "Shanti how can you do this, how can you go away without informing . . . without taking my leave . . . how can you go?" And she opened her eyes.

'It was as though a miracle had happened. She opened her eyes, smiled, did not say anything and then again closed her eyes. Then we brought her and kept her here in this room.'

For a long time we kept quiet. This room must have witnessed such greatness and love that it is no wonder there was such peace and warmth in this room, I mused.

'Sadhu Vaswani was fond or influenced by Ramakrishna Paramahansa?'

'Yes. He had great reverence for Ramakrishna Paramhansa. He said that it was His misfortune that when He went to Calcutta, there was neither Ramakrishna Paramhansa nor Keshub Chandra Sen, the great orator—who even the Queen of England visited to hear him speak. He was a staunch Hindu who fell in love with Jesus Christ.'

'Sadhu Vaswani also held Swami Vivekananda in high regard?'

'Yes. But Sadhu Vaswani did not have an occasion to meet Vivekananda because Vivekananda had just passed away a little while before Sadhu Vaswani went to Calcutta. But with the passage of time, Sadhu Vaswani felt drawn more and more to Guru Nanak and other disciples of the Lord. Sadhu Vaswani has written and sung on bhakti. He used to utter the Name Divine and keep awake at nights and chants used to flow out. The whole of His composition is this masterpiece called the *Nuri Granth*. It is His utterance and there is hardly a page which does not carry the cry of a bhakta's heart. All these four thousand songs and two thousand slokas have been composed by this noble, divine man.'

'Why do all Sadhu Vaswani's songs end with Nuri?'

'Once Sadhu Vaswani was in Hyderabad, I think it was in the year 1933. He was advised by the doctor to go to a hill station. In Sind, we did not have a hill station but we had something like a hillock called Jhirkan. During His sojourn in Jhirkan, Sadhu Vaswani saw a vision in the middle of the night, a glimpse of a heavenly form, Nuri Nimani. Nuri was a fisherwoman whom the king made his queen. But Nuri never ever forgot her humble background; she would look at the mirror and say to herself again and again, "Never forget that you are a fisherwoman, it is the king's grace that has made you a queen." Nuri Nimani in Sindhi literally means "the radiant and the humble one". He adopted this name Nuri as His pen name. That is why in every one of His songs, His Nom de plume, Nuri, is mentioned. And the compilation of His songs and verses and slokas is known as the *Nuri Granth*.'

'And your songs and slokas are compiled in the *Anjali Sangraha*. Why *Anjali*?'

'Anjali means an offering. Anjali is the one who has completely and totally offered himself to the Lord.'

'You are Anjali. Okay. During the last six years of Sadhu Vaswani's life, after He had that fall, was He in a lot of pain?'

'Oh yes,' Dada grimaced as though reliving that pain, 'He was in terrible pain. He used to lie on this cot silently with the pain tearing into His body. The femur bone, the hip bone of His right leg, was broken. And the doctors were of the view that He should get a surgery done. When we used to appeal to Him, His answer repeatedly was, "If you get the surgery done, you will lose the bone and you will lose the man." So that was ruled out and then He started to get twitches and shooting pain every three to five minutes, and that twitch would pull the leg. He could not control it as it was broken and it caused Him pain. But on His lips there was the word: "*Shukur! Shukur!*" Shukur means gratitude or thank you. He believed that suffering had a place in the life of a seeker.'

'He believed that?'

'He believed it. And we used to feel that He takes upon himself the suffering of others.'

'You feel that was the reason why He didn't get himself operated?'

'I don't know but this was repeatedly the answer. He would give us the impression that we would lose Him and that tied our hands . . . because almost every doctor who visited would wonder and speak aloud, "Why don't You get the surgery done?" and He would refuse saying the surgery would lead to us losing Him. The irony is that He was beyond fear and death was for Him something that would bring Him closer to The One. Thus it was very frustrating, but we could do nothing but see Him in pain which He bore with such calmness.'

'How would He pass his day for those five years and three months?'

'He used to lie on the cot. There were times when His room doors were closed and then when the door was opened, people would come in. They used to wait for the door to open.'

'Would He sleep alone here?'

'No, all of us used to sleep here but we slept on the ground.'

'So for all those years He went through that suffering?'

'Five years and three months, to be exact. But it was terrible.'

'Which meant for five years and three months He barely slept.'

'He used to sleep for not more than ten minutes at a time because even when He fell asleep, the twitch would come after ten minutes. What these twitches are I don't know but they would come. I too get these twitches and they come after every three minutes, but in my case it wasn't painful. But He used to feel pain. His bone was fractured and left like that for so many years.'

'So He kept waking up through the night which meant even you must have barely slept?'

'Yes, we did not let Him sleep alone ever. We were always there to rub His leg. So someone or the other was massaging His feet through the night. We would take turns.

'Not having an operation was just an excuse. Because that was not the only time that He suffered. His entire life was like that. We always saw that when someone dear to Him was sick or carried to the hospital, the sickness would be transferred to Sadhu Vaswani. We saw lots of cases of that type. We saw quite a number of such instances all through our lives we spent with Sadhu Vaswani.'

'Sadhu Vaswani's last five and a half years and your seven years seem to be very similar, at least where health and physical limitations are concerned?'

'You cannot compare Sadhu Vaswani's experience of pain to mine. I am not in pain or at least I am not in perpetual pain. I can sleep. I have the luxury of modern medicine. He went through much more. Far more than any man I have known. Also you must understand that a True Master allows and welcomes pain as it is through experiencing and embracing pain that the Master feels a great kinship with the Lord. Apart from sharing the burden of His flock, He feels a greater intimacy with the Lord as the pain has a power which draws the Master further within Himself.

'Let me tell you something. It is not easy for the disciple to see the pain of the Master but the Guru has realized the blessings of pain. The Guru prays for pain. There was a Guru who prayed to God and said, "God the whole week has passed but you have not given me a painful experience, have you forgotten me?" The Guru knows the value of pain. He knows the value of suffering. Therefore, it is not easy to understand or take on the pain of the Guru. The Guru does not want to leave it.

'Sadhu Vaswani called Rabia, the woman saint of Islam, the Meera of Islam. Once She had an attack of fever. The fever would not leave Her. Then a friend, Sufian by name, said to Her, "Rabia, Allah comes to You every day and You speak to Allah, why don't You ask Him to cure You of this fever?" And Rabia said to Her friend, "Sufian, don't you know who has sent me this fever? God has sent me this fever. This is a gift of God to me. If a friend gave a gift to a friend and the friend who was to receive the gift refuses to receive the gift, how would the friend who had brought the gift feel? This is a gift which God has given to me. Let Him continue to give it." Thus Sadhu Vaswani made sure He went through those five and a half years of excruciating suffering. I would like to believe He did this to lessen the suffering of His flock and also to let the pain bring Him closer to God.'

We kept silent for a long while. It was humbling and exasperating. Before Jesus Christ and after Him, how many Masters had taken on the suffering of a lost mankind and our tortured planet, till it bore witness to such souls, would continue to spin on its axis, solely because of the selfless love of our Masters.

'What was His last communication with you?'

'The last communication was when He went into sleep on the night of the 15 January. I was pressing His legs when He held me by the hand and the words that He uttered were, "Be by me, my child!" Those were the last words that He uttered and He then went off to sleep. He rarely slept more than ten minutes at a time but that night He kept on sleeping. And of course none of us realized it but Shanti told me that this is not natural, something must be the matter. It was at her insistence that we sent for the doctor. I did not want to trouble anybody at night as I did not realize the seriousness. Dr Hathiramani came and he arranged for a group of doctors, including Dr Grant, Dr Wadia, the neurologist and others. And they all said that nothing can be done now. It was a matter of time. This was after two at night. But I think at ten minutes past eight in the morning, the nurse said we should turn Him over as it's not good that He is made to lie in the same position. As we turned Him over, the breath left the body. Then we kept Sadhu Vaswani's body for that day in the hall downstairs and the next day we took His body out in this part of the city. And at about 5.20 p.m. or thereabouts, our beloved Guru's body was cremated. Two days earlier, he had said, "Bring all my clothes. I want to give them away to the poor; keep only two pairs for me. They will suffice." Not one of us got the hint that He was saying to us that he would be with us for just two more days. During those last days, He repeatedly said, "The boat has left and it will soon arrive and take me away. Then you will not be able to see me . . . this *drisht* (visible) form. Then I will not be visible to you but I will be close to you, I will not be far from you, I will not leave you."'

'Did He ever, in his last days, talk about your responsibility?'

'No.'

'What gave you the strength to go on after he left the body?'

'When He passed away I was deeply moved and grieved. Then I went to my room upstairs, sat in silence and I heard those words again, "Be by me, my child!" That gave me strength. Then I came down, and they say there was a smile on my face.'

'He has kept his word.'

'Yes. He always keeps His word.'

That day when I bowed down to Sadhu Vaswani's Samadhi, I looked up at His statue. How much They do for us. And we continue to lounge in the dark alleys of the soul. They must either love us a lot or they haven't got in their Divine Heads that no matter what They do, we human beings will never change. And They did all this with so much of silence and humility and grace. I wonder how They did it, truly?

I had asked Piya if Dada had ever mentioned how one was supposed to inculcate silence for going within?

'The first thing He says is to be natural. The main thing is to be spontaneous and we should always have God in the background of our consciousness. This is what He says. If you are holding on to God with one hand, and with the other you're doing your normal work, naturally you're not going to move away from the path. Always have God in the back of your mind while doing anything, because God is always there to guide you. So your actions are bound to be somewhere on the right path.'

'You've spent so much time with Dada, is this the philosophy that drives Him?'

'Yes! He walks His talk. And He doesn't believe in anything superfluous. Come forth from peace. If you are calm within, then all is well; otherwise there is something wrong at some core level. I feel God is guiding each one of us separately; it all depends on our nature, our karma and the like. And each one has a different way and capacity to receive God's grace. Dada's teachings are like an ocean. You can take a spoon or take a bucket or a truck full—it all depends on how much you can take and how sincere you are. And most importantly, I have seen Dada go down to the level of the individual who has come for guidance or help. He doesn't wish to look or sound as though He knows too much. With you, He is talking and sharing such wisdom, but most often He will give basic examples, depending upon who is going to receive it. He makes you feel as though He is one of us. But that's not true. It is His ability to come to our level.'

'To make us understand . . .'

'Exactly. I've seen Him talk to saints several times. His language is different. When he talks to children, He speaks in their language. To those in pain, in their language.'

'So if you were to give five teachings of Dada which you can incorporate in your life, what would they be?'

'First of all Dada says that in whichever situation you find yourself in, there is always a chance of turning back towards God. You may be on any path, but you can never be far away from the hands of God. However far away from the truth you may travel, God's hands will come and hold you because we can't live without God. A part of God is within us so there is always an underlying, everlasting oasis—God's arms upholding us. No matter if we be good or bad; every human being has a spark of God within each one of us.'

'God will never abandon us and no individual has gone so far away that he or she can't turn back to God?'

'Yes. Turn back to God. Also we cover ourselves with so many things because we are somehow led by our karmas or by our thinking or any path which may not be right. But we can always turn back and go God-ward and become perfect. He keeps urging all to go within and by going within, slowly but surely, all the debris and karma will slowly be removed. So every time we move our debris, our consciousness or our vibrations becomes more refined. So once we have such vibrations naturally, we can get attuned to our Lord who is within.'

'Have you ever felt, maybe not with words, but felt Him look at a particular individual and indicate that the individual is beyond redemption?'

'Oh honestly, never ever. For Him there is no individual who is beyond redemption. He truly believes that. In fact, if there is somebody truly off the path, He takes care of that person even more. He will love and honour him even more. And we will be wondering why? Because we see only the negative part. Because all those things are within us. I guess He doesn't have those negative emotions, thus He can't understand how anybody can have those emotions. He's a saint, He knows better.'

'Do you feel that by His honouring that person or giving that person more attention, a positive change takes place in that individual?'

'Honestly speaking, may be not. But we do hope that the person might come to some realization that "If a saint can say these things about me, maybe I have to become that one day." Maybe it could help an individual clutching at straws, who wants to turn around but does not know how, a certain confidence or hope.'

'Could be that He's seeing the potential of what an individual can become rather than what he has become?'

'Yes. He's giving vibrations of love.'

'Also, He has the ability to make each individual want to become a better human being.'

'Yes. He loves people. You cannot put on an act for ninety-seven years of your life. His love comes forth. And the best part is that He makes everybody feel special as I guess He sees His Master in everybody. He makes you feel as though "Dada loves only me and I am only for Him and He for me". Or "He thinks only about me or He cares for me so much. I'm special. I will not let Him down". Each one of us feels we are special and He makes us realize that in reality each one of us is special. But He has attachments to nothing. He loves books. He's such an avid reader. He must read every day. In His childhood, He used to read one book a day. In spite of that He's not attached to His books. If anyone comes and says, "Oh Dada, this book looks interesting", you can be sure He will give that person the book, no matter if He is truly enjoying it or is special to Him. He says, "Please take it." Even though He wants to read it. Though He wants to see what's in it. He will immediately give it away. And this is the case with everything. Not just books. I am a witness of this day in and day out,' Piya concluded.

I left the Samadhi with the realization that forget everything, if one can come forth from selfless love and Oneness, the spiritual realm shall bow down and the very Heaven will roll out the red carpet. We all know this. But we are going to spend lifetimes tying ourselves in knots, chasing our own illusionary tails, getting more and more entangled in the karmic merry-go-round.

8

Dada and I met after a few days. He had been insistent throughout that we meet often and complete our taped conversations as fast as possible. He would tell Krishna and me, "Let us complete the interviews at the earliest," and every time He said that, my heart would sink.

I had met Him about twenty odd times, but the very thought that there would come a time when I would not breathe the same air as He did, made the void within grow slightly deeper. Dada reminded me of my Swamiji Naik, sage and medium of Maa Mookambika, on whom, through Their grace, I had written *Devi's Emerald*. I am sure it is no coincidence that both Dada and Swamiji were born on 2 August. Swamiji had taken Samadhi a few years ago. He too had suffered immense physical suffering for the last few years of His life. I still miss Him.

Thus in Dada, I saw Swamiji and my elders and teachers who had passed over; the same kind of love, care, wit and the reassurance that till they are there with you, all is well with God and the world.

And then one by one, they get wings and soar away. Their bodies battered with life and age and their consciousness in another dimension where blessings pour down in deafening silence.

I always wondered how Dada Vaswani continued to function and perform His duties after His Master took Samadhi. Also, how easy or difficult was the transition. I had asked Piya this question.

'I feel in some way Sadhu Vaswani laid the foundation. He was virtually laid up in bed for the last five years and three months and slowly He created a platform for Dada to head the Mission in His own way.'

'Yes, for sure,' Piya replied. 'Sadhu Vaswani beautifully laid the foundation for our Dada. There were some people who could have created unnecessary problems but Dada is a very courageous and brave man. I have never seen anybody as brave or courageous as Him and most importantly, He does it with humility but firmness. He was not afraid of those who were trying to speak ill of Him because of their jealousy. But the most sublime part of it all was how beautifully He treated those same people and won them over. Everybody knew that after Sadhu Vaswani, it was Dada. That was understood and Sadhu Vaswani made sure everyone understood this. But once again let me tell you that nobody can compare with the life of Sadhu Vaswani. No one. Underlined. But Dada's life is very spectacular. And the way He speaks, behaves, handles Himself and all those around Him, His humility, His wisdom, His courage and fearlessness, His way of life—there was no doubt that it was naturally Him.'

'What are the similarities between Sadhu Vaswani and Dada Vaswani?'

'I think They are reflections. One of each other. He reflects Sadhu Vaswani so much that sometimes I get confused whether it is Dada Vaswani or Sadhu Vaswani.'

'Do you think Dada loves Him so much that He's actually merged His entire personality into Sadhu Vaswani's personality? It is as though He is most happy walking in the shadow of Sadhu Vaswani and therein lies His real greatness. Being a perfect disciple has made Him into a Perfect Master. It's as though before every action, thought, word or deed, Dada puts a simple question before Him—what would make Sadhu Vaswani happy and proud of Him?'

'He doesn't have to think. He abides in His presence, so there is no question of forgetting Him. Sadhu Vaswani is always in front of Him and present with Him.'

'I've a very strong feeling that being a perfect disciple has come in the way of Him playing the role of a Perfect Master and thus prevented the exposure that was so needed to spread Sadhu and Dada's great philosophy and divinity to a greater number of seekers.'

'Yes. I'm a nobody. The Guru knows all. But I agree cent percent with what you are saying. All I can say is that I have never seen anybody so detached from everything and anything. He truly is the most generous human being I have ever known. So much so when He was young, while doing His post-graduation or PhD, all He had to was just submit His work and get a doctorate. But He was with Sadhu Vaswani all the time and thus He didn't want to do anything about His research. So one of His friends asked Him if he could use the entire study and put his own name on it and submit it. Dada told His friend that He would give him His research. What he wanted to do with it was up to him and His God. So He gave His hard work away. Fortunately somebody came and told Sadhu Vaswani what a wonderful disciple He had, somebody who can give away His research just like that. Sadhu Vaswani called Dada and told Him that by doing so, He was following the path of untruth. "How could you do that? Go now and submit your papers in your name." Poor Dada had to go back for fifteen days, brush up, submit the research and then rushed back to Sadhu Vaswani. He's not attached to anything. He doesn't want His name anywhere. He doesn't want to say that I said this. There is no question of I in His life. It's always My Master,' Piya concluded.

I stayed at the Samadhi and then took Sadhu Vaswani and Sister Shanti's blessings. I didn't talk much with Them. It is humbling to be in the presence of such love and devotion.

I was moving out when a couple walked in. They began to take snaps with Sadhu Vaswani's statue in the backdrop. I looked at Him and I couldn't help but grin. Sometimes even God, Goddess and Guru become nothing, but a good photo op and Sadhu Vaswani looked at the couple with love.

I got a call.

'Dadda, can I have coke?'

'No. You can't.'

'Ok. No problem, but please buy me this new computer . . . by the way where are you?'

'Dada Vaswani . . .'

'How much do you both talk! Your interviews are not getting over only. Did you ask Sadhu Vaswani about His finger pointing to the sky . . .'

'I was going to ask but a couple came and began to take photographs inside the Samadhi.'

'Dadda if they ever make a statue of you and a couple would try to take a selfie of theirs with you, you would begin to start throwing things at them for sure. You would be the most irritable angry statue ever . . .'

'See you soon . . .'

'So coke or computer . . .'

I entered the Kutiya and Naresh heaved a sigh of relief seeing me.

I sat on my spot and shut my eyes. Today was a good day not to be. Dada entered. He looked more exhausted than me. His body showed His tiredness. He was somewhere far away. Oh boy and I thought I was in bad shape. Today was going to be a short interview.

But like always, the moment we both began to speak, at least where I was concerned, my tiredness left and everything else stopped existing. May be it was Dada's energy or the vibrations of the Kutiya or both, I don't know. But it was as though somebody had switched on the light within me.

'Don't you feel there is a lot of similarity between Sadhu Vaswani and You? I know you will say no.'

'Not in the least, He was a man apart, really. You cannot describe Him. I am a nobody.'

'No, You need to understand this. You may always come forth as being a disciple but You cannot stop your disciples treating You as a Master?'

'No, no. They are my friends. We are all fellow devotees. Believe me. I am not a Master. I have not even become a true disciple yet. Who is a Real Master? A Real Master is He who has mastered himself. He who was mastered His lower self of passion and pride, of anger and lust, of greed and hatred and strife, of averse and arrogance and self-love and miserliness. When a man masters His lower self, then He becomes a Master. I recall a very amusing little incident in the life of that great king known to history as the world conqueror, Alexander the Great. Alexander the Great came with his huge armies to India. On arriving here, he found that the people of India were so brave and heroic.

'Yes, there was a time when India's people were brave and heroic for they believed in the teaching of the Gita that every man is immortal, is deathless is eternal. These teachings sank into the hearts and souls of India's people and they became fearless. And coming to this country, Alexander said, "I shall not wage a war I shall not wage a battle with this country. I shall befriend them."

'And then he decided to return to his homeland. He remembered how his people asked him to bring an Indian yogi with himself as he returned to Greece. In quest of an Indian yogi, he goes to a Tapobana, a forest of meditation and sure enough, there, underneath a tree, he finds a yogi sitting in meditation. Alexander the Great goes and sits by his side. And after sometime, the yogi opens his eyes. The eyes are lit up with a wondrous light—the light of peace, the light of love. And Alexander says to the yogi, "Here I have been waiting for you, for I want you to come with me to Greece. I shall give you whatever you need. Come with me to Greece. The people are anxious to hear you and be blessed by your holy hands." But the yogi smiled and said, "I have no desire to leave this place. I have everything that I need, I need nothing besides."

'And Alexander the Great becomes very angry. This was the first time that anyone had said no to him. He unsheathes his sword. And showing it to the yogi says, "You dare say no to me. Do you know who I am? I am the great king, the world conqueror. You dare say no to me. I shall kill you. I shall tear you to pieces." The yogi smiles once again. He is calm and unruffled and gazing straight into Alexander's eyes, says to him, "You said you are a king, may I tell you who you are? You are only a slave of my slave. And you said that you will tear me into pieces, that you will kill me. No, you cannot kill me, you can only tear my body to pieces and my body is but a garment that I have worn. You cannot tear me to pieces. You cannot kill me for I am deathless, I am eternal, I am immortal, I am immutable."

'Alexander is amazed at the calmness and the serenity of this great yogi. And he feels ashamed of his conduct. And now he says to the yogi, "O yogi, you said to me that I was a slave of your slave, pray explain this to me." And the yogi says to him, "You become angry easily, you are a slave to anger. Remember I have mastered anger. I am a master of anger. Anger is my slave and you are a slave of my slave.'

'Thus true Masters are those who have mastered themselves and their senses, their minds and transcending them all have entered into the universal self. They can be called Masters. I am not a Master. As I told you, I am still striving, still trying to be a disciple and I ask you all to bless me.'

This is Dada. He doesn't say all this for effect. For over fifty years since He has carried forth the work of His Master, He has maintained this philosophy. In this time and age, He stands out as something so sublime, surreal, humane, that one can only whisper, Jai Baba.

9

I couldn't enter the Samadhi Temple today. There was some gathering and too many people were present. I bowed down from afar and then walked towards the Kutiya. I had a number of interviews to be done, with Dada too. I had fired Naresh today though I know it could not have been his fault. Eventually He has to follow what is told to him. As mentioned earlier, those working in spiritual organizations, Missions and Ashrams, especially renowned ones and those who are close to a Guru or working in close proximity with the Guru, are so lost in their world of *seva* and their Guru that they assume that the world revolves around their timings. Appointments are either shifted at the last moment, postponed or preponed, people for interviews added on the list at the last minute and one barraged with calls and messages to adjust. I would like to think that just as I do not take anybody's time for granted, I would expect the same consideration and then I say things which I on hindsight feel a sense of remorse. I don't take things well, to say the least. I was not present in the queue when the Lord was handing out calmness and maturity. Come to think of it, I wasn't standing in line when most of the sensible qualities were being dished out.

Anyway, after interviewing more of Dada devotees, it was time to speak to Dada. He first enquired if I had had tea. He apologized for coming in late every day. The time for our interviews was set at five. The interview usually began earliest at five thirty, often closer to a quarter to six. For some reason we rarely met on time. Often I had been told by those close to Him that when it was our day to meet,

He would tell those near Him to hurry up and plan the day so that we could meet undisturbed. A number of the inner circle mentioned to me that "Dada enjoyed and waited for the interview to begin. He, for some reason, enjoys talking to you."

'Dada, did Sadhu Vaswani ever talk to you about who or what is God?'

'Not that I know of. I do not think He ever spoke to us of God. He never spoke to us of the creation of God or the entire universe; we took all those things as granted. But it is a good question that you have asked me. What I did not ask of Sadhu Vaswani I will ask of you. Tell me something about God.'

'You are the Master. You have to tell me. What is your childlike concept of God?'

'As children we used to think of God as a creator . . . He has created all that which exists. That is what we thought of God. And we always thought of God as the nearest of the near and as of the dearest of the dear. One who is always with us, one who is watching us, one from whom nothing can be hidden. That is how we always have been thinking of God. In fact we take God for granted as we take so many other things for granted! And I remember in those days, we were told there were two schools of thought—there was the English school of scientists who believed in God and their leader was Newton. There were a French group of scientists who were given to atheism; they did not believe that God exists. One French scientist came and visited an English scientist and said it is a wonder that you are a scientist and yet you believe in God. The English scientist heard him quietly. When the time came for them to part, the French scientist passed through the living room of the English scientist. And there in a corner he saw a beautiful globe, with the map of the world on it. And immediately he asked the English scientist, "Who is it who made this beautiful globe?" And the English scientist said quietly, "Nobody built or made it, it came out of itself". The French scientist looked at his English counterpart and said, "How can a thing come out without anybody making it?" And the English scientist said to him, "You believe that this whole universe can come out of itself but you find it impossible to believe that this tiny globe could not come out of itself but had to have a maker."

'So God was taken for granted, that is how we thought of God. And it is a comfort to know that God is love. He is watching us, He is noting down everything that we are doing but He does it with understanding. That is how we thought of God. God is within you, that is what we were told and if you want to contact God, if you want to have what they called a darshan . . . a vision of God, you must practice silence, try to go deeper and deeper within yourself until by the grace of God you will arrive at a stage where you will have a vision of God. And we always thought of God as energy, as Light, the Light that illumines the whole universe. Gradually we came to know that we could have some intimate relationship with God. God could be our father, He could be our mother, He could be our brother, He could be our friend, but that came gradually.'

'Which means it is in the hands of every individual to try to at least connect to the God within?'

'Yes.'

'Are we our own enemies here when we prevent self-realization or God realization by our own need for material things rather than spiritual things? Do we stand between God and ourselves?'

'We were taught that it is our ego that stood as a wall between us and God. God was very near and dear to us, but why is it that we were unable to see God? It was because of the ego— there was that wall of the ego. All we had to do was to break that wall.'

These Masters are too cute. If only breaking the wall was so simple.

'How does one do that? How does one break the wall?'

'Therefore the need of a Guru. It is the Guru who knows how to break the wall of the ego. If I did something to you, you would feel bad, but if the Guru did the same thing to you, you will accept it without a question and hence the need of the Guru.'

'Dada, in today's time, in all probability, if I were to pick up a stone and throw it on someone, it would hit a so-called Guru or a real-estate agent. How does a simple common man know whether the person whom he has surrendered to is a true Guru?'

'That is what is happening in the world today. A true Guru will never speak of Himself as a Guru and so the people are drawn to those who are not true Gurus but who call themselves Gurus.'

'How does one recognize the divinity in the Guru?'

'There are certain marks but it is very difficult. Recognizing those landmarks are very difficult. For instance, a Guru is one who wants nothing. He is a man of utmost purity. The Guru is a lover of silence and is pure humility. There was a German theologian called Rumer who studied the lives of hundreds of saints. He said that there was this one common quality in all the saints. They differed in many other things but there was one quality which was common and that was humility. But I think that this relationship between a true Guru and a disciple has existed through birth after birth. And the Guru comes and finds the disciple. The Guru can find the disciple, the disciple cannot find the Guru. On the other hand, the disciple can make anyone his Guru, the Guru cannot make anyone His disciple. That is the privilege given to the disciple. The disciple says, "You are my Guru"—that power the disciple has, not the Guru.'

'Did Sadhu Vaswani ever talk about any such personality that he looked up to?'

'Sadhu Vaswani's reverence went out to all and more to Krishna, Christ, Buddha and Nanak. He revered every saint of every religion. I know of no other saint who has written on the lives and teachings of saints belonging to different religions with such understanding, reverence and love. He has written on Christian saints, on Buddha and His followers, on the Holy Prophet of Islam, on the Sikh Gurus, on Hindu bhaktas and has urged that they all belong to One brotherhood. In His heart, there was no sense of separation.'

'Why is it that nowadays among the so-called new generation of Gurus, this basic attribute of silently going about their work is not present? Like Sadhu Vaswani kept saying, He wanted to be the lowest of the low, to serve. He would avoid being in the limelight. Are these the trappings of one's environment now? Is the need of the hour to market one's own spirituality?'

'We live in an age of commercialism. And everyone likes to take advantage of it as far as he can. There are few, very few—you can count them on your fingers—who are detached from this way of living. Most of us get attached and the glamour draws us. There are three things that appeal to people today. Ramakrishna said there are two things that attract . . . *kamini* (lust) and *kanchan* (gold). But Sadhu Vaswani said there are three that draw us . . . *kamini*, *kanchan* and *kirti*. Kirti is the applause, the recognition.'

'Yes, the need for applause is growing.'

'Growing like anything. It is as though there is a competition among the so-called saints. How many people have become their disciples? Very often, when correspondents come and interview me, this is the question they ask of me—How many followers do you have? I tell them I am trying to be a follower myself, there is no question of me having followers. I have not yet become a true follower.'

'I guess it is working both ways, there are very few true Gurus and there are very few true disciples too.'

'Fewer than true Gurus are true disciples. There is a proverb, *Guru mile lakhe lakhe, shishya ek bhi na mile*! Gurus are found in abundance, but it is difficult to get even one true disciple.'

'Why?'

'It is because the ego is becoming strong these days. It is the ego that keeps me away from the life of the spirit. This is the type of education that we receive, it makes you feel that you can take decisions yourself about what is happening in your life. In olden days, why, in our own days, if a Guru sent a word, it was immediately followed. Now they come and explain to the Guru, "Gurudev, you have not understood the situation, it is like this." So the disciple now becomes the Guru of the Guru.'

We both began to chuckle. 'Sadhu Vaswani said to us, "He who loses himself in His teacher is the true disciple. He who follows his own will and his own desires is not a true disciple; he who entertains doubts in his heart and is dominated by personal ambition may be intellectually strong; he who argues endlessly and emphasizes the rightness of his own point of view may be an able debater, but a disciple he cannot be for he is a worshipper of himself."'

'What is the greatest obstacle to overcome the false sense of ego? Intellectually we are aware that for spiritual growth ego has to be annihilated, but why is it that we are still stuck in it?'

'The reason why traces of ego remain in the best of us is this false sense of how people perceive us. Perhaps the greatest obstacle is, what will they think of me? What will they say about me? Sadhu Vaswani once gave a lecture on the topic: They say, what do they say, let them say!'

'So is being beyond the so-called worldly honour and dishonour the first step?'

'The first step I think is to stay connected with God. Then all qualities come naturally. But the first step is to have that connection. The first step is to realize that you are not what you have been thinking about yourself, that you are an immortal spirit. That is the first step. Even staying connected comes after that. Today's spirituality is more of psychology than spirituality. In ancient days, we did not have psychology.'

'Why do you think this shift has come from spirituality to psychology?'

'There was a time when man was regarded merely as his body. Then they came to the mind and said man was a mind contained in a body. Then they went a step further and came to intellect. The intellect influences the mind which was contained in the body. But beyond it all is the spirit. Spirituality is essentially of the soul—the immortal spirit—it has nothing to do with the intellect or the mind, it is the master of the body, the mind and the intellect.'

'Why do we shift from spirit to the other things?'

'I think that is because of the Time Spirit, the different yugas. To be in touch with the immortal spirit you have to make many sacrifices because you have to bear witness to the truth. And as you so rightly put it the other day, people are scared of going within, being silent, meditating; they feel it will take them away from their responsibilities, their worldly pleasure, their fun.'

'Let me tell you, obedience, surrender and service are not marks of servitude; they are the means by which we cultivate self-discipline and learn to conquer the ego. The spirit of true surrender to the

Guru is born out of humility, faith and devotion. It is faith that gives the disciple absolute confidence in the Guru; it is faith which makes him repose all his trust in the Guru; it is faith that gives him the firm conviction that the Guru's words are the highest truth. This faith and devotion find their best expression in obedience and service.'

Krishna once mentioned to me, as a young seeker, Dada had argued, discussed and debated freely with His Master. If the questioning spirit had dominated one phase of His spiritual growth, there came later, a phase of absolute and complete acceptance. At that time, Sadhu Vaswani was ailing and in severe pain. All night long, Dada would be awake, administering whatever comfort He could to the Master. Finally, overcome by exhaustion, both Guru and disciple drifted into sleep.

'When Dada woke up with a start, it was midday. The Master was awake too, and enquired of Dada, "What is the time now?" "It is past twelve in the afternoon," Dada replied. "Should I bring you something to eat?" "You're mistaken," said Sadhu Vaswani. "It is past midnight now."

'Without hesitation,' Krishna continued, 'Dada agreed. "The Master is always right!" He said to himself. Dada tells us that with faith in the words of the Master, he went out to the veranda and looked up at the sky. In His mind there was no doubt that it was midnight, as His guru had said. And believe it or not, on that memorable cloudy afternoon, Dada did, indeed, behold the stars!' Krishna concluded.

'Sadhu Vaswani used to speak about city of light and city of God. What did He mean by that?' I enquired of Dada.

'He used to say to us that even as you have a universe outside of you, there is a bigger universe within each of us, but we are unable to see it because inwardly we are blind. When light comes—the inner light—then we will be able to see that inner city of light. And that is a luminous city.'

'That can be reached only through silence.'

'Yes, through silence. Therefore in His teaching, his emphasis was on silence. Whenever we had a question, we went to Him and asked Dada, "What does this mean?" He said, "My child, go and sit in silence and you will get the answer. The answer will come to you from within, that answer will satisfy you and will always be with you. If I give you an answer, you will forget it in no time." There were some answers which He gave verbally but for most of them, He would ask us to go and sit in silence.

'We used to have satsang in the morning in Karachi. One morning he was explaining the teaching of the Gita and He said that there was one sloka in which Krishna says: "Think of Me and fight." So when the satsang was over I put to Him the question, "How is it possible to do two things at the same time—think of Krishna and also fight?" He didn't answer. After about an hour or so, He said to me, "Take me out. I want to see how people are living." I took the car and He sat next to me. When I was driving, He was talking to me. Then he said, "Did you get your answer?" I went blank. I had even forgotten the question. I said, "What question?" He said, "You asked me a question this morning." But still I could not remember. Then He said, "You are doing two things at the same time, you are being very careful to see that you do not run over any one when you are driving the car and at the same time you are giving me an answer to the questions that I put to you. If that is possible, why is the other thing not possible?" So there were certain questions to which He gave answers but mostly He would say to go and sit in silence.'

'Now when we talk of "go and sit in silence", what does it really mean?'

'He said that there are two types of silences; there is the outer silence and there is the inner silence. He said for outer silence, you must find a corner where the noise of the city does not reach you. But then He said, there is the inner silence. That inner silence, He said, is karma *mauna*. Mauna means silence, karma is work. He said that when you sit in silence, work will come and disturb you—I had to do this work but I have not done it. Another type of inner silence is *smriti* silence. Smriti means memory. Things that had happened in the past will come and disturb you. So He said that you must have all kinds of silences. External and internal. In other words, the mind should not be distracted. You should take one word, one mantra, one incident and concentrate on that one without the least distraction—that is silence. He used to spend hours in silence and we dare not disturb him.'

'He would just sit quietly?'

'What He did we don't know.'

'Why is it that most of us don't follow this–something so simple to actually get us closer to God?'

'We want to follow it but we postpone it to tomorrow. That is the difficulty. Many of us want to, people come and tell me that we are going to start sitting in silence from tomorrow, and that tomorrow never comes. As you said the other day to me, people are afraid of sitting in silence. When you sit in silence, you arrive at a stage where you have to take a leap, from this to that. And there the seeker becomes confused and he withdraws. Because it is at that point that he needs the help of the Guru but he does not remember the Guru at that point and so he gets confused . . .'

'What I have been told by a number of people who were practicing silence was that it begins to make them detached from everything around them. But they cannot afford to get detached because they have certain responsibilities. So they are afraid that the more they go into silence, they might not be able to live up to their worldly responsibilities. Is that true?'

'But there are forces. If you practice silence, there are Angels–I love to think of them as Angels—who come and do your work. Truth and silence both have these angels. This is the difficulty of so many who wish to speak the truth but who cannot for certain reasons. There are situations in which they cannot speak the truth.'

'Our education system and the modern family set-up have moved so far away from silence. I don't think our children have a fighting chance, it's an alien concept that they need to be occupied the whole time with something or the other.'

'Yes. True. Therefore in our schools here, I do not know what they do now, but when I used to frequent them regularly, every hour a bell would ring and all work would stop and for two to three minutes, there would be silence. In those days, school was for six hours, so for around eighteen minutes in the day, one could get the taste of silence. And once you get the taste of silence, you really hunger for it.

It is because they have not tasted silence that our youngsters do not know its value and its power. When you go into the depths of silence, you don't wish to come out. In the beginning, it is true they perhaps feel bored but once they get into the depths, there is nothing like silence. Silence is its own reward. And it is in silence that the powers of the Spirit are realized and released. It is because we are lost in noise all the time that we have no idea of the powers of the spirit that we carry within us. I often say, "Silence is the mother of God. It is in the womb of silence that you get to realize God."'

'Sadhu Vaswani has mentioned that after an individual reaches the state of renunciation there comes a deep state of loneliness. Why?'

'Gurudev Sadhu Vaswani repeatedly pointed out to us that it is indeed significant that the very first chapter of the Gita is entitled "The Yoga of Depression". Perhaps the very first step on the path of spirituality for many seekers is depression, darkness of the soul. Our greatest saints and sages have gone through this period of loneliness, wandering and quest. What is the meaning of life? Why are we born here upon this earth? Where do we go from here? Some call it the dark night of the soul.'

'What is the dark night of the soul?'

'It is actually the title of a beautiful Spanish poem by the Catholic saint, St John of the Cross. Here, the darkness represents the hardships and pain that the soul must face before it attains to God. Here the darkness has two functions: the first is to purify the senses; the second and more difficult process is the purification of the spirit. When you feel that you belong nowhere, neither here nor there, in that utter loneliness, you are tempted to go back to worldliness. Otherwise you thought you belonged to the spiritual family of the Guru, but the Guru leaves you. He does not even look at you, rather He tries to put you off, but if you can cross this stage—the penalty stage—you become a member of the family.'

'Is it a very important stage?'

'Yes. But you might ask, "Why do such periods of darkness occur?" Some mystics attribute this to "spiritual fatigue" or the enormous transition we have to make from the worldly to the spiritual way of life. Others feel that this despair is the outcome of acute consciousness of our own imperfections and the ecstasy of the union with perfection which we wish to attain. There is also the profound sorrow of the consciousness of the separation that has been our lot until now. It is this state of psychic isolation, negativity, despair and misery that is described as, "The Dark Night of the Soul".'

'Everyone has to go through it. It is like being stripped absolutely naked. There is a mystical book in Christian literature titled "The Cloud of Unknowing". In it is given a full description of the dark night. I think this idea of the dark night of the soul emanated in Spain. There were Spanish mystics who described it as the dark night of the soul.'

'And each one on the path has to go through it?'

'Each one has to go through it. You have to be stripped because otherwise you can't reach the goal. Some little attachment to the body remains and that keeps you tied. You have to be absolutely free. Spain threw up wonderful mystics in that period. I think it was the sixteenth century—St John of the Cross, St Teresa of Avilla, Raymond and others. It is not correct to say that bhaktas and gyanis and mystics have appeared only in India. They have appeared everywhere. But in India they were received by common people and their message went out to common people. But there have been wonderful mystics. Hence, Sadhu Vaswani said that there is a brotherhood of mystics, saints, seers, and sages. And He used to point specially to Jesus, Krishna, Guru Nanak and Buddha, I think.'

'What was so different in these four?'

'We never asked Him, but we found Him gravitating towards Them. And the beauty about it was that suppose it was the month of May, when Buddha Jayanti falls, He would become like Buddha. We would feel as though we are sitting at the feet of Buddha. If it was December, He was like Jesus. In the days of Janmashtami, He would be like Krishna.'

'Dada, tell me more about the dark night of the soul?'

'It is a period that comes in the life of a pilgrim when he feels despair and pessimism and begins to harbour serious doubts whether his higher aspirations will be fulfilled. It may happen in a variety of ways—he may lose faith; he may feel that God is not listening to his prayers; or it may be that his Master, who at one time showed him what it was to live a life of love, now disregards him, does not pay attention to him and turns away from him. When that period comes, the disciple, at first, feels that it is no use living in this world. Many a times the desire wakes up within his heart to perish, to leave this life. But he has received that training according to which suicide is a great sin. So he does not resort to suicide. The next possibility is to turn back to the worldly life which he has renounced. But the entire world appears to him as insipid, tasteless. He tries to move in the company of people but he feels like a misfit, he cannot understand them. He says, "What are they talking about?" He has to pass through this period to be purified, because the very first experience that every pilgrim must have is the experience of purification. It is then that he steps on to the second stage, the stage of illumination. Then the light shines within him and he knows that he is the light unto himself. He does not doubt—he moves forward, onward, upward, inward, Godward.'

'So this is mandatory for all on the path?'

'May be he has passed through the stage or through one of the stages in a previous birth. Then, he need not do so in the present life. The repetition of the experience is not absolutely necessary. But even though he has passed through such a period in his earlier life, a sort of shadow passes over him in this life.'

'So it does touch him in this life, even if he has gone through it in the past?'

'Just a shadow.'

'Is there a possibility of the pilgrim turning his or her back on the path?'

'There is, because Satan too has been given power which he tries to exercise as far as possible. Transformation means both ways—a transformation which elevates you, or a transformation which drags you down. But even if he is dragged down, a stage comes when he is again lifted up. If you recall, even a great saint like Augustine fell from grace, several times, for several years, before he could find that crucial turning point . . . it can happen to the best of the great souls.'

'Did You go through the dark night of the soul? Did You go through this testing time?'

'I do not know if I passed through this stage, but I passed through a stage in which my entire soul rebelled. I actually wanted to run away from My Master.'

'Why?'

'Because a time came, when after lavishing all His attention on me, He just seemed to ignore me. He would not even look at me. Once, continuously for fifteen days, He did not even utter my name or mention me. I was used to a different way of life, and this really was too much to bear. But looking back, I realize that it was really a period of purification. It was what taught me to go deeper and deeper into humility.'

'I recall a particular incident; UNESCO was about to set up a new centre in Hyderabad and they requested the Master to preside over the inaugural function. For fifteen days before the event was to take place, Sadhu Vaswani used to say repeatedly, "At this function I will take only Jashan (that is my name) with me; no one else will come with me. No one will be able to understand what is going on but I will take him and him alone." That was so till the last day. But when the day arrived, He took all the other people in the ashram but didn't take me. So they said to him, "Jashan is standing here, you have not asked him to step into the carriage in which you are going." He acted like he did not hear. He did hear, but He showed as if He didn't hear. Somebody again told him, a third person told him. But I knew that this was deliberately done to me. They all went, but I was left behind. And maybe I shed a tear, I was all alone. But then the understanding dawned upon me that perhaps He was trying to give me some sort of training. The Master knows best what the disciple needs. This happens in the life of every Guru—he has to train the disciple. This is what happened in the life of Sri Ramakrishna.

'Sri Ramakrishna loved Vivekananda so much that if Vivekananda did not come to Dakshineshwar for three or four days in a row, Ramakrishna Himself used to go to him. He did not have the wherewithal to hire a carriage. He used to borrow money, fourteen *annas* or something—the fare to reach Vivekananda. He used to do it. But a time came when Ramakrishna, if He saw Vivekananda coming to meet Him, would shut the door.'

'I think Sai Baba of Shirdi did the same thing with Upasini Maharaj. Bhagawan Nityananda did the same thing with Swami Muktananda.'

'Yes. The list is long. Now that You mention Swami Nityananda, though I don't think I have met Him, I feel as though He was close to me. So much so that I sometimes feel that I saw Him sitting in the veranda, in his cross-legged posture.'

'In Ganeshpuri?'

'Ganeshpuri, yes. Nityananda too had kept His foremost disciple away.'

'Swami Muktananda . . .'

'Yes. Swami Muktananda used to have an elephant and He had trained the elephant to place a garland around distinguished guests if they came to the ashram.'

'Ok. So Dada, back to the dark night of the Soul. Why does the dark night fall upon the disciple or pilgrim when he has renounced everything?'

'Yes it does enter after the stage of renunciation. It is as though you are two, one of those two, who wished to cut itself off. Sadhu Vaswani's emphasis was on light, "*Tamasoma jyotir gamaya*". When the college began functioning, they came to Him and asked for a motto, He gave them this, "Kindle the light". Which light, they asked Him. And He said, in every act kindle the light of love.

'Also, where the dark night of the soul is concerned there is no logical reason for it to take place. And then too, it is not for the disciple to ask why or how. Many people ask me, "Why is there no help or grace even after we surrender?" My answer is simple. "If you have truly surrendered, how can you have complaints and grievances? When you surrender truly, you must be able to abide by the will of the Guru, and not insist on what pleases you."'

'And Your dark night went on for how long?'

'I cannot say how long but there was one thing—it comes through in a natural way, it goes as though it did not exist. It is not like a train moving from one station to another . . . no, it just comes and goes. But that coming and going in terms of the calendar may be quite long.'

'And how was Sadhu Vaswani's behaviour towards you when this was going on?'

'As though He did not know me, that is what kills a person. The Guru tries all methods to crush the disciple's ego. In my case, there were quite a few of us who were very close to Him. And He would shift His attention completely from you to somebody else to bring about your transformation but somehow or the other in my case I found that when He shifted His attention from me to you, then automatically I came closer to you. I rather helped you. It is like this. He used to give me dictation for two to three hours every day, then suddenly He would give dictation to another just to bring about some sort of conflict within me but my attitude towards the other one became more intimate.'

'That happens one out of hundred times. Otherwise ninety-nine percent of people would have issues with the other person?'

'Yes. So the Guru tries all types, all methods to bring about these emotions. But in my case, perhaps, I was not prepared yet.'

'Is it because the Guru wants you to face every emotion and every dark side? And that He will reserve this only for his special ones?'

'Yes. As far as I could see, that is what He did.'

'And He will reserve this only for His disciple and not for his devotees.'

'Yes. Devotees will run away.'

We both began to chuckle. It was truly so beautiful to see that broad smile, those eyes twinkling, His body shaking when He laughed.

'This was one of the first things that Shanti told me. She said to me that to live with a saint is like toasting a bar of butter. She said it is not easy. And she said, "You have to be very careful because you belong to His family." So I was always on guard to see that this thought did not enter my mind that He is my uncle.'

'Avatar Meher Baba has said, "God is all merciful but the path to God is merciless."'

'Oh Yes! That is perfectly true.' He said it with the complete wonderment of a child.

'But Dada, tell me one thing, suppose the disciple is cracking up because of all the emotions that are coming about, does the Guru stand back and watch?'

'Yes.'

'He will not intervene in the process?'

'Sri Ramakrishna Paramahansa would often tell His disciples, that "there is no magic in turning milk into ghee". If you want ghee, as every housewife in those days would tell you, you have to go through the process of making ghee. First you have to boil the milk, then remove the cream, store the cream and make it into curd, then separate out its whey, churn the solid into butter and then melt it to get ghee. The same is true of an aspirant. He has to put in his own effort and go through a process. "The bliss" is to be earned. There is no magic wand or magic formula, which will bring it to you "in an instant". The same is true of this process. The disciple must go through this cleansing and purification, all by himself. It is not that the Guru does not know what he is going through. But He will not intervene obtrusively. At least, He will show that He is not interfering, although He has himself brought about this state, this condition, for the good of the disciple. That art He has, He is doing it purposely. He is doing it but He will act as though He does not know. And He will let the disciple churn as far as it is humanly possible to churn.'

'I guess the Guru knows how deep to put the knife.'

'But at times a disciple may not be ready and in this birth the person may fail. There was one young man who completely dedicated his life to Sadhu Vaswani for quite some time. He worked like His secretary. Sadhu Vaswani said, "I have no secretary, I am a simple man." But this young man used to work devotedly. Then there was a conference in Lahore when we were in Sind. The two of them—Sadhu Vaswani and this young man—went to Lahore. And there they had arranged a wonderful reception for them. On return, the train stopped at the Montgomery railway station. Here in Montgomery dwelt a girl with whom this young man was in touch before He came to Sadhu Vaswani. So that girl happened to know that they were passing. So she sent a word to this young man, "I am lying sick and as the train is going to halt here for three quarters of an hour, would you not come and meet me for a few minutes?" So leaving Sadhu Vaswani at the station alone, this young man went and did not return. Now from Montgomery to Hyderabad, Sadhu Vaswani came all alone in the train. We were all surprised how this young man could do this. And later we learnt that they had decided to marry each other. He sent an invitation because he had links in Hyderabad. Sadhu Vaswani Himself did not do anything but He made a remark which was conveyed to this young man that "marriages are made in heaven". In other words, Sadhu Vaswani did not wish that he should get married. But it had no effect on this young man. So there were cases like that.'

'When you were young, how many true disciples or intimate devotees were around Sadhu Vaswani?'

'The beauty of Sadhu Vaswani's life was that if He came in contact with anyone, that person thought that he was the one who was loved the most and the cynosure of all eyes. So, in that way, there was a group.'

'And how many remained?'

'Then there came Partition and so they were all scattered. They may have gone to different places but they had the same reverence for Him. Whenever they used to come here, they had the same reverence. But we were all scattered.'

'Do You feel Sadhu Vaswani has got that kind of mass reverence like many other saints and sages of His time? I know He didn't seek it or want it but just a question to you . . . do You think He has or was it His humility that did not allow that kind of mass adulation?'

'People who knew Him would say He is Krishna. And to answer your question, the fault lay in us. We failed to bring it out. That is the work of the disciples. In Sind, it was like that.'

'Because from reading a lot of your work on Sadhu Vaswani, it is obvious that He was a tremendous seer, saint or sage—whatever you want to call Him.'

'You are right. It has been our fault and the flaw lies with us. But He refused to cooperate when we wanted to highlight His greatness. But still I think we could have done better from that point of view. But the conditions through which we were passing were not favourable.'

'And I believe the country was passing through its own transition?'

'Yes. Now He and Mahatma Gandhi were friends but we did not take advantage of that situation. We just knew that all these leaders who were close to Sadhu Vaswani would have done anything for Sadhu Vaswani but He was so humble and He didn't see the point of spreading His glory or name or the work we do.'

'I remember the man in charge of Pandharpur Ashram had once come and told Sadhu Vaswani that they were celebrating something and that all the leaders, including Nehru and Patel, have consented to come and that He must also come. I felt tempted when I heard this and I said to Sadhu Vaswani, "This is a good chance." When that man went, Sadhu Vaswani told me, "Let the cobbler cobble his shoes. Don't get tempted."'

The problem with the world now is that there aren't such cobblers around. There are marketing geniuses and networking professionals; psychologists and life coaches but genuine cobblers have shut shop.

I bowed from far to Sadhu Vaswani's statue. Dada as usual had given me prasad for Meher. Fortunately, it was a bag of chips she would like. Or both Dada and I would have been told things about having absolutely no taste where picking up stuff for young eight-year-old girls was concerned.

10

'Dada, when did You know that You wanted to just live a life of being a disciple of Sadhu Vaswani? You were brilliant in academics and a promising career was open to you, wasn't it?'

'I have a feeling that I always knew I wanted to spend my life with Sadhu Vaswani. The realization came about when I was in the intermediate class of the college. But then Sadhu Vaswani stipulated that "you must complete your studies before you come to me". So I had to complete my post-graduation before I could go and stay with Him. However, during the vacations, I was allowed to be with Him.'

'So you were quite sure this is the path you wanted to take?'

'I did pass through a period in which I was not sure. While I was with Him, someone came from Karachi, the place where we used to live. Hyderabad was the place where Sadhu Vaswani used to do His work. So a man came from Karachi and told Sadhu Vaswani, "I have met Jashan's mother and she said to me with a heavy heart, 'I brought Him up, I have given Him the best education, and now my brother-in-law (that is, Sadhu Vaswani), has taken Him away.'" When Sadhu Vaswani heard this report, He said to me, "Pack up your things and go back to your mother." I had to obey. I packed my belongings, went back and said to my mother, "Ma, I have come to do what you would bid me to do." She said, "Jashan, my son, after the death of your father, I have pinned all my hopes on you. I want you to get yourself a good job and earn a lot of money so that we all can live a comfortable life." Coincidentally, that was the time when they needed appraisers for customs. There was a common friend of the family who had some influence in the customs. He told my mother, "If you give me an application from your son for the job of collector customs, I could get him the job right away." Otherwise they used to have competitive examinations for applicants, but he said that he will be able to procure the job for me directly. I obeyed my mother and wrote out the application. I was with my mother for three days. On the morning of the fourth day, as I was sitting in silence, my mother came and said to me, "Jashan, I know you will not be happy if you are with me. You will be happy only if you are with your uncle, Sadhu Vaswani. I give you permission to go to him." I told her, "Now He will not accept me, after what He has heard."'

'She said, "Jashan, my child, do not worry. I am going to give you a letter and He will definitely accept you." She gave me a letter in which she wrote, "Gladly and with all my heart I permit Jashan to serve you and be with you." Sadhu Vaswani preserved that letter with Himself till the very end.

'So, I too had to go through that period. For those three or four days I was sure that I would not be with the Master because my mother was quite strong-minded. I was the eldest son of the family and it was perfectly natural for her to want me to be with her and the family and get a job and start a family—the usual things each mother, I guess, expects out of her son.

'Earlier, I had an offer from the college to join the teaching staff. This was just after I finished my MSc and the college reopened after the holidays. At that time, I was with the Master in Sri Lanka. He had been invited to preside over the Pan Asian World Conference for Peace. Hitler had pounced upon Poland and the conference was called in this connection. The climate of Sri Lanka happened to suit Sadhu Vaswani. Thus, He decided to stay on for some more time. That was about the time when my college reopened, and the head of the department of physics, Dr Paldhikar, sent a word to me that there was a vacancy for a lecturer and that they would keep the job open for me so that I could come any time and take up the position. Once again, Sadhu Vaswani said to me, "You should ask your mother about what she wants you to do." This time, I wrote to my younger brother and placed my dilemma before him; I told him that it was my personal wish to stay on with Sadhu Vaswani. He wrote back to say that my mother had no objections if I stayed back with Sadhu Vaswani. So the Master felt sure that my mother had permitted me.'

'It must have been difficult for your mother too, to let go of her eldest son.'

'Should have been, but there was a smile on her face when she finally permitted me to go. But it must have cost her a lot, because we were not rich. My father had a good salary but he used to spend it all. There was rarely a day when he did not bring some hungry one or some guest to the house for meals. He was like that, he was a giver. He passed away at the age of fifty-three. He did not leave anything behind, there were no savings. Strange enough, the savings came when Sadhu Vaswani left the college and resigned from his post. Somehow or the other, the impression that He created among the family members was that He had nothing with himself. But it seems He had some savings. So when my father, who was His elder brother, learned that He had nothing, he sent him a month's salary for His private expenses. But Sadhu Vaswani returned the amount saying that he did not need it at that time. And my father put that amount in the insurance. That was the first and the last premium that he paid and soon thereafter he passed away. So I think my mother got quite a large amount by way of insurance. That is how we were brought up.'

'In a strange way, Sadhu Vaswani, knowingly or by default, helped your father to pay the first and last insurance premium and thus helped Your mother get a decent amount as insurance. Strange. How old were you?'

'Just eleven years old.'

'How did Your mother take care of Your family?'

'She became a teacher. Because my father was a social worker, he had built up certain institutions of service. So he had friends who felt for the family. And they created a post for my mother.'

'When You look at it, both Your parents, in their own way, have contributed tremendously to make You who and what You are.'

'Yes. Without them, we would have been lost. My mother, especially, empowered us. Otherwise, I would have had to enter some professional service and this life with the Master would probably never have happened.'

'How old was Your mother when she passed away?'

'She was born at the turn of the century; I think she died in her late seventies. She came with us to India and was a strong presence in our lives.'

'Krishna told me the other day that during one of Your birthdays, You disappeared?

'Yes, an accident took place. There was a cyclist who was coming in the opposite direction and just to save him, I went off the road . . . it was more of a slope. And the car actually turned. But nothing happened to me. Just that I got a feeling that perhaps God does not want me to behave like this. I guess I wanted to spend a quiet day with myself. But over here, a lot of things were planned and I didn't want to go through all that. So when the small accident took place, for me, it was like a lesson that when your loved ones give you love, never run away from it.'

'But what I found more interesting was that you found yourself in the pilgrimage sanctuary of Alandi and You narrated how You were visited by a number of avatars, Masters and saints who blessed You profusely. How was the feeling? Was it a vision, was it in the mind or did You actually see Them? Because You rarely write about all this and You rarely talk about all this. Since You have revealed this incident, it must for sure have made an impact on You.'

'That is where I found that there is only One God or One Creator and He can put on any form that He likes. He can appear to you as Ganesha or He can appear to you as Hanuman. He can appear in the form of Sant Dnyaneshwar or Sant Tukaram.'

'And They give you one supreme message to "always embrace love".'

'Yes. Give love but the love that you give should be selfless. I remember there was a dharamshala near where the accident had taken place. I won't be able to recognize it now. It was years ago.'

'How old were You at that time?'

'I don't remember, but it is quite some time ago.'

'Was Your mother in the body then?'

'She was there.'

'So did she fire You for disappearing?'

'Oh Yes!'

He had such a childlike expression that my heart melted. He was like a child now. A saint? Yes, always, but the childlike quality was so evident.

'Do you feel when an individual has to walk the spiritual path he is born into a family that allows that growth?'

'Yes. The family will play an instrumental role. Either positively or negatively, they will push the person towards spirituality.'

'So the cosmos is making things ready for him or her?'

'But in spite of that, very few take advantage of this. But the forces of good cooperate to elevate the person.'

'Who did your parents pray to? Who was your *ishta deva*?'

'My revered father was influenced more by Dr Annie Besant. He was a theosophist. My mother didn't care for anything so long as my father was in the body. After he departed, she felt drawn to Guru Nanak. And she used to pray to Him for hours together; she used to read the Guru Granth Sahib regularly.'

'There are many times when an individual prays and suddenly the name of another God, Goddess or Guru comes about and often the devotee begins to feel some kind of guilt. As though he is fearful or ashamed or saddened that the Name which was always chanted was replaced by some other Name. Is it necessary to chant only one mantra?'

'It is not necessary but it is helpful. Because ultimately the entire universe is One; it is we who have differentiated it. We have created the difference between Shiva and Vishnu when both are actually One.'

'I have been told that as we chant One name, that power of the name or mantra starts building up into our aura and becomes One with the aura.'

'Yes, it does take place.'

'Why is it mentioned in virtually every religion that the best time to pray is, what we call the *Brahma muhurat*, usually from four to four thirty up till sunrise or at mid-day or twilight or after midnight? Why are there these timings?'

'For two reasons—one, if you are particular about the timings, it makes one disciplined and helps the practitioner. And the second reason is that these are periods of the day and night when it is believed that there is a descent of vibrations from above that helps the seeker.'

'So the first slot is around 4.30 A.M. to sunrise, the second is mid-afternoon and the third would be twilight. The fourth would be . . . ?'

'Ideally, just as you go off to sleep. It does not matter what time it is. I request the sangat, "The one thing that you should do is to remember the Lord at least for a minute after every hour." But after every hour it becomes difficult, as you are busy working and easily tend to forget; the hour is over and you are not aware of it. So I tell them to do it at least five times during the day; once when you get up, once when you take breakfast, lunch, dinner and once before going to bed. Five times becomes very easy. The Muslims offer *namaz* five times.'

'Even Zoroastrians are supposed to pray five times in a day. If you are staying near a fire temple, you will hear the bell toll five times in the day. We have specific prayers for each time of the day. What is its significance?'

'If your religion has specifically suggested five times for prayers, like Zoroastrianism and Islam, and you hear the fire temple bell or the holy call for namaz and you don't pray, you will feel guilty. It is not that God is a toll collector. No. But if something is apparent, it helps one to become more disciplined.'

'You have mentioned that while meditating one should face either the east or the north direction?'

'It is said so in our ancient scriptures. I am sure it has got to do with the vibrations emitted from these directions. And when one gives a specific direction to one's prayers, it creates a mystic hue around everything.'

'In Zoroastrianism, if you are not facing the east and you don't know where the sun is, then one is asked to face the south as according to me, and I could be wrong, when you face the south, your back is never to the sun.'

'In those early days, when Zoroastrianism and Hinduism were one, the sun was regarded as God. They said you must not turn your back to the sun. Zoroastrians and Aryans were brothers. Then there were some differences and they parted ways.'

'Dada, have you ever felt fear, have you ever been fearful of something?'

'More than once. But the good thing was that when I was young, a holy man gave me a mantra. He said whenever fear enters your heart or it is bound to enter your heart, then I can repeat this mantra. My faith in the mantra saved me. It was not the mantra, but my faith in the mantra. The mantra was: "Satnaam mushkul aasan!", which means "the holy name of God makes the difficult things easy". Mushkul means difficult and aasan, easy. In Zoroastrianism, you also have a prayer called "Mushkhil aasan". It is dedicated to . . .'

'Dedicated to our angel called Behram Yazad.'

'Yes. When I was small, I often could not fall asleep due to fear. The fear would overpower me, leaving me trembling and shaken. One day I placed a chair by my bedside. When I lay on the bed, I began speaking to God. I told God, "Sit on this chair and stay awake and watch me while I go to sleep. Why should both of us stay awake? If you stay awake, I can go to sleep. In this way, one will sleep and the other will be awake."' We both began to chuckle. Like two kids. 'From then on, this was my attitude. Whenever I felt overwhelmed or frightened, I would imagine a chair placed beside myself, on which God was seated, watching over me. This enabled me to totally eradicate fear.'

'So eventually it is one's faith in a mantra or faith in the Guru that really, really helps us cross the worldly ocean.'

'I think ultimately it is faith in the mantra, because the mantra may be recited by a hundred people, but it works only in the case of five people. Why? Because the remaining ninety-five don't have that faith. I think it is faith that matters.'

'Have you ever grappled with the issues of anger?'

'Yes. In my early years, if something was not done as I wished it to be done, I used to get angry. Until the grace of God came on me and I realized that there are two wills—there is my will and there is the will of God. Surely the will of God is better than my will, so why get angry? It is always good to be patient. As the Chinese say: "If you are patient in one moment of anger, you will escape a hundred days of sorrow."'

'Many people tell me that they don't get angry over little things but get angry when somebody does something that really displeases them. But according to me, anger is something that must be avoided always. You can't have a reason to get angry. It is like somebody telling me, "I never take a bribe unless it is a very big bribe. It should be above one crore rupees and only then do I succumb to bribery." But at the end of the day you have succumbed and thus you are as guilty or corrupt as the person who took a hundred rupee bribe. A bribe is a bribe. Anger is anger. You cannot have reasons for either.

'The very first thing that you must understand is that when you get angry, you only harm yourself. You don't harm the other person. When I feel angry with you, you may just pay scant attention to me. But when I get angry, I harm myself because I circulate poison throughout my blood system, through my body. Therefore, once I understand that I harm myself, when I become angry, I'll try not to get angry as far as possible and hopefully, soon get over anger and not get angry over anything.

'But there is one type of anger that is permitted. That is why God created anger, otherwise He would not have created it at all. If every type of anger led to harming the person who became angry, He would not have created anger at all. There is one type of anger that is permissible. It is called righteous anger. When you are angry on occasions when you find that the rights of others are being trampled upon, when you get angry in defence of an innocent person, when you get angry when you find a girl is being molested by someone—those are the cases of righteous anger. Anger is permitted, but in those occasions too you must be careful to see that you don't take the anger within yourself. That anger should be on the surface.

'Now, when you find that somebody is not speaking in the right spirit concerning your parents, you've every right to be angry, but be angry only on the surface. What is meant by being angry on the surface? There was a holy man of God who he entered a town, and in that town there was a snake. This is only a story told to us, but every story points to a deep truth. This snake came to the holy man and said to him, "O holy man, I've lived for so many years and I've bitten so many people but now I want to change, I want to become a new type of a snake. I don't want to live the old life. I've repented for the wrongs I've committed so far. Won't you initiate me in the Name Divine so that I can keep on repeating it and cleanse myself of all the undesirable karma I've entered into. Before I leave this body, I want to be thoroughly cleansed. Will you not initiate me in the Name Divine?" And this holy man said, "Why will I not initiate you? I find that there is true aspiration in the heart within you. There is a true longing for the Name Divine." So, he passed on to the snake a Name and told it to keep on repeating that Name. The snake kept on repeating that name. When the little children of the town found that this snake did not want to get angry or hurt anybody and had begun to chant a Divine Name to control itself and mend its ways, they started pelting stones at it. They said, "Now is the opportunity, now is the chance. He is not going to do anything to us. We are going to take our vengeance." So, they kept on pelting stones at him. After some days, when the holy man entered the village, this snake could hardly crawl. He was so badly hurt by the stones that were pelted at it. So, the snake came and from a distance it said to the holy man, "This is what has happened to me. You initiated me in the Name Divine. I keep on repeating the Name but this is what has happened to me because you told me if I repeat the holy name, I must not bite anyone. And because I don't bite anyone, all these little children have taken advantage of me." So, the holy man said to him, "I told you not to bite anyone but I did not tell you not to hiss. You must keep hissing. When a snake hisses, everybody gets frightened and flees. You can hiss but you must not bite. And the test of that is, when you hiss, it's only on the surface; it's only superficial anger. It is projected anger, not real anger. This is also called righteous anger."'

'Sri Ramakrishna Paramahansa was one of the mildest, gentlest and loveliest of men that India and humanity have produced. And His teaching to everyone was never to be angry. Never to speak roughly to anyone. Then one day, one of His disciples came and told him, "Sir, I was going in a boat, and there were some people who started speaking bad words concerning You." "Then what did you do?" asked Sri Ramakrishna Paramahansa. "Sir, Your teaching was that I should not speak rudely to anyone, I should not speak harshly to anyone, so I was quiet." He said, "Fie on you! Why didn't you show that you are angry? Not in the heart within. Is that clear? Just show it." That type of anger is permitted when it becomes your duty to be angry.

'There are occasions when the mother pretends to be angry with the child, otherwise the child will not understand his fault. The child will not reform. There are occasions when the teacher has to be angry with the student. There are occasions when the employer has to be angry with the employee, otherwise they will not be able to get the work done. But, you have to only make a show of being angry. Thus, the focus on what one can call "seeming anger", but avoiding "real anger". You must keep away from real anger. Real anger will harm you. But if you just show anger, it will not harm you. Your Guru Sai Baba of Shirdi used to show anger. He would shout, scream and even threaten to hit a disciple, but the next moment He would behave as though nothing had really happened. He was a Master in showing anger. He never really got angry, just showed it. You have written about it in your books on this quality of Sai Baba.'

I nodded, humbled.

'Remember that God is in each one of us. Remember that when somebody slaps you on one cheek, don't get violent. You can show anger but don't let anger consume you. Eventually we have to offer the other cheek.'

'Dada what happens is, in the real world, when you go out to work, if you were to use this philosophy that God is in each one and that is why I shall behave in that appropriate manner of humility and calmness, you can be taken advantage of. Your calmness can be treated as weakness. How does one handle such a situation?'

'There was a time when on occasions such as Sadhu Vaswani's birthday or Mahayagna day, there used to be distribution of charity money; five or ten rupee notes. A particular amount would be given to each one of the so-called beggars who came in a row. I don't know how the word would go around. There used to be some beggars who were between twelve to fifteen years of age and they used to come over and over again. Somehow or the other I realized this. So when they would come twice or thrice, knowing that they are images of God, I would give them the note again. But when they came the fourth time, I used to give them nothing and acted as though I was giving them money. They would understand that I had caught them. In my heart, I would say, "Lord you are playing with me, I too want to play with you."'

'So they got the message without saying anything. But Dada, in the teachings of the Gita, Lord Krishna tells Arjuna that to do evil is wrong and to allow someone to do evil to you is wrong too. Where the philosophy of eye for an eye was prevalent, you had Jesus Christ who said if someone slaps you on one cheek, give him the other cheek also. They are two very different philosophies. Even the Old Testament and the New Testament philosophies are so different; eye for an eye was the philosophy of the Old Testament.'

'The essential teaching of Krishna is that you must first become a man of self-control and then do what is needed to be done. Krishna went so far as to become a messenger of peace; He went to the Kauravas and told them, "Don't give Pandavas their share. Take the entire kingdom and give only five villages to the five brothers and they will be happy with it." But Duryodhana said that he would not even give the space occupied by the point of a needle. So the teaching that Krishna gave us was that if your right is being completely denied by the other party, you can stand up and fight. The teaching we get is first try and resolve the issue peacefully, but if there is no other option, then peacefully stand up for your right.'

'So you can stand up for your rights after trying to handle the situation calmly and even if that means entering hell for a heavenly cause.'

'Absolutely, this is very necessary.'

'Like prophet Zarathustra used to say, "Go in the world with peace in your heart, a smile on your face, but a big club behind your back."'

'Or like my maternal grandmother kept telling me, "When a situation can be resolved by a spoonful of sugar, why do you want to use a bottle of vinegar?"'

'Similar teaching was given by Sadhu Vaswani to a military official who came to meet Him and asked for His advice. And the guidance which Sadhu Vaswani gave the military official was, "Love and peace in the heart, but keep the gun powder dry." This is what we need, the blend of the two.'

'So basically what you are saying is, if one has to fight, one does it with calmness and compassion. From the point of dharma.'

'Yes.'

'You are not fighting the person, you are fighting the cause.'

'There was a case which came to Sadhu Vaswani. It was a family matter. When Sadhu Vaswani's mother passed away, she gave her daughter's hand to Sadhu Vaswani and said to him, "You should take care of your sister." Years later, there was a problem which was brought forward to Sadhu Vaswani. I do not want to go into the details of the case, but his sister was sure that Sadhu Vaswani would favour her and He would give a judgment which would be in her favour. But Sadhu Vaswani didn't do so because He did not think it fair. And this displeased the sister. But as soon as the case was closed, Sadhu Vaswani, who was also a shareholder in the matter, told His sister, "You take away my share so that you get much more than you would have got if the case was decided in your favour." He resolved the issue in a dharmic manner and because of His love and compassion, gave His share to His sister.'

'Dada, in today's time there is so much of suffering, largely man-made suffering. Or let us take for instance the Second World War where six million Jews were tortured and killed. How does this fit into the whole concept of retribution, karma, grace?'

'That is why life is said to be a mystery, and the teaching given is, "You do your duty, you play the part that has been assigned to you in the cosmic plan. Give your best and leave the rest to the Lord's wisdom."

'God realized souls will never question the workings of the cosmos.'

'But Dada, even Sadhu Vaswani Himself has written that, "Sometimes when I see what is happening around me, it makes me want to question."'

'Yes. And He said about Guru Nanak also, on more than one occasion. Guru Nanak began to question the wisdom of God as to "How is it that You permit these things to happen?"'

'Have You ever felt this desolate feeling?'

'I am a dull person, I don't think of many things. I know this work has been given to me and I keep on doing it. These questions are philosophical. It is for philosophers to understand. Ruzbeh, we are workers, our role is to serve our Masters.'

'What is the meaning of God being a servant of the suffering ones? Sadhu Vaswani has mentioned this time and again that He wants to be the lowest of the low and that God is the servant of the suffering ones?'

'God is in everything, this is true God realization. To the realized person, everything is God. He sees God in the lowest of the low, he sees Him in the highest of the high. So He means to say that you must not forget that the hearts of those who suffer, in that experience of suffering, are touched by God. Otherwise suffering will have no place in life.'

'So you mean that even the reason for suffering is to open our hearts to God. But suffering so often has a reversal effect. It makes people bitter, negative, despondent.'

'Yes, very true. Some become more bitter. But if one is calm and silent within, slowly they begin to realize that we need to go beyond those testing experiences. When we open our hearts, we realize that our God is not unjust and that every experience with an open heart will takes us closer to Him. Than we realize the value of the open heart.'

'What is the secret of You embracing the pain in such a beautiful manner?'

'I don't regard it as pain. I regard it as a gift from the spotless hands of God and I offer it to the Lord so that the pain of some others is lessened. That gives me joy.'

'How does the common man embrace pain?'

'The common man firstly finds some sort of physical reason for that pain which is not the right way. But that is the first thing he does. "This is the reason why I have got pain." The right way for all of us is first to accept the pain gracefully. Nature wishes to teach us this lesson of acceptance right from the time we are born. I am born with a dark skin and I have to accept it. You and I are both born at the same time, in the same maternity home, yet you are of fair complexion while I am of dark complexion. But I have to accept it, I cannot enter your body. I am born with only one eye, you have been born with two eyes. I have to accept it. So from the very first day, life wishes to teach us this lesson of acceptance. And as life goes on, this lesson becomes more and more intense.'

'Dada how does one embrace pain gracefully?'

'Firstly by explaining to oneself that pain applies to the body. I am not the body. Practice detachment from the body, so that when you feel excruciating pain in the leg you say, "My dear leg, you are feeling the pain, I am so sorry but I can't help it. You have to go through your karma." This detachment gives you the strength to face pain. And secondly I should accept pain. Pain too is a gift from God. Pain too comes from Him, to teach me a lesson that I need to learn. Thirdly, I should accept pain and offer it to the Lord. "Lord, let this pain be with me, but let others be free of pain." These are the three things that I do.

'We should always look for something for which we may feel grateful to God. A man had lost a leg in an accident. When he regained consciousness and discovered what had actually happened, he said to those around him, "Thank God it was the leg with arthritis."'

'You have gone through much more than Your share of pain. You feel these are the three philosophies, the three ideas that helped You to . . . face pain gracefully?'

'There are people who say there is no pain. But the fact is that pain is there. I have never denied that there is pain.'

'But it is very real. What You are saying is one should not fight the pain, one needs to embrace it.'

'And one needs to use it in the service of humanity.'

'Has this pain taught You anything?'

'Pain has taught me to go closer to the Lord. Years ago, I used to put a nail in my shoe at the heel of the right foot. So every time the right foot pressed on the ground, there used to be pain. It was a reminder that, "You have forgotten your God." You must repeat the Name and so that pain became a reminder. Thus, what nothing else could achieve, pain succeeded in teaching me to keep on chanting the Name.'

'I guess all this can happen if one's priority is God, Goddess or Guru. Otherwise, I don't think folks are going to put pins in their shoes like You, Dada, or prick themselves with pins when a wrong thought enters like Sadhu Vaswani.'

'Yes. But that has to happen sooner or later, either today or tomorrow. And that is how you use pain.'

'Convert pain to prasad?'

'Well said. Yes, Ruzbeh. Convert pain to prasad.'

'How come none of us really learn from pain?'

'We are meant to, Ruzbeh, but not many learn from anything. We need to make God one's priority.'

'Making God one's priority is the final culmination for a human being, but the only problem is that it can take centuries to walk that path.'

'Human birth is only a station on the way; the journey is long.'

'I have never understood whether Buddhism recognizes or does not recognize God and the personal soul?'

'Buddha said to His disciples, "There are so many leaves on the tree under which we are sitting—more than the number of these leaves are the things that I have not told you about. I have told you only a few things, concentrate on them." Now He didn't want to go into theology, therefore He didn't use the word God. But surely He believed in God. It is the most practical religion. Other religions talk about a hundred things, but Gautama Buddha focused on a few things and asked to concentrate on these things and leave the rest.'

'And what about Jainism?'

'Jainism and Buddhism are almost the same. In fact, Gautama Buddha and Mahavira worked together. I believe Gautama Buddha was close to Mahavira's heart. They disagreed on one point—Gautama Buddha said that if a *bikhu* went out to beg and got food of non-violence or food of violence, he should not differentiate. But,

Mahavira said that no food of violence should ever be accepted. They disagreed on this one point. Mahavira was senior in age to Gautama Buddha. If I am not mistaken, Mahavira too was from a royal family.'

'Yes, He was. He gave up everything.'

'Trishala was His mother.'

'Yes she was from a highly aristocratic family. But he was very hard on Himself.'

'Not on Himself, but on His body.'

'But when you are hard on your body, isn't that violence too?'

'Therefore violence has a place; all these *vikaras* that we wish to avoid have a place in life. But we do not use them in the right way. Anger has a place in life; I should be angry but at myself. Greed has a place; I should be greedy for the true treasure.'

'So anything that is used to help us on the path and furthers our quest is fine?'

'Yes.'

'Sadhu Vaswani has mentioned that when you give, you don't see whether the person is deserving or undeserving? What does that mean?'

'He would say, "God does not see whether I deserve to have what I have, therefore, who am I to look into what one deserves or not?" Thus Sadhu Vaswani would give selflessly, never seeing whether the person to whom He gave deserved it or not. A number of people would complain quite often that Sadhu Vaswani was being fooled or cheated as He never saw the credentials of the one who sought something from Him. There was one who looked like a beggar and seemed of unsound mind, though some thought he was pretending. He received money from Sadhu Vaswani till the last day of His life. The day Sadhu Vaswani left His body, that man also dropped his body. I don't know what we used to call him. Gopal was his name but we used to call him Mastana or something. Now most people never understood why Sadhu Vaswani encouraged that man by giving him money but Sadhu Vaswani was beyond such logic. He gave and gave.'

'What is your opinion about giving to people, whether they seemingly deserve it or not? Do you believe in this same philosophy?

From the spiritual point of view, yes, it is right, but what about from the practical point of view?'

'I believe in the same philosophy. But if it is a large amount, I do make enquires.'

We both began to laugh. Dada giggled and His eyes twinkled.

'When does a Guru become the happiest with His or Her disciple?'

'We asked this question of Sadhu Vaswani and He said the Guru becomes the happiest when His disciples decrease in number. We were all surprised because we thought that the Guru should feel happy when the number of disciples increases. Then He explained to us that when one disciple has attained perfection, when the disciple himself becomes a Master, this makes the Guru the happiest. Sadhu Vaswani once told us the story of a saint who was about to pass away at the age of eighty. They found tears in His eyes. And they said to Him, "Master, You have always told us that death takes you to a better, nobler, more fragrant and a more beautiful life. How is it that You are weeping?" He said, "I am not weeping because I am moving on to my home, I am weeping because God gave me a treasure to go and distribute amongst the people but I did not get even one to whom I could pass this priceless treasure. That is the difficulty of Kali Yuga."

'There is a story of Raja Janak. It is said that one day he was taking a walk in a garden when a man came and said to him, "When shall I be free of this bondage, they call it *chaurasi ka chakar*?" Janak happened to pass by a tree at that time so he caught hold of a branch and he said: "Oh please free me of this branch. It has caught hold of me!" And he began to cry. And the man said, "Why are you crying, you have yourself caught hold of the branch." Janak smiled and said, "You have bound yourself."'

'Sadhu Vaswani spoke a lot about awakening the longing for God. I can understand longing for God but how can one awaken that longing for God?'

'Awakening comes in a variety of ways. Sometimes one can work for lifetimes and then in an instance the awakening can come forth. Sometimes it is God's grace. Or perhaps something happens to you,

you get a shock and in that shock you awaken. Sadhu Vaswani used to give us the example of Raja Bhartrihari. Bhartrihari was a noble, virtuous, kind and compassionate king. His subjects were happy under his rule.

'Once, a group of holy men visited him. They brought to him an Amarphal. It is a fruit that bestows immortality. "O Raja, king of our hearts, please accept this rare and precious fruit from us. In the whole world, there is only one Amarphal; and we wish that you, our noble king, should have it. We have brought it to you because you are the one person who deserves to live forever and ever more."

'Bhartrihari accepted the fruit. But as he was about to eat it, he said to himself, "Of what use is life to me without my beloved? Let me give this Amarphal to my wife, whom I love more than my life. Let her live forever and ever more."

'So the king passed the Amarphal to his wife saying, "This is the fruit of immortality, eat it, and you, my beloved, will never die." The queen accepted the fruit. But as destiny would have it, she was secretly in love with the coachman. She said to herself, "Of what use will this fruit be to me if I live on, but my dear coachman perishes?" So she passed on the fruit to the coachman.

'As for the coachman, he was in love with a prostitute. He handed over the fruit to the prostitute. In a moment of rare introspection, the prostitute said to herself, "Of what use is life to me? On each day of my life on earth, I draw so many to a life of sinfulness. If there is anyone who deserves to live eternally, it is our great, good and just king, Raja Bhartrihari."

'So the Amarphal back came to Raja Bhartrihari. The king was amazed, he was dumbfounded! How did the fruit get into the hands of this prostitute? He made inquiries. He found that his wife had been unfaithful to him.

'"What a fool I was to have placed my trust in the world and in a creature of this world!" he said to himself. "Let me lay all my trust in Him who never faileth. Let me set out in quest of the One and Only One Beloved, the First and the Only Fair, the Purest of the Pure, the Spotless, the Stainless." Raja Bhartrihari renounced the world, became a *jignasu*, a seeker of truth.

'Now if you get a shock like this, your sleeping soul wakes up. Or sometimes if you are sitting in a satsang and you hear a song, there might be a line which penetrates your heart and you say, "What have I done with my life." So this awakening can come in a variety of ways, said Sadhu Vaswani. But awakening is very necessary. That, according to Him, is the first step on the path. We are all asleep, we take the first step when we are awakened, when we regard the world around us as a dream or as a play. It is then that we start moving forward.

'You asked me the other day what defined Sadhu Vaswani? It is love. It was as though He was an ocean of love. His eyes were radiant with love, His words were vibrant with love. The very tips of His fingers thrilled with love. He used to touch us and we used to feel those vibrations. On one occasion, He was asked to give His teaching in one word and the one word He used is love. I remember there was a period when He was ailing and He was lying down on bed. He could not get up, He could not walk. I think after six weeks or so, He had a desire to go and meet the devotees downstairs in the hall. So we carried the bed on which He lay and placed it in the hall. And some of the satsangis said, "Master, You have come to us after so very many days, pray give us a message." And He said, "My message is to love God with all your heart and mind and soul. And give the loving service of love to all who are in need of it." He went a step further and said, "Even animals, every creature that breathes the breath of life, is sensitive to love." But before we can love in the right way, our hearts should be pure. Therefore in His teaching the emphasis was always on purity of heart.'

'How do you reach that stage of purity of heart? How does one work towards that?'

'It comes through inner cleansing. But it is not possible to do inner cleansing on my own. I need somebody else to come and cleanse me. So once again we come to a point where we need the grace of God and the Guru.'

'How does one earn that grace from the Guru?'

'Grace and earning, the two don't go together. Grace is just grace. One day I had asked this question to Sadhu Vaswani, "Is it possible to quicken the process of receiving grace from the Guru?" He said, "You can't do that, but there is one thing that helps. If you are good to your enemies, if you return good for evil, it draws the grace of the Master."

'Therefore keep on doing good all the time, to as many as you can, on as many occasions as you can, in as many ways as you can, and as long as you can.

'There were people who spoke ill of Him. These things happen in public life, you know. Those very people, when they were in need, came to Him and He never remembered the wrongs, the slander, the hate or their behaviour towards Him. I remember there was an editor who they had bribed and he had written all sorts of nasty things about Sadhu Vaswani. He printed them in a newspaper and that paper was given free to every household. The disciples and devotees of Sadhu Vaswani approached Him and said to Him, "Gurudev, this is what the editor has done. If You will very kindly permit us, we will boycott the newspaper." Sadhu Vaswani said, "No, my dear one, don't boycott the paper. Truth will soon be out." After about two years, this editor's wife was diagnosed with tuberculosis and it was in a very advanced stage. The editor did not have the money to purchase medicines for her. The people who had bribed him did not want to help him. Sadhu Vaswani came to know and He sent for him and said, "My brother, whatever you want you can take from me, but take very good care of your wife." The man broke down. Later, he and his family members became staunch followers; they came to the satsang every day.

'There have been several such incidents in His life. In fact, the very first incident that created an impression on me was when Sadhu Vaswani came to Karachi and stayed at our house. In Karachi, fruit sellers would go from house to house. When they came to our house, my mother was not present. But, Sadhu Vaswani was there. The first thing He did was to give the fruit seller a ten rupee note. In those days, ten rupees meant a lot of money. Sadhu Vaswani then took whatever fruit He wanted. When the final calculation was made, the fruit seller, it appeared to me, was taking advantage of Sadhu Vaswani's goodness. So I spoke to the fruit seller roughly. I said to him, "Just because Sadhu Vaswani has trusted you, is this the way you behave?" He heard the tone of my voice and when the lunch hour came, He would not take lunch. He said, "Today I don't feel like taking lunch." We thought perhaps that He was not hungry at that time. After an hour we again asked him and got the same answer. After another hour it dawned upon me that perhaps something has happened which has upset Him. So I asked him and He said, "Did you not see Shri Krishna in that fruit seller?" I had forgotten all about the incident.' Dada, like a child, bit His tongue to express what a mistake He had made. He looks like a child when He does this. 'I said, "Which fruit seller and which Krishna?" Then He told me about how rudely I had spoken to the fruit seller. That was the first lesson that I learnt from Him. To see the Lord in everyone, not just the fruit seller, but in the sinner too. And that I think is the basis of true humility. When I see God in you, I will deal with you in a humble way. I have no option but treat you with respect.

'He even saw God in a stone. We were walking on the roadside when there was a stone in the front and I kicked it to the side lest Sadhu Vaswani's foot trips. Immediately, His hands went to His heart. I said, "Dada, did I do something which hurt you?" He said to me in Sindhi, "*Jey poothiya mein parmeshwar ta pathar mein ko biyo*?" Translated into English, it means, "If there is God in the scripture, is there someone else in the stone?" Therefore, He said, "Touch everyone, everything with reverence. Treat everyone with love." This was His teaching not only in words but in the deeds of His daily life.

'They brought to Him a girl who had gone astray. Sadhu Vaswani looked at her and her eyes were filled with tears of repentance. He blessed her and said, "Forget what God hath forgotten, go and live a new life." The girl's life was changed. He was love personified.'

'Sadhu Vaswani had mentioned it, in fact you yourself have written it, that God is the secret of man. What would that mean?'

'That means that you are God but you don't know it. You have to unveil that secret—*Tat Twam Asi*! That thou art *Aham Brahmasmi*! I am the Brahman! That is the secret. These are also known as the Mahavakyas of the rishis. Vakya is utterance and Mahavakya are

Great Utterances. In fact, it was the duty of every rishi to teach to the young people who came to him that Thou art That.'

'But, the process of eventuality of self-realization would be dependent on grace and according to You grace has no laws, right? No true foundation? More like a divine whim?'

'It is like being taken from a dark room into a well-illuminated room. So somebody has to take you. That process is grace. *Tamasoma Jyotirgamaya!* That was the constant prayer of the ancient rishis. Take me from darkness into light. All the good things that I am doing have no value because they are in darkness. They have no value whatsoever. But they are helpful in the cleansing process. Your inner instrument, the *antahkarna,* is being cleansed.'

'And the foundation of all this is love and silence?'

'Oh yes. Silence and love includes selfless activity.

'There was a young man who was in quest of such happiness. He said, come what may, I want to be happy. I don't want to give up happiness, which I regard as the greatest treasure of my life. But let me tell you, we are here not to be happy ourselves but to make others happy. It's only when we make others happy that part of the happiness which we give to others comes back to us and we become truly happy.

'This young man did his very best to be happy. He tried all methods but he found that there were always occasions when he was not happy. Someone suggested to him to go and meet the hermit who stays on the outskirts of the city, "Why don't you ask him how to be happy permanently because he is always happy. We always see a perpetual smile on his face."

'So he went to that hermit and he placed his difficulty before him. And the hermit said to him, "Young man, let me give you the secret of happiness. The secret is that you must want what you have. You must not try to have what you want. You must want what you have.

'There is no end to our desires, and desire, if unfulfilled, makes you unhappy. Actually, even if desires are fulfilled they make you unhappy. But we will consider that point later. Every desire, whether fulfilled or unfulfilled, makes you unhappy. If you want to be happy permanently, do not desire anything.

'Who is the truly happy man? He who desires nothing, he who expects nothing, he who claims nothing and he who accepts the Will of the God. He merges his will to the Will of God. The motto of his life is: Thou knowest everything Beloved, let Thy Will always be done. In joy and sorrow my Beloved, let Thy Will always be done!

'This is the secret of true happiness. It is not that the man who has the greatest wealth is happy. Millionaires and billionaires have met me with tears in their eyes and have said to me, "We have whatever we want and yet are not happy." The secret of true happiness, I believe, is not in any outward things. The secret of happiness is in peace of mind. If your mind is at peace, you may have nothing in the world yet you will be truly happy. It was Jesus who said, "Nothing in the morn I have and nothing do I have at night yet there is none on earth richer or happier than I."'

'Dada how does one incorporate this or try to bring about happiness when an individual has a family, goes to work where s/he is treated badly and has been given a raw deal in life. How does one still try to bring about this feeling of happiness?'

'To be truly happy, we have to rise above the conditions that are around us. Conditions should not affect us at all. That is why I said, "*Tum hi saab kuch janat*". "The Lord knows the conditions in which I am and yet He has kept me in that condition. And God is my father, He is my mother and He doesn't want me to be unhappy and yet He has deliberately kept me in that condition. Why? Because He wants me to learn a lesson which I need to learn. I often think of this earth as a school, a school in which we all have to come to learn the lesson of happiness. The more we try to be happy ourselves, the farther we move from the spirit of happiness. But if we make others happy, a part of that happiness comes to us.'

'Sadhu Vaswani had said that one should avoid overwork on the path of spirituality. What does that mean?'

'Because work is not an end, work is only a means. Work is the means to the end. Work purifies and the very first step on the path is the step of purification. We need to purify our inner instrument, what is called the antahkarna in Sanskrit. It is only when the antahkarna becomes clean and pure that the Lord himself comes and stays there.

Where the Lord resides, there is divine happiness. So work is only a means. Most of us take work to be the end. This is our mistake. Therefore we keep on working, working and working all the time with the result that we have no time to sit in silence and try to enter within ourselves.'

'How does one purify oneself? How does the whole process of purification start?'

'It starts through experience. Let us suppose we are working together and I do something which irritates you. You get irritated again and again until a stage comes when you say to yourself, "This irritation has not helped me at all. Why be irritated at all? I must rise above this irritation." You have conquered irritation, you have become purer. Work purifies; it is only a method of purifying our inner instrument. I may work for the Lord but work does not appeal to the Lord. It is said that work will take you to the gates of the mansion where the Lord dwells, but it cannot take you inside to the bedroom of the Lord.'

'But what about the belief that work is worship?'

'Yes, but work becomes worship when we work on ourselves. Then we automatically stop seeing flaws in others as we get to see our own flaws. There were occasions when people came and offered their services to Sadhu Vaswani telling Him that they wanted to dedicate their entire life to His service. But He said, "You are not yet ready, you must go through the cycle of work." He had His own way of training us. I think I told you on an earlier occasion that once I spoke roughly to a fruit seller and on that day, He would not eat anything. He starved just to teach me a lesson that the Lord resides as much in the fruit seller as it resides within Him. And it is a lesson I remember even today. If He had not done what He did on that day I would not have learnt that lesson.'

'He has also spoken of repentance. But he says that there is a higher meaning of repentance. That there are two kinds of repentance . . . one is the normal kind that we know of and then there is a higher meaning, a higher form of repentance. What is that?'

'The higher type of repentance is when you will not repeat the same mistake again. We say we are sorry, but we do the same thing again. When you truly stop doing something for which you have repented, it becomes a very high kind of repentance.'

'Is there a difference between remorse and repentance?'

'If there is a difference, it is only a difference of degree. Otherwise, there is no difference. With repentance comes the resolution not to repeat the same thing again. It's only a question of degree. Remorse is a slightly lighter emotion than repentance.'

'For You, what does renunciation mean?'

'Renunciation means treating nothing as your own, that is all. Nothing belongs to you— it's that simple. When I say, "He is my friend", it is not renunciation as nothing is mine. We are like logs of wood. I am told that near Kashmir, they have a river where they just throw logs of wood and the logs go and reach the destination. Perhaps they write the names of people to whom they are sending those logs. I don't know the details but this works. It is so natural for a family man to regard his children as his own. It is here that we need to correct our entire attitude. No one is mine, nothing is mine. This body itself is not mine. This is the first line of the *Isho Upanishad.* It is a small Upanishad and the entire Upanishad can be written on one page. And the very first sloka is, "*Ishyavasyam idam sarvam, tena tyaktena bhungita magridha!*" (All are vestures of the Lord. Be not greedy, renounce, renounce, if you want to get the true joy of life.)

'I was a boy scout and we had gone for an outing to Quetta once. Our scout master was asked to arrange for our stay. So we were supposed to be guests, but when we reached there, we found that his wife was not in Quetta as she had gone to her parents' house. So the man in charge arranged to get our meals from a hotel. I was the only vegetarian in the group. All the others ate non-vegetarian food to their hearts content. They ordered the most expensive and fancy food. They kept on eating as they said it was free. We were there for about eight days. On the eighth day, when we were just entering the train as we were going to leave, the police came and stopped us. "We will not allow you to go; you must first pay the bill to the hotel." I was the only one who had taken simple vegetarian fare and so my bill was very reasonable. The others had to pay through their noses. And I could see the difference in attitude between me and them. So in renunciation, one abstains from greed and thus in renunciation there is joy.'

'Dada, You have time and again said that it is only with His grace that everything takes place. Thus, with that surmise, is it only with His grace that even qualities of renunciation, surrender and silence can come about?'

'I should think so.'

'But then there is the law of karma which says that if you have worked in your past lifetime towards this state of renunciation, you will get it in some lifetime. There is a huge difference between grace and working towards something . . . on the one hand, it is the grace of God and on the other hand, it is the sheer hard work of individuals through several lifetimes. The use of free will, I would assume.'

'It is like this: A wealthy man distributes money. There is one amongst the receivers who is in great need. He virtually pleads and gets down on his knees to be given just a little more money as he is in urgent need of money. The rich man takes compassion and gives him that extra money. The other beggars too clamour for that extra money but the rich man refuses the others, as he has seen the true need of the first one. Thus, the heart of the wealthy man has been touched by the first one and so he gave him more than what he would have given him otherwise. It is something like that. We cry out to God because we know it is only His grace that will give us what we want. Now this cry is a cry for grace. We will all get a mandatory amount, whether we plead or not. But the extra benefit or extra amount will come only through grace.

'I think it was Jesus who gave this parable to His devotees: He told them that there were masons who were given an amount for the work they did during the day. But there was one who came virtually at the end of the day and worked for just an hour. But all the workers were given the same stipulated amount. The other labourers objected to it and said, "Why is this so? He worked for only an hour. Yet, you have given him the same amount that you have given us." The employer replied, "But you all got what you were promised and what you deserved. What I give this man is none of your concern." Grace, in a very crude way, works like this.'

I thought it was a rather partial and unfair way of functioning. It went against the reap-as-you-sow logic and the laws of cause and effect.

'For a normal person, how does one get such kind of grace?'

'We put this question to Sadhu Vaswani, "What is the best way of getting grace?" He said, "The way is to do good for evil—somebody does evil to you and you return it by doing good." He said, "This draws the attention of the Lord and he pours His grace." That was his answer.

'We are given the story of Shri Krishna taking Arjuna for a walk. As they walked on, they came to the house of a rich man whose house had a big, beautiful garden. They knocked on the door and the wealthy man opened the door. They said to him, "We are pilgrims. We have travelled a long way and we are tired. Will you let us spend the night in your mansion? We will go away the next morning and you will not even know that we spent the night here." The rich man fired them, "What do you think this is? A *dharmashala*? Get out from here. If you speak more, my dog will come and bite you."'

Dada and I began to chuckle.

'And Sri Krishna blessed the man, He said, "You are rich, you are wealthy, may you grow more and more in wealth and in riches."

'Then they came to a hut, a cottage of a poor man, who was a devotee of the Lord. He didn't know that it was Shri Krishna who had come. "Will you take us in for the night?" The poor man said, "O I will be so happy. I am all alone as all my relatives have died. I have only one cow and this hut; that is all that I possess. I shall do my best to keep you comfortable and happy." And he served them so much that he helped them to sleep by pressing their legs. In the morning as Shri Krishna took leave of the bhakta, He said to him, "May your hut be burnt and may your cow die a natural death."

'When Arjuna heard this, he became very agitated. He was not happy because Shri Krishna had blessed a man who had been so rude to Him and virtually cursed this poor man who had served them with all his love and selflessness. So he said to Shri Krishna, "Krishna, what has happened to you? You blessed that man who treated us so rudely and cursed this noble soul who served us." Shri Krishna said,

"I did it for the good of both. I wanted the rich man to grow more and more rich in order to come to a peak of wealth because it is only when he comes to the climax—the peak from where he cannot go up any more—that he will start moving down and by moving down, he might realize his faults and then hopefully change for the better. And this man is already living a life of detachment. His relatives have passed away and only two things stand in the way of his complete detachment . . . the cow and the hut . . . once these attachments that cling to him are taken away, he will then be truly free. Thus I blessed him to be free of both of them." So that is the way of the Holy Ones.'

Dada, though he looked tired, still remembered that I was given a box of prasad for Meher. He looked at me and said, 'My dear Ruzbeh, you have no idea of the happiness you have brought to me through these talks. Thank you for all the joy you have brought me.'

I could only look at Him and kiss His hand.

11

After bowing down to Sadhu Vaswani and Sister Shanti, I went to the Kutiya with my friend Samir. It was a Sunday. November felt as pleasant as the month of May. As pleasant as watching the proceedings of our ministers disagreeing in Parliament. Global warming is last week's news. The poor globe has been cooked properly. It's now global meltdown.

For a week or more, Dada was not in Pune. Dada had gone to Goa to take rest as the next few weeks were going to be truly hectic for Him. Preparations for Sadhu Vaswani's birthday on 25 November were on. Every year, in connection with Sadhu Vaswani's birthday, a *rath yatra* is organized in Pune. Dada would be seated by Sadhu Vaswani's statue in a chariot and he would travel through the streets of Pune blessing one and all.

Sadhu Vaswani's birthday is celebrated the world over as International Meatless Day. I still think the day should be called The Day of Compassion. Millions of people pledge to abstain from the food of violence and resolve to go meatless on that day. There are even some who turn complete vegetarians on that occasion.

Then He had to go to Mumbai and record His lectures which would be telecast on television. He would record as many as possible in the ten days. He was ninety-seven years old, with a body thrashed by illness and age and He just kept at it with a smile.

Dada entered and after bowing down to Sadhu Vaswani and after Piya had settled Dada with the mike, I knelt at His feet holding His hands. We both expressed our feelings of having missed each other. I really did and the way Dada expressed Himself, I knew the feeling was mutual. He looked fresh, like a baby just out of a bath and powdered—all the sweet stuff that one associates babies with. I looked like an eye sore. In short, we both looked our part.

The set was ready. Piya wanted to hear if the sound was okay. She looked at Dada. Dada turned towards me. I smiled.

'Dada, today I would like to speak to You about Your educational and medical institutions and inherent tendencies.'

Dada nodded.

'According to the teaching of the Master and according to the teaching of Sri Krishna, we must attend to our duties honestly, faithfully and sincerely. But we must not forget that our work doesn't stop there. We have to go a step further, do our duty, do our work and a little more. This little more the Gita calls *lok sangrah.* Lok is people and sangrah is welfare; we have to do something for the welfare of the people. We have to make the earth a better place when we leave it than when we entered it. Each one of us is required to do as much good as we can, to as many as we can, in as many ways as we can, on as many occasions as we can and as long as we can! People feel that they have come to this earth to be happy. No, we have not come here to be happy but we have come here to make others happy. The emphasis should be on making others happy. The happiness that we give to others will in due course return to us, but we should never think of that while we are trying to make others happy. That person is truly happy who regards making others happy his very religion. They asked an ancient rishi, "Where is your home and what is your religion?" He said, "The whole earth is my home and to do good is my religion." This should be the ideal before every one of us.

'I am reminded of an incident, a very touching incident, in the life of that great German philanthropist Oberlin. Oberlin believed in sharing everything that he felt God provided him with. He went on giving and giving and giving, without in the least feeling that he was the one who was giving. One day he was caught in a fierce snow storm. He cried for help, but his voice could not be heard by anyone. Until finally exhausted, he fell down on the snow. A little while thereafter, a peasant happened to pass by and finding a fellow human being on the snow, he carried him to the warmth of his hut. There Oberlin revived and looking into the eyes of his saviour, said to him, "You have saved my life, I shall give you a big reward." And this simple poor peasant said to him, "Reward for what? I have done nothing great. I saw a fellow human being on the snow. I just brought him to my hut. How can I accept a reward for doing what everybody would have done?" Then said Oberlin to him, "At least tell me what your name is." And the peasant said to him, "Has the name of the Good Samaritan been mentioned anywhere in the Bible?" "No," said Oberlin, "his name has not been mentioned . . . there is only the mention of a Good Samaritan." "Then?" said the peasant, "let me withhold my name." Here was a true disciple of Gita though he did not know the teachings of Gita. He was not even aware that there was a book, a scripture like the Gita. But he bore witness to the teachings of the Gita. Devotion to duty is very necessary, but we must go a step further and do lok sangrah.'

Dada finished and then turned towards me. He was a sage seconds before. Now He looked at me as though a child was inquiring if all was well.

'Beautiful Dada, now please tell me how did the educational institutions and hospitals come about?'

'All this work is dedicated to Him and He is doing it. Things are happening on their own. We don't think of doing anything in particular, but then some donor comes along and says, "Why don't you start this project? I can keep aside so much money for it." For me, that money is a signal from my Master and God that we should try and serve people through the means of healthcare too. Thus came about the heart hospital. Then someone came and said to us that we should do something for the sight of the sightless, and that is how the eye hospital was started. So it keeps on growing. If there was one institution which Sadhu Vaswani Himself wanted to start on His own, then that was the St Mira's College for Girls. He said girls should have their own atmosphere. People here advised Him against it; they told Him, "Please don't start any college for girls as three years ago we had started a college for girls and the college had to be shut down because the girls would not come." But Sadhu Vaswani didn't listen to them. We started with seventy-two girls and now I think there are around three thousand students.'

'Why was the name Mira chosen?'

'Because He believed that the coming civilization will be built by women and He wanted women to have a role model. And in Mira, he saw devotion to the Lord and love for the poor. He admired this combination the most and so he got the college named after Mira.'

'Dada, You have mentioned the Zen Masters who advised that "the true wisdom of life consists in the elimination of non-essentials". But for such a philosophy to come about for children, even before the educational system, the environment at home should be fertile enough for it to take root. So before the educational system comes the foundations laid at home?'

'I could not agree more, Ruzbeh. Once, Sadhu Vaswani was addressing a meeting of wealthy bankers. Many of them, of course, were millionaires of those days. The Master had the courage and the moral force to tell them frankly: "You are busy gathering silver and gold; but you must not neglect your richest treasure—your children! Let us give time and attention to our children! Let us be careful to see that they receive the right type of training and atmosphere at home, and the right type of education in school and college. Let us make sure we make the right choices for our children!" And over here, the mother plays the most important role. While taking care of the home, the priority has to be the well-being of children.

'Emperor Napoleon was once discussing the future of France with his trusted advisers and friends. "What is it that we need to do to ensure a bright future for our youth?" he asked them. Pat came the reply: "Good mothers!"'

'The Emperor was so struck by this that he remarked, "Here is a whole system in a single word, a single human being!" In the days gone by, our mothers played a major role in shaping our lives and influencing our minds and hearts. They told us wonderful stories from the ancient scriptures. They taught us prayers which are enshrined in our hearts. They inculcated faith in our lives. They took every care to point us in the right direction, to indicate how life must be lived in the right way. That is true education. The foundation is laid there.

'It is only the mother who can blend discipline with love so that the child has the assurance that he is not alone—that there is someone that he can turn to, anytime of the day or night, all through his life!

'Let me repeat that what our children need most from their parents are not lavish gifts, toys, gadgets and money. What they need above all else is time, attention and love. Without love and care, no child can grow up in the right way and realize his true potential.

'Today I find that parents are doing many things, but they have neglected the one needful thing: setting right examples and being good role models for their children. May I offer a few practical suggestions in this connection?

'Always find time for your children. Do not allot specific time for them—be there for them when they need you. If a child needs to talk to you, if he wants an answer to a question, a solution to a personal problem, don't put him off. Do not say to him, "I shall attend to you later", "I will answer that question tomorrow," or "I will talk to you when I am free". Children live in the now. Don't give them anxieties about the past or fear of the future.

'Every child is a human being with a heart and a soul. We must not treat our children like clones, a pet or a personal possession! We must not forget that every child is an individual, with his own personality, innate talents and his own life to lead. Let us make an attempt to understand our children and encourage their creativity and originality. We must not seek to impose our ambitions and goals upon them: let them flower and bloom in their own way. If you are a doctor, your son does not have to be a doctor. If you are a businessman, your daughter can choose to become a singer or a writer. Do not enforce your mould upon them.

'Let your children learn to respect the value of work and the dignity of labour. Therefore, allow them to participate in household chores. Encourage schoolgoing children to polish their own shoes, pack their lunches, and tidy their work and play areas. Let them cultivate reverence for all forms of manual works. If you employ servants in your household, treat them well—be courteous to them and do not take them for granted, for you are setting live examples which your children will emulate. Pull up your child when he speaks sharply or rudely to a servant.

'We must not indulge in idle gossip and slander before our children, lest they should pick up these negative tendencies from us.

'Teach the children to respect the value of money. Do not let them indulge their every whim and fancy, just because you can afford it! Money is no substitute for love and the child must be taught that the best things in life cannot be bought with money!

'Do not treat the TV and electronic gadgets as the governess, companion and baby minder—all rolled into one! Today, many parents have 'handed over' their children to the care of TVs, computers and phones so that they may be free to pursue their own personal interests.

'The fathers also have a vital role to play in good parenting. They cannot neglect their responsibilities or relegate them to the mothers. Business cares and work responsibilities are no excuses to neglect the children.

'Parents must get into the regular habit of praying together with their children. As we have all heard, "The family that prays together stays together".

'Children are the builders of the future! They are the greatest blessings conferred upon us by God. They give meaning to our life, so we must take good care of them. Let us teach them the virtues of compassion and understanding, caring and sharing. Let us give them a healthy, happy and harmonious atmosphere at home so that they grow up to be good children, good citizens of the world, and, above all, good human beings!'

'The very fabric of the home lies in shambles. Could it be the reason that our children have no real role model to look up to?'

'Our difficulty is we have thrown God, both out of our homes and out of the educational institutions. I remember when I was a child, we lived in the love and fear of God. We felt that even when we were alone, we were being watched. We were afraid of doing something which would offend the Creator, whom for want of a better word, we called God. Today, they don't believe in God. The fear is gone and they think they can commit the most heinous crimes without compunction. We need a new type of education.'

'What is the need of the hour as far as education is concerned? It is obviously going wrong somewhere.'

'I think there are two things that are very necessary for education. The first is the root of education. The root is reverence. "Let knowledge grow from more to more, but more of reverence in us dwell." But there is no reverence—no reverence for elders and no reverence for teachers. I read of a student telling a teacher, threatening him, "Come outside and I will show you." Sadhu Vaswani said to us, "The root of education is reverence, the fruit is service." Today both are missing.'

'What are the simple ways in which every educational institute can start helping the children focus on the "root" and the "fruit"?'

'By having the right type of teachers. But that again is a difficulty. Teachers are teachers just because of their salaries. The teachers of old were *acharyas*. An acharya is one who lives the life that must be emulated; a true role model. It is easy to start anew but more difficult to replace one system by another. Now we have to follow the second one as we already have a system. That system should be stopped and a new system should come over. It is a difficult process. Experiments are being performed in different places by different organizations. The great Thomas Carlyle received a letter from a young man who wrote, "Mr Carlyle, I wish to be a teacher. Will you tell me the secret of successful teaching?" Carlyle wrote to him, "Be what you would want your pupils to be! All other teaching is unblessed mockery."'

'But can we create such an environment at home and in our educational institutions? It seems insurmountable.'

'Yes, we can. The time spirit is very strong. Twenty five years ago, if you uttered the word "vegetarian", they used to laugh and scoff at you. There was a joke around that time about a man who goes to a doctor and says, "I cannot sleep, what shall I do?" "Then count sheep." "But I am a vegetarian. How can I count sheep?" "Then count carrots." But today, vegetarianism is a force to reckon with, a powerful worldwide trend. So until the time spirit takes it up, we have to keep our little candles aglow.'

'What do you think should be made mandatory in schools?'

'The first lesson that should be taught is that God is watching you. The second lesson that needs to be taught is that you must always speak the truth because you are being watched. If you have taught these two lessons to the student, he will grow in the right way. Also it is very important that they learn how to control their anger.'

'What if an individual wants to better himself or herself as far as anger is concerned? There must be something he or she can follow.'

'Prayer. There are certain things which I cannot do on my own; I need the help of a superpower. I can ask for it, and asking is prayer. Our children have lost faith in prayer. There is no faith. Norman Vincent Peale has in his books given us such stirring proofs of the power of prayers. It was the great scientist and statistician, Babson, who said, "The greatest and the most unused power in the world is the power of prayer."'

'But eventually it is not just about prayers. It is also trusting one's Creator that s/he knows best which prayer should be answered for the larger good of the child.

'I think it was Dean Inge who said, "I have lived long enough to be able to thank God for not having answered many of my prayers." I like Plato's prayer. Plato was Socrates's disciple. He used to pray, "God, grant me the good, even though I do not ask for it and refuse to give me the evil, even though I ask for it."'

'You have also mentioned that a little time be kept aside for silence in schools?'

'Yes, otherwise we will not be able to think of God. If you are busy with other things, you have no time for God at all. That is the condition today; they have no time for God. God gives us 1440 minutes in a day-and-night cycle every day. With folded hands I tell people to give just one minute, out of those 1440 minutes, just one minute, and thank God for the greatest gift that He has given you—namely the gift of the human birth. Everything will then fall into place automatically. Once you thank God for having been born as a human being, the next question arises, "What is the purpose of this human birth? Why have I been born as a human being? What are the duties of a human being?" The way is simple but we keep on postponing it. I told you the other day that in our schools, for two minutes every hour, everybody, including the principal, teachers and children, have to maintain two minutes of silence. It is mandatory.

'The great Emerson learnt about Carlyle. Both of them were contemporaries. Carlyle was in England and Emerson in America. And Emerson felt a pull towards Carlyle. He said he would love to meet Carlyle and so he came all the way from America to England. It is said that both of them were together for three hours, but not one spoke a word. And when they took leave of each other, someone asked Emerson, "You met him but you did not speak to him?" He said, "We have spoken volumes." A similar thing is told concerning one of the disciples of St Francis of Assisi. He and the Emperor were classmates. One of them became an Emperor and the other a *fakir* who joined St Francis Order. One day, the Emperor came and called upon the fakir. They were together for quite some time but not one of them spoke a single word. "But we two are talking."

'When we went to meet Sadhu Vaswani, we came with questions in our heart. Sadhu Vaswani was seated on His bed and we used to come and sit on the floor. And without putting forth the questions we got the answers. Though He spoke not a word, the questioner spoke not a word, he got an answer. I remember there was a man . . . I don't recollect his name . . . who came to meet Sadhu Vaswani. He came and just sat at His feet for a few minutes. I went to see him off and as he was taking leave, he told me, "I am thirty-five years of age and married. But the love that I have received from Sadhu Vaswani in these three or four minutes is unique. Nobody has given me so much love." So in silence, one can communicate many things.'

'But how do we instil this in our children as most often we are consumed by noise within our own selves?'

'It is the atmosphere that we create. The child is not influenced by the words that we utter. The child has an indirect influence, as it were, of the environment. The emphasis in everything today is on words. It means nothing. Words are not remembered, words are forgotten. True silence remains, nurtures and heals.

'The ancient texts say that the highest type of *daan* or charity is that of *vidya* daan or imparting education. And now the most profitable business has also become the business of imparting vidya.'

'Yes, now the government is controlling everything . . . the control of the government has taken the spirit out of education.'

'The issue of loneliness and depression has become a major force amongst children?'

'Loneliness is a great psychological disease. People are lonely because they build walls instead of bridges. In our days we were taught that we are not alone and so we never felt alone. Gandhi as a child used to fear the dark. He was eight or nine years old then. When his maid servant, who was in charge, told him, "Why are you afraid? There is Rama with you. Repeat His name and go in the dark and He will accompany you. You will not be alone." Gandhi said that just that one line "made me what I am". People used to point pistols at him. He was unafraid. He said, "If it be God's Will, the pistol will work. Otherwise, you may fire a hundred pistols at me and not one of them will show any result."'

Dada kept silent. There was eventually one bullet with the Mahatma's name on it. I sighed.

'Did you meet him?'

'I was not fortunate enough to meet Gandhi but I have an impression that I saw him from a distance. The Congress had a session at Karachi and I was one of the volunteers. In those days, they used to have what was called lathi charge. Freedom fighters were beaten with sticks. As volunteers, we used to carry the injured to hospitals for treatment.

'As I have told you, Gandhi and Sadhu Vaswani were friends. Most of His early books carry tributes to Mahatma Gandhi.'

'Do You believe that the right kind of education, from home and school, could change the very fabric of our life and society?'

'Oh yes! My Master believed that if the world is to change, it is through education. It is the child of today who is the builder of tomorrow, provided he is given the right type of environment and the right type of education at home and at school. Therefore the very first thing that Sadhu Vaswani did when He started His work was to start a satsang and a school where that type of education is given to one and all—children and elders. Then soon, He started the schools. Remember, He was the principal of a well-known college when He renounced His career for the path of being a seeker and for doing seva. Thus, when He began His education institutions, in addition to academic subjects, he concentrated on character building and bearing witness to ideals which give a meaning and significance to life. Now we have the St Mira's College for Girls, Sadhu Vaswani Institute of Management Studies and Sadhu Vaswani College of Nursing. The third thing that He did after starting the school was to open a charitable dispensary. These three things were dear to him. The dispensary has grown into a hospital. And the satsang, of course, goes on.'

'Dada, you met Mother Teresa. What were your feelings when you met Her?'

'If I were asked to sum up that experience in one word, that word would be "love". She gave love to all and most of all She loved Jesus. But she did not get the response that she expected.'

'Response from whom?'

'Jesus.'

'You mean she didn't get Jesus.'

'Her conscious effort was to see Jesus in everyone whom she served. But she did not get the assurance that Jesus has accepted her service.'

'Why?'

'There are cases in which Jesus or Krishna or Rama, whoever you believe in, gives you Their glimpse at the last moment when your body is being separated from the spirit. At that moment you can't talk or speak of your experience. But They come and receive you. I believe that was the case with Mother Teresa. Jesus could not have abandoned Her though She wrote in some of Her letters to Her confessors that she feels abandoned. But I believe He must have come at the last moment to Her. For the love of Jesus, She renounced everything. He had to come to receive Her.'

'She inaugurated the hospital, right?'

'The Inlaks and Budhrani Hospital, yes.'

There was silence once again. All those who I have looked up to have left the body. I looked at Dada. He was ninety-seven. It would be a matter of time before He too would leave His body. The giants had all but gone and soon the maggots would inherit the earth.

'I think the greatest reality of Kali Yuga is that as time passes by, one's role models become fewer and fewer.'

'Yes. The true role model is one who is happy in all conditions and circumstances of life. He is a man of *ananda*, divine joy. You may be blessed by Brahma, Vishnu and Mahesh and yet not get ananda. It is only when you are free from the clutches of the ego that you get ananda. Because Mahatmas have no ego, they have no pain. Pain is in proportion to the ego. It is the ego that creates all the trouble. Just to take an example, if your spouse yells at you, and if you are egoistic, you will retaliate and you will create more karmas. But if there is no ego you will smile and handle the situation. The problem is not that there are no true role models. The issue is that the real role models have hid themselves from us.'

'But why consciously do they hide themselves from us?'

'Why, because the master of Kali Yuga is the ego. And They do not want to fall into the trap of the ego. So many of the so-called religious leaders are slaves to the ego. They don't know it, but they have been inflamed by the ego. There are those who don't want money, who don't want pleasure—theirs is a life of utter simplicity but they want numbers. They call it *panth* or their following, They say in my panth, I want so many followers and this is sheer ego talking.'

'I think the panth or the path of spirituality is filled with landmines.'

'Yes. But these landmines will not kill you but will kill your spirituality.'

'Yes, that is the worst kind of death. Death that cripples the soul.'

'Yes, the worst kind of death.'

We again sat in silence for a long time. Then Dada looked at me.

'Dada, we were talking about Mother Teresa who inaugurated the Inlaks and Budhrani Hospital. What was the seed that germinated into the well-known hospital it now is?

'The seeds took root in Bombay. I was in Bombay and was due to return to Poona when on the last day I passed through a street and found a man lying in the centre of the road. They told me that he had been lying there for three days. Cars were rushing to and fro; men were walking by, but nobody paid any attention to him. For three days, he lay there almost in a comatose condition. He had not eaten anything, he had not even had a drop of water. So I took him to the nearest hospital. The hospital would not admit him. They said they want his address. I did not even know his name. I then moved from hospital to hospital until a friend of mine, who was with me, said, "You must leave for Poona. I will attend to this." He sent me a word two days later that no hospital was prepared to admit him because he did not have an address. Probably he had come from the south in search of a job or was a vagrant. This made me sad and I said to myself that if ever I get a chance, I will take it up on a firm footing. Coincidentally a friend passed away and his wife brought a crore of rupees. In those days it was quite a lot of money. She said, "This is for the hospital." I said "Which hospital?" She said, "The hospital which the Mission is running." I said, "We are not running a hospital as of today, but we want to. So if you will permit, we will start the hospital." So that is how the idea of the hospital came about. In my simplicity I had assumed a crore rupees was sufficient to start a hospital. I was hugely mistaken. I was in Kenwood Park in London when Mrs Budhrani came and said to me that they were going to give a crore of rupees, provided the hospital bears their name jointly. The first donor was Inlaks Foundation and the second was the Budhrani family. I said I would have no objection but that she will have to talk to the first donor. And the first donor said they too had no objection. That is why the hospital came to be called Inlaks and Budhrani Hospital. And it has done a lot of work, a lot of good work. Then came the Morbai Nariandas Cancer Institute, K.K. Eye Institute and finally the Fabiani and Budhrani Heart Institute. We also have a diagnostic centre at Khandala which caters to many villages.

'The K.K. Eye Institute has done wonderful work. It has really touched my heart. There are people living in the villages who lose their sight due to simple cataract formation. The loss of vision makes people feel that they have become useless and unproductive; and nobody pays them any attention. In the family, they sit in a corner; sometimes they get food to eat and sometimes they don't. Our K.K.

Eye Institute runs this service programme through which poor people from remote tribal areas and villages are brought here to Poona by bus. They are given free travel, accommodation and food during the course of their treatment. Their eyes are tested beforehand and then they undergo cataract surgery. They stay overnight after the surgery and are sent home with glasses the next day.

'So you see, giving sight to the sightless is, I think, one of the noblest things that a man can do. And this hospital has crossed over a hundred and twenty thousand free operations. That was two years ago; I think the figures must now reach over a lakh and thirty thousand operations. Then we started the Fabiani and Budhrani Heart Institute. I think we have four hospitals—the fourth is the cancer institute.'

'What made you start the cancer institute?'

'Chandru Budhrani donated towards it and wanted it to be named after his mother; it is called the Morbai Naraindas Cancer Hospital. The cost of treatment is exorbitant and when cancer is the illness, the cost could cripple a family. Similarly, for every heart patient, it costs us over eighty thousand rupees to carry out a simple cardiac procedure. The same operation in another hospital would be over a lakh and a half. But from where are the poor people going to bring that amount of money? Now this month, that is November, when we celebrate Gurudev Sadhu Vaswani's birthday, anybody, whether rich or poor, can get free treatment at the hospital. There is a friend who is donating the expenditure in memory of his father who passed away two years ago. He passed away in the month of November and so he said he is going to take up this seva.'

'But it must be a huge expense to run four hospitals?'

'Oh yes!' He exclaimed like a child seeing the ocean for the first time, awed and mystified. 'The expenses are astronomical. Just one instrument, the linear accelerator, costs over eighty million rupees. But the Lord inspires generous hearted people to donate the money which is needed. Sadhu Vaswani used to say, "The Lord provides where He guides."'

'So far we have not taken even one rupee by way of a loan. A new building for an educational complex is being built. So far it has cost us a hundred crore. The entire project may cost another fifty crore. The Lord gives us inspiration and then He gives us the means to make inspirations a reality. It is all up to Him. The Lord taketh and the Lord giveth. One needs to follow and obey with complete love, faith and humility.'

'Unfortunately, the profession of doctors has become more like a business now.'

'Yes, that is what we find in all hospitals today. There are consultants who lure the patients to their own private clinics. We had experienced this in our hospitals too. We thought that was just going against our very principles. We want to provide the best possible medical service at the lowest cost, if not free. Therefore, we now have paid professionals. They are there for eight working hours and they have no private practice of their own and we pay them the good remuneration.'

'You feel giving them the current industry rates makes them more settled and dedicated?'

'Yes. The salaries are huge but at least the mind is at rest. The *bhav* of seva can flourish only when the heart and mind are at peace.'

'What is your opinion on organ donation?'

'I think it is a very good thing provided it is not misused. In a number of cases, it is misused.'

'But if it is not misused?'

'Oh it is wonderful. The Bodhisattva says, "I will feel happy if after my death my skin is used by someone." It's a wonderful thing. But several associations that exist today working in this field of organ donation . . . they are not honest.'

'Does it matter spiritually how the body is taken care of when an individual dies?'

'No, it does not matter spiritually. There was somebody who came and asked me that he had a desire to donate his eyes after death. And he said that his friends told him that if he donates his eyes in this birth, he will be born blind in his next birth. I said that nothing of that sort will happen, rather his third eye too may open.'

For a long time we had a hearty laugh. Dada laughs so beautifully that one can't help joining in. And for some reason, we laughed at the silliest of things.

'But Dada, it is a fact that this fear of organ donation has got its seeds through the wrong spiritual guidance given by those in the scheme of things. This is a very genuine fear amongst people where organ donation is concerned.'

'The greatest good one can do where the body is concerned is organ donation. Imagine if through your eyes a blind person can see. Imagine. Families are saved through organ donations. What a beautiful seva we all can do. It is really something wonderful.'

'Dada, unfortunately, the most noble professions, be it the medical, educational or legal professions, have got caught in the money and power trap.'

'Yes, because money is the God that is worshipped in this age. In this age, the three Gods that are worshipped are . . . money, pleasure, power.'

'How does one come out of this situation? How does one make oneself or one's children get out of this sickness because it is deep-rooted now? Do you think we can get out of it?'

'The more I think of it, the more I believe that what we need is a new type of education. But then again the difficulty arises; you must have the right type of teachers. You can't get those type of teachers today. The teachers we had in the olden days were men and women of sterling character.'

'When the child is in the mother's womb, what can the mother do for the child's spiritual well-being?'

'It is believed that love and care for the child begins even when it is in the mother's womb. The mother's state of mind, her living environment and her spiritual attitude during her pregnancy will influence the child in the womb. It is said that when bhakta Prahlada's mother was carrying him, she had been left in the care of Maharishi Narada. His constant chanting of the Name Divine, "Narayana, Narayana, Narayana," so influenced the unborn child that Prahlada was born a Vishnu bhakta, despite being the son of the Vishnu-hating asura, Hiranyakashipu. We also know that

Swami Vivekananda's mother was a great devotee of Lord Shiva, and earnestly prayed to Him to bless her with a divine child and thus was born the great soul, Vivekananda.

'We believe that the mother-to-be must be surrounded by peace, calm, serenity and beauty; that she must hear and speak good, holy words and prayers; that she must think thoughts that are pure and noble so that she may bring forth a child with these pure and noble qualities.

'The very first thing a mother should do is to ensure that there are no negative thoughts or feelings in her mind, because negativity works faster and sooner than positivity. So she has to be very careful. No thought of hatred, no thought of jealousy and no thought of envy.

'In short, all these dos and don'ts are meant only to ensure that her yet-to-be born child receives the best influences and the best vibrations even while in the womb. The young mother is constantly enjoined to remember that the little baby that she is moulding within her is also an immortal soul and her every word, thought and action will affect the child.'

'You mean, despite the child's destiny and inherent nature, what the child in the womb experiences can shape the child's temperament and his/her process of going through life and how s/he reacts to situations?'

'To an extent. If a child has the destiny to be a saint, the child will become one. But the influence the child has had while in the womb will decide the journey. The journey could be calmer or more aggressive depending upon what the child has experienced while in the womb. You are right, it will not change the destiny or the inherent nature of the child. May be the reactionary process might differ. Because now the life to be born is part of the mother; once the child comes out, it gets its independence. So she has to be very careful.'

'Which means a mother has the power to enhance the child's spirituality when the child is in the womb?'

'Yes, the mother has that power. Not the father.'

'Not the father? Only the mother?'

'We read of queen Madalasa in the Markandeya Purana. She started speaking to her children even while they were in her womb, telling them, "Don't forget that the world in which you are coming is a transitory world and a world of temptations. You have to have self-control." One after another, the children who were born to the mother became sanyasis or yogis. Remember, they were children from a royal family—sons of a king—and in the normal course of things, they would have inherited the kingdom. Her first three sons were ascetics. When the fourth child was in her womb, the husband told her that we must have someone to take charge of the kingdom when we are gone; otherwise the kingdom would suffer. She agreed. She blessed the fourth child in her womb and tells him, "You are blessed my son because you will rule the earth without obstacles. Now cultivate in your heart the desire to do well to others. Never cast your eyes on women other than your wife. Always contemplate on Sri Krishna to destroy the evil thoughts in your heart.' And she gave birth to a prince who would uphold dharma and rule his kingdom wisely.

'Now the question to ask is this: Was it the karmic pattern of the first three sons to take up sanyas or was it their mother's influence on them?

'Apparently, it was the mother's influence. The reason why they came to that mother may be karmic, but apparently it was the mother's influence which dominated.'

I humbly do not agree with this. Most mothers pray that their children, when born, turn out to be noble, upright, happy, healthy and successful human beings. Good human beings. I have seen the worst of the scum born to noble parents. I would rather go with, 'If there is a God, then the laws of karma rule.'

'Dada, what about the inherent nature of each one of us? What according to you is inherent nature? Where does that come from? There are certain people who are angry by nature. Some people are greedy, some are lazy. What is inherent nature and where does this come from?'

'In the beginning, we are all pure. But the choices we make eventually make us a part of that choice. We choose to be angry or greedy and eventually get controlled by anger and greed.'

'So inherent nature is the ramification of our free will. How does one go beyond one's inherent nature?'

'Surrender. The only way out is through surrender.'

'Surrender will take us beyond the beyond?'

'Yes. Surrender means that for whatever I do, my Guru or as you say, God or Goddess, is responsible for that. Therefore, on the one hand, I have to be very careful about what I do and on the other, a ray of the Guru's strength and power goes through me and makes me a different man from what I was before I surrendered. Therefore, there are men who are born that way and some have to work towards it.'

'But Dada, even surrender has to be part of one's inherent nature. If it isn't, I doubt it will come about on its own?'

'Yes, but let us say one has surrender as part of one's inherent nature. Even then, one has to accept it, bow down to it and say, "I am ready to surrender." There was a man . . . I have forgotten his name now . . . who told me, "I am very obedient to the Guru." When the Guru tells me to do ten things, I can at least do eight of those ten things exactly according to what He says. Then I told him, "This shows that you are obedient to yourself and not to the Guru because you choose those eight things—eight things which you like to do. It is those two things that will prove whether you are obedient or not." Milarepa is regarded as the ideal disciple. He was the son of a rich man. But he was just two or three years old when his father passed away handing over his charge to his brother. The brother and the uncle cheated them and ate up all the money, and the widow and the children could not even get food to eat. Ordered by his mother, Milarepa went and learnt black magic. And with that black magic, he completely destroyed his uncle's family. Then repentance awoke in his heart, "What have I done, after all, what have I got!" Then he goes to Marpa and becomes his disciple. Marpa shows him the way, but, in the process, tells him to build speaking podiums or platforms. He tells him, "I want platforms from which I can speak to all the people who come to listen to me." Platform after platform is made and rejected for no fault of Milarepa. Marpa either wanted the karma of Milarepa to end or to do something. I don't remember the exact number, but about twenty-seven platforms were made by

Milarepa by carrying bricks on his shoulders, moving from one place to another, until he got tired. He then told his Guru that he was tired. The Guru, though spiritually very evolved, is a harsh man and very difficult to please. Then the Guru's wife tells Milarepa, "Don't leave, your Guru knows everything and you are just on the point of being accepted." Still he runs away, but comes back and begins to make the platform which, eventually, his Guru accepts. He is known as the model disciple. Marpa tells him that to be a true disciple, you have to surrender completely to the Guru. You don't have to have an iota of the ego.'

'Thus, though surrender was part of the disciple's inherent nature, while reconstructing the podium for the twenty-eighth time, he decided to abandon surrender. But wisdom prevailed and he embraced surrender again.'

'Yes. So you are right that surrender should be part of one's inherent nature but one has to surrender to that aspect of one's inherent nature for it to come about.'

Ironically, the only way one can go beyond one's negative inherent tendency is by "not surrendering" to its pull and destructive tendency. Make note. It eventually all comes down to what you are surrendering too.

'Now there are many people who want to walk on the right path, they truly want to walk on the right path, but somehow their inherited tendency is far more overpowering than the desire to walk the right path. How does an individual go beyond that craving or tendency or negativity?'

'Therefore the necessity of prayer. If there is something which is to take us beyond karma, then it is prayer.'

'So you do believe that prayer can take you beyond your karma and your tendency?'

'More than belief, it is the complete faith in the power of prayer. Ruzbeh, prayer is of different types, but if you pray for others and not for the self alone, that prayer shows you wonderful results. Therefore we should pray for all.'

'Where do we get the tendencies for anger, hate, jealousy, lust, calmness, happiness, selflessness and the lot?'

'As we move on the pathways of life, we get a number of experiences and the same experience would unfold a good quality in you or the same experience would unfold a not-so-good quality—that is how these things creep in. Karma opens the door and past-life tendencies, desires, frustrations, joys, etc. will mould the individual's temperament, which we term as inherent tendencies.'

'Dada, a lot of times our environment is not in our control and it is very difficult to choose one's environment. Often it is the environment which eventually chooses one's friends and role models; so what does an individual do at such times?'

'You don't have to choose, you have to accept. The word "choice" should not be in your dictionary, only the word "acceptance" should be. God has placed you in a particular environment that must be the best environment for you; thus one needs acceptance.'

'But Dada, one's environment could be soul numbing and even morally questionable. It could lead to harbouring negative inclinations.'

'You should first accept your lot and then, instead of fighting it, try to go beyond it. Try not to let the negativity consume you—that can start when you do not fight things but face it with calm wisdom.'

'So basically, most often, the only free will that we do have is how we accept what is in store for us, which has been decided by our karma of our past lives, which was in turn decided by how we chose to use our free will.'

'We have free will all the time. That is how some of the most wicked people in the world have become saints. They take advantage of the free will that is given to them. At every step, at every round of life, free will belongs to us. All we have to do is to will to become better. Karma binds us, it is true. What I do and what I have done in the past determines the tendency in which I move. It does not compel me. People feel that karma is a compelling force; karma does not compel, but it indicates. I have done so many things in the past which I should not have done. They are supposed to take me in a particular direction but I can put a stop to it. At any given moment, I can put a stop. There is a connection, as it were, between karma and free will. And there is also the grace of the Guru or God, which is a tremendous force. In one of the songs which was sung by my beloved Master Sadhu Vaswani, this line is repeated again and again, *"Ik kano kripa jo kafi!"* The words mean, "Just one grain of Thy grace O Lord is sufficient for me, just one grain." Grace is such a tremendous force.'

'I know we have discussed this before, but You still don't think karma has anything to do with receiving grace, as I still am not comfortable with the concept of God granting something just on a whim? That would make God, Goddess or Guru extremely partial or temperamental.'

'No, if karma had anything to do with grace, then it would not be grace at all. It would be the laws of cause and effect. How can one earn grace? One can earn blessings and one can earn spiritual growth, but grace, Ruzbeh, by definition, is something out of the ordinary, out of the box. Grace cannot be earned. It is like creation, it just came about.'

'Ok, let me ask You a question. Is Krishna, through Your grace and will, calling me to write this book and make this documentary . . . is it destined, is it grace or is it my free will to write it?'

'It could be karmic or it could be the beginning of some karma, because karma too gets generated. I know what you mean, but remember that our duty is to give our best and be in a state of complete gratitude. We are asked at every step, in every round of life, to thank God. Results may appear to be favourable or otherwise, but we have to thank the Lord. The sixteenth century monk, Meister Eckhart, was the one who said that if in your entire life you have offered this simple prayer, "Thank you God! Thank you God! Thank you God", it is enough.

'In the Sindhi language, the word is shukur. One day, Sadhu Vaswani was explaining to us the meaning of the word. He said, shukur is built up of three alphabets . . . "shu", "ku" and "r". The alphabet "shu" is *shah* . . . shah meaning the king, the king of all kings. "Ku" is *karye*, meaning whatever He does, whatever the king of king does, and the last alphabet "r", means *razi*, meaning, "I have to be happy or I have to accept gracefully" or "I have to be filled with the sense of satisfaction". Perhaps that is the difference between a holy man and an ordinary man like me. The holy man offers gratitude to God for everything that happens to him, but I don't. Perhaps that is the difference.'

'Your feeble attempts at humour are much appreciated, Dada. So basically what You are trying to say is that one should not bother about karma and free will and that one should do one's work and leave the rest to God, Goddess or Guru as that is not only the most sensible and wise thing to do but also because everything is truly complicated otherwise.'

'Yes. It is complicated on one hand, while on the other, it is more like clockwork—you just switch it on and it goes on.'

We kept quiet for a long time. Then He looked at me.

'You still want to ask about inherent tendencies, right?'

'Dada, I am flawed. Therefore, bear with my questions on inherent mess-ups.'

Dada smiled. Waited.

'Can traits like selflessness, generosity, kindness and purity be cultivated or are you just born with these?'

'It can be cultivated. It should be. The first way is through contact with generous people if you want generosity; calm people if you are seeking to learn patience and calmness; selfless people for selflessness; kind people for kindness and noble, pure people if you want purity.'

'So what you are trying to say and it makes complete sense is if one is amidst such people, slowly their vibrations envelope us and their traits begin to work through us. Thus the need to be close to spiritual people. Their spirituality rubs off on those who are close to them, but only on those who truly want to grow. If the intent is not there, then no change takes place.'

'Yes. It is all about wanting to change for the better and to move on the path.'

'Dada, what if in one's orbit or for whatever reason, one does not have access to such noble people or saints? Then what is to be done?'

'The next best thing would be to read about the lives of such noble people and imbibe their nobleness through their words. And then most importantly to begin to indulge in selfless activities as through selfless activities, one can acquire many virtues. Through giving of oneself, one is blessed with so many virtuous traits.'

'So however angry, mean, rude or selfish a person may be, can actually cultivate something noble that we don't have as our inherent nature?

'Oh yes! For sure we can cultivate every noble trait if one truly wants and works towards it. That is why we are here and that is why we have different types of people on earth. It is not only that we can but we have to and it has been done by countless individuals and they have gone beyond their flaws. How is it that a man becomes a Guru? He has to transcend his lower self and nature. India is full of Gurus. They all have gone beyond their lower selves and have embraced the highest of the high.'

'Do You think the five elements which control us can make a difference to an individual's spirituality?'

'It depends upon the will power of the individual; if he has worked on himself and built up his will power, then nothing can shake him. But if his will is weak, than he can be influenced and that is when problems arise. Most of us can be influenced and led astray.'

'The five elements which were present, let us say a thousand years ago, are not the same as the five elements which are present now. The food we eat, the water we drink and the air we breathe are not the same. Corruption and pollution have set in virtually all the elements. If the elements make the physical or gross aspect of the individual and if they are affected or degraded, would it have an impact on one's well-being and through that, our spiritual progress?'

'Yes, but remember the same element has a different effect on different people. If you and I drink the same water, that water may elevate you, but I could remain indifferent to it.'

'How does that happen?'

'It is action and reaction. That is the rationale behind medicines—the same medicine you and I were to take would affect us differently.'

'We cannot change the elements . . . for instance, we cannot change the air that we breathe.'

'True, but we can change the effect of the air we breathe.'

'How?'

'That would depend upon your attitude towards all that you imbibe. Depending upon your attitude, the element will affect you. If you change your attitude, you can change the effect. There were two beggars sitting side by side. A man gave a rupee to one of the beggars. This beggar said to him, "Sir, you better keep it to yourself. It will be useful to you." The man offered the same rupee to the other beggar and the other beggar said to him, "God bless you abundantly." It depends upon the attitude. You have the power, but you don't make use of it. That is the issue. You are a tremendous powerhouse; but you don't know it and you don't make use of that power until you come to that level when you become conscious that you are God and then magic takes place. But when you get this consciousness that you are God, you simultaneously get the consciousness that you are nothing. That is the beauty of self-realization and spiritual growth. True spiritual growth leads to the realization that we all are One and that as an individual we are nothing.'

'So the best way of going about is being silent and calm within, moving towards the light and doing one's dharma in the most detached and selfless manner.'

'Yes. If you face the light and do your duty and good karma, karma itself is going to bless you.'

'How does a common person, who wants to walk the path, sincerely do so as there are so many obstacles within as well as outside the individual? How does that individual continue living up to the ideals of the Perfect Ones? There will be issues in one's personal life, career and relationships. How does s/he get up every day with the resolve of not reacting and just living a life that makes his or her Master happy and proud of that individual?

'Therefore the place of faith in our life. If the common man has the faith that there is a meaning of mercy in everything that happens, his life becomes different. It is because we don't have faith, because we are mind-dominated and not spirit-dominated that the mind always finds faults and the mind will always suspect.

'Bulleh Shah, the Sufi saint, goes and meets Inayat Shah. Inayat Shah was a gardener and He was working in a garden, transferring plants from one place to another. It was while doing gardening that Inayat Shah says to Bulleh Shah, "Like how I transfer a seedling from one place to another, you have to transfer your heart and mind to the spirit." It's very much like a man walking towards the light. As he walks facing the light, the shadow is behind him. It is all luminous in front of him. But if he turns his back, then the shadow is in front of him and he walks in darkness all the time.

'In your book, *The Fakir,* this has been explained. Baba tells Rudra that darkness does not come because the sun has moved away from the earth. Darkness comes as that part of the earth has shown its back to the sun.'

'But why do we make our journey so difficult? What is in mankind, in us, that makes the path so dark?'

'Because in darkness we think nobody is watching us and we can do what we like. There was a time when we were taught that there is One who is watching us and we dare not do anything wrong. You and I, weren't we taught this?'

'Yes, my maternal grandmother used to tell me that once a day, for just one moment, God says "*Ameen*". The only problem was that nobody knew when it is said by God. So, we were asked to be very careful of what we were thinking, saying and doing.'

'I was taught the same thing, the only difference being that instead of Ameen, we were told the word is *Tathastu*. So be it. Thus, be very careful, we were told, as who knows when the angels might say Tathastu.'

'Now with the nucleus family system, we have almost made our elders redundant.'

'It is in a period in which they can give the very best and we throw them out.'

'Sometimes I feel the deterioration of society started with the disintegration of the joint family.'

'Yes. The breakup of the joint family, coupled with false attachment to one's children, has been the cause. If the grandparent was strong, he would not allow pampering to go on to the point of spoiling the child's future. It is this attachment that is the cause of all the rigmarole that we have.

'There was a woman who used to come to the satsang every day; one day, she came and wept. I asked her, "Amma, what has happened?" She said, "My husband passed away leaving his entire wealth to me because he knew that my son, our son, was not moving in the right direction." And she said, "He has spent almost all the money and now he comes and even beats me if he wants something. I have very little left now, but he comes and beats me." I told her, "Amma, why do you worry about it? There is a police inspector who comes often for the satsang. I will tell him to call your son and a good talk will settle everything." "Oh no, no, don't talk of the police. I don't want the police to get involved." Now it is attachment which has brought about this condition. That is the very first lesson that the Gita teaches us, "Be detached. Be detached!"

'Yes, one must be certain that one's detachment is also not without compassion; the two must go together. If it is without compassion, the detachment can be very cruel and that again would create other problems. So the two must go hand in hand.

'A lot of spiritual people are beautifully detached but they don't have compassion and thus become very cold individuals. But I knew of a man who was most detached but had such rare compassion that I always remember Him with warmth in my heart. Like Sadhu Vaswani, who was the most detached and the most compassionate human being I have ever met.

'There used to be a holy man in Sind. There was a small area there which was known as Khairpur. They called it Khairpur Mirs as it belonged to the Mirs of that place. And this Mir had great regard for this holy man, a Hindu. Someone had done something or not done something and was ordered to be hanged. So he came running to the holy man, and pleaded that the holy man to intervene on his behalf. "Oh sage, you have influence over the Mir. Kindly get me a pardon as I am truly innocent." So this sage goes to the Mir and seeks pardon for the accused man and the Mir says, "I cannot say no to you. Since you have come, it has to be done. But please promise me that you will not come again with another request." The sage says, "You can take whatever promises you want, but save the life of this man." After sometime, another similar case occurs and another innocent man comes to the holy man. And He once again goes to the Mir and says, "I know I have promised you I would not intervene, but here I am. Call me a liar, an untruthful man, a man who breaks his promise or anything you want, but please save the life of this man too."

'This holy man was shot in Sind by two people who were His followers . . . if memory serves me right. His name was Bhagat Kanwar Ram. So one day, the sage was travelling by train for returning to His hometown. He had to change trains and so He got down from the train and sat for a while on one of the benches at the platform. Two people came to Him and said to him, "You are a holy man, bless us so that the work we have to do is successful." I have a feeling this good man knew what they had in mind, but so filled with compassion was He that He blessed them by saying, "May you succeed in what you have undertaken." Those two fired at him and killed him.'

Dada went silent. I went silent. For a long time none of us spoke. The satsang had begun. Somebody down there was belting out another bhajan. I knelt at Dada's feet. He told me, "Come soon, I miss our talks." I nodded. Smiled. He gave me prasad for Meher. Blessed Samir too.

I entered the Sacred Samadhi. Took Sadhu Vaswani and Sister Shanti's blessings. Then turned again towards Sadhu Vaswani.

'Dear Sadhu Vaswani, please make note. Bless me with detachment and compassion but retain a bit of common sense in me and yes, please don't make haste. I am in no hurry. Take your time with all this business of detachment and compassion. Love you. Jai Baba.'

12

I bowed down at the Samadhi of Sadhu Vaswani and Sister Shanti. I had a strange sadness within me. Though nothing was spoken, I had this feeling that today would be my last interview with Dada. I was really going to miss these conversations with Dada, The Samadhi Temple, the Kutiya, the team, the inner circle and the gentleness and the kindness that enveloped me every time I was here. I sat for a while just looking at Sadhu Vaswani.

Then I remembered I had to pass on a message to Him from Meher. She had eventually understood why He had His finger pointing to the sky.

'That is because Sadhu Vaswani is saying that in life you can only love one thing. If you try to love more than one thing, it creates a lot of problems. Tell Him that. And also tell Him to tell Dada Vaswani that the *mawa* cakes were awesome.'

I sighed and found myself on the first floor just outside the Kutiya. Naresh got me a hot cup of tea and biscuits. I, for the fortieth time, told him I could not eat those biscuits. For the fortieth time, Naresh said, "Have one!"

I sat in the Kutiya and zoned out. It was truly peaceful inside the Kutiya. The vibration of Sadhu Vaswani, Sister Shanti, Dada and all the disciples and lovers was very soft and peaceful. Dada entered early. He prayed to Sadhu Vaswani and then turned and saw me and smiled.

'Where have you been? I have missed you.'

'I thought you must be tired with the recordings in Mumbai, Dada, therefore didn't want to tire you out further.'

'But you don't tire me. I enjoy our talks. I hope you too.'

I nodded. I looked at Him and smiled. Boy, am I going to miss Him. I truly am going to miss our conversations and our time spent together. I put the thought away and got ready for the shoot. Piya adjusted Dada's shawl making sure not a crease was out of place. There was some function to be held that day and we had to complete our shooting by six thirty. Piya offered Dada and me a mint to ease the throat.

Dada spoke about His recording and then enquired if I had had tea. He never ever forgot to ask me this. Never once forgot to give me Prasad for Meher. Never ever. It is something astonishing. Even once when I was leaving at ten thirty at night and He was in His room and I had gone to just take His blessings, He enquired of my health, whether I was taken care of and made sure I was handed the holy offering. He always made me feel special. I am sure He made one and all feel special. But I was told by a number of Dada's disciples that He truly enjoyed our conversations and looked forward to it. These are the little things that make the ludicrous ups and downs of life worth its while.

'I had forgotten to ask you this question when we were talking about life after death. According to spiritual Masters, Sai Baba of Shirdi and Meher Baba, there is a community or a band of spirit helpers called *Abdals*; a band of spirit workers who help the Master's work in all dimensions. What do you think of that? Every perfect Master, it seems, has a band of spirit workers, who assist the Master in His or Her work, be it in the physical plane or beyond.'

'I believe so. But it is only the Masters who know how to draw help from that group. You and I cannot do it, we can pray.'

'But how does it work? Who are these people? Are they what we would call spirit guides who had lived here and moved on?'

'I should think so, yes. Even insofar as spirit messages are concerned, supposing I wish to contact somebody who is on the other side, I must have a spirit guide. Otherwise, I will be cheated. Because there are so many wandering spirits that when the line is opened—the line of communication between this and that world—the spirits rush through that open line wanting to come and communicate. You need a spirit guide, somebody who will open and close the line, who can protect you from mischievous spirits with ignoble intentions. There are people who know how to open the line, but they can't close it. It is dangerous terrain and thus it is best to have a Master to help you through this process. Masters know how to make the spirit brethren work on the path of light.'

'Who are these so-called wandering spirits with not-so-good intentions? How come they are wandering?'

'They are wandering spirits because at the time of death, the last thought that they carried was worldly . . . thoughts and emotions predominantly worldly and of the gross world.'

'You mean their focus was still on worldly things and centred around the material?'

'Yes. That keeps them from going out of the orbit of the earth.'

'So you mean the spirit becomes earthbound?'

'Yes exactly, the spirit becomes earthbound. But they don't have a physical body through which they can fulfil their desires. There was a woman who came and said that her husband had married four times—one after the other. The first wife died, followed by the second and the third. She was his fourth wife. After he passed away, she had been feeling a sensation in a particular part of the body. The man must have carried some unfulfilled desire.'

'So what you mean is if a man, at the time of passing away, is still controlled by the need for sex, money, power, material objects, hate, etc. he can get earthbound?'

'Yes. So the husband needed to be liberated. Therefore, they need our help. We must pray for all such souls.'

'So what you are trying to say is that power of prayers is so magnificent that if we made it our priority to aid all of creation by simply praying for all of creation, that aid would reach those in need and our prayers would help not only those in the physical body but even in the spirit realm?'

'Yes, for certain. There is not a doubt in my mind that the power of true selfless prayer can move mountains.'

'Are these souls looking for an entry in a body to release their desires, to live their desires?'

'I assume this must be their main agenda. Because they are not happy, they are restless and are seeking a release.'

'Would prayers from a truly sincere heart be able to create some kind of a shield to protect one from such earthbound entities?'

'I believe so. Prayers create their own vibration and those vibrations act as a shield against negative influences and energy.'

'What is your take on spirit communication?'

'If you don't believe in spirits and want to know if there are spirits, you can try it out once or twice. But it is not good because spirits, people who have passed over or the departed ones, have their work to do on the other side and every time we call them, we are disturbing them in their work. They don't want to be disturbed.

'Secondly, there is so much of impersonation. Supposing there are people who say they want to call the spirit of a great one. Now, instead of the great one, some other spirit connects with you pretending to be the great one. How would we ever know who is on the other line? It is like getting a wrong number on the telephone. Now, the person who gets that number doesn't want to leave you and wants to talk to you. So there are spirits like that. You will think you are talking to the great one and that it was the great one who told you all those things, but it was not. It was some other spirit. May be a lower spirit, and therefore, it's not good to call spirits. It's only when you have a spirit guide on the other side that you venture into this world. There are spirit guides who are very careful to see that the spirit you contact are the right type of spirits. Otherwise, they tell you not to do so. But that will be only when you evolve—not by the use of the planchette or these ordinary things.'

'So now we are entering the realm of what is popularly known as the dark world or even black magic, where certain people are aware of how to control these earthbound spirits and get work done through these spirits? Is that how it operates?'

'If we believe in the power of prayer, that would mean I believe in white magic. The power of purity. But if the power of purity exists, then logically, the presence of evil, which is generally called black magic, could exist too.'

'Zarathustra is considered the first known Prophet and it was He who said that if there is heaven, there must be hell as if there is light, there has to be a shadow created. But the common perception is when an individual dies, the person gets wings and goes up to either hell or heaven, or remains earthbound. But nine out of ten people must be dying having some worldly want. What would differentiate those who pass away and those who are in limbo?'

'Most of the people who die don't enter the astral world immediately. They have to pass through what is called a purgatory. In purgatory, they keep on fulfilling their desires with others looking on. Now suppose I die with a desire, I am sent to purgatory. It's all open there. Here on earth if I have to fulfil a desire, I do it in such a way that no one comes to know of it. In purgatory, it is all open. Everyone is looking at you while you are fulfilling your desire and knowing that your secret desire or your intentions that fuel you are out in the open, most often, a certain sense of shame enters the individual spirit. The shame leads to a realization that one would rather not fulfil those desires than indulge in them shamelessly in front of one and all. When the individual shakes off the desire, it is then admitted to the astral world.'

'So you die, land up in purgatory, realize you are making a fool of yourself, feel ashamed and slowly slip into the astral world. So who are the wandering spirits? How come they don't go into purgatory?'

'I think it is the degree of the desire which would allow you to move upward, even if it means going to purgatory. So I guess if your desire is all consuming, you are earthbound and locked in the orbit of the earth.'

'And are guides from the astral world?'

'Yes.'

'So for how long do they remain in the astral world? And do they come back to Mother Earth or do they move someplace else?'

'From the astral world they go to the causal world. Then the astral body dies and you come to the causal body. It is in that body that you know your entire destiny. What is to be and what has been. It is there that you make the right decisions for yourself. Then you come back to earth. When you come back, you have forgotten that you have made the decision yourself. Now suppose I am given to anger and the slightest thing makes me angry or irritates me, it is in the causal world that I know that if I get married to such and such a person, I will be tested and may learn how to manage my anger.'

'So the logic is if the individual can conquer anger through such a prolonged time living with a person whose very agenda may be to provoke, then for sure, the individual will have succeeded in conquering anger.'

'Yes, but I forget that upon coming here and we fight for the rest of our life to escape the situation by filing for a divorce or separation. That is why sages discourage divorces.'

'Dada, what happens when there is no option; may be the woman is being traumatized or violated or physically abused by the husband? Wouldn't one be encouraging the man to abuse the woman more? Even spiritually, wouldn't one be creating more karma, first by going through the abuse and secondly by allowing the power of abuse to grow?'

'I know what you are saying. There are women who are virtually kicked by their husbands. Brutally violated by their husbands.'

'So wouldn't divorce be the rational move for everybody, including the children involved as their entire childhood goes in seeing their father abuse their mother?'

'I agree, Ruzbeh. On this plane, yes, but then a number of issues come about. There is karma. There is individual karma and combined family karma. Sometimes an individual has chosen a life of being subjected to abuse to see one's own level of compassion and patience. It is complicated.'

'But so many times in a marriage, because of the animosity of the husband and wife, the children suffer the most. Wouldn't the best solution be to get the children out of that situation?'

'As I told you Ruzbeh, there is combined karma. The children who are born to such couples are the ones who may karmic-ally have to go through that experience. That is why they are born in that family. To tell you the truth, often life is beyond the ordinary intelligence of man.'

'What about miscarriages which take place? What is the karmic link between the child and the parents?'

'It is possible that the particular soul has almost reached its goal and maybe there is some pending karma and through the miscarriage, that pending karma is mitigated. The soul has to pass through that experience to reach where it wants to go.'

'And kids who live for a few days or pass away very young?'

'Yes, they too had to go through that experience for a particular time. It was needed for their journey. There are babies that are born and live for only twenty-four hours. You might think there is no logic to this whole process, but, Ruzbeh, the whole process has its own divine logic and justification.'

'So they have to complete their karma, most often with their parents or family, and then move on. Okay, it seems heartless but then whoever said living was either easy or made any sense? What do the terms *moksha* and *mukti* mean, are they the same things?'

'Yes, the same things,'

'Great. So what do they mean?'

'Moksha means freedom from desires; you desire nothing, you expect nothing, you claim nothing.'

Dada went silent. We waited. Then after a while, He looked at me and smiled.

'Dada, the normal concept of moksha means merging with the Creator. Does that happen?'

'It would if you and the Creator were different. One believes that you and the Creator are different. In reality, you and the Creator are One. Moksha could mean that the ignorance of duality is removed.'

'So you mean it is self-realization that you are the One and that The One is you?'

'Yes.'

'So you don't go anywhere? You don't kind of merge into oblivious divine ecstasy?'

'I don't think so. You come to the realization that you are One with the Creator. Thus you go beyond all desires, all wants and all needs. You are free.'

'What happens to us when we sleep? Apart from the body being repaired and all that medical stuff, does something take place spiritually? You have talked about the silver cord.'

'If you want to experience what the sliver thread is, you must go into the depths of meditation. You will have an out-of-body experience when you are not aware of this body. You carry the silver thread with you as you move out of the body. As the silver thread leaves the body, there is a "twin-g" sound. It is a wonderful sound. Even the best singers amongst us cannot repeat this sound. It is musical. Again when you enter the body, this sound is there. It is this silver cord that keeps the body and soul together. If the silver cord is intact, the soul can enter the body again. If it is broken, the soul cannot enter the body. It is very elastic and can stretch up to thousands of miles. You can keep your body here and go to America if you like. If this link is broken, you will not be able to enter the body.

'The silver cord remains intact. The silver cord is that which connects the physical body with its etheric double. So if the etheric double were to travel, the silver cord gets it back to the body. But a man passes through four states or *avasthas*. The states are awakening (*jagrat*), dreaming (*swapna*) and deep sleep (*sushupti*). That is a state of dreamless sleep. Man has to enter this stage without him being conscious of it. Beyond the state of deep sleep is *turiya*, the fourth state of supreme consciousness, when we are actually able to see into the Truth of existence.'

'So when does healing takes place?'

'Healing may be taking place all the time because every cell of the body is a chemical factory. Every cell of the body contains the healer or the healing process. The cell is incomplete without the healing part. The healing goes on.'

'This state that you are talking about, blissful sleep, does it have to take place? What if a person is very worked up before sleeping?'

'Still he must have it.'

'Only the time duration might change.'

'Yes.'

'The greater period of blissful sleep means more energized the individual. So does this fourth stage or state of sleep called turiya, the state of supreme consciousness, when we are actually able to see into the Truth of existence, fill you up with divine energy?'

'Yes. It is as though the soul returns to its home. During the rest of the day and night, it is separated from home. Now it returns home and comes back filled with energy.'

I assume the longer time we spend in that state, the greater the amount of Divine Energy we are filled with and vice-versa. If one is harrowed or restless or stressed or preoccupied, the time spent home could be less than a few seconds, which would explain why on some days we feel so blissfully relaxed even if we slept for just a short while and on some days when you wake up you feel as though a regiment of healthy men have walked all over you wearing spiked shoes. Hmm. Is that why our elders would keep telling us to pray and sleep?

'This etheric double that you keep talking about . . . is it one's higher self?'

'No. The etheric double is actually a subtle body which connects our physical form to higher bodies or higher selves within us. So it is like a conduit. A catalyst.'

'But are we connected with it during the day?'

'It is connected with us all the time. Because if it were not connected then this body would perish and pass through the experience we call death. It is what we call the *pranamaya kosha*, the sheath made of *prana*, subtle breath or life force.'

'Okay, got it. It is the covering that absorbs the life force and pours it into the physical body. The moment when it can no longer channel the life force into a physical body, that physical body croaks. Okay, got it. Now coming back to the soul going home. When you say that the soul goes home, are you trying to say that it rests in the etheric body rather than the physical?'

'No. Man is essentially the soul, not the body. It is the soul that has been separated from the source. Yoga is the science that shows you the way for the soul to be united with the source. Now this process of union of the source with the individual soul takes place every night but we are not conscious of it. Yoga is that which makes us conscious of it. Consciously, we return home.'

'I know this may sound a bit odd, but the soul is within the body right?'

'According to me, the body is inside the soul because the soul is far greater. Far, far greater. Just because I am not acquainted with the soul I feel it not–that is my ignorance. Most of the people feel that the soul is inside the body, but the soul is so vast that it cannot be contained by this body. When you touch the state of Samadhi or even earlier, when you are meditating when you lose your body consciousness, you realize how vast you are. Now all that vastness cannot be contained in this tiny five-foot body.'

'It is also said that when one is sleeping, the astral body moves around, visits places, you know, becomes a cosmic traveller?'

'Yes. It can.'

'So does this astral travel take place on its own or are there people who can consciously make their spirit or soul leave their body and travel. Like yogis?'

'Yogis move out of their body consciously every day. And the oftener you move out of the body consciously, you understand your own spirit better and the workings of the creation better. Once you return to the body, you are conscious of all you have learnt and experienced and thus you can help your own spiritual evolution in a quicker manner.

'When you travel unconsciously, you don't remember all that you have done when out of the body. But conscious or not, the etheric double, with the help of the silver cord, is connected to the physical body. Thus, the body lives. But once the silver cord is snapped, the body will not be revived. Energy flows through the etheric double, through that silver cord, into the body. Thus astral travel does come with many dos and don'ts and if one doesn't have a Master to guide and protect you, all this is not advisable.'

I have often been told that when one is travelling astrally in a conscious manner and the physical body is left unprotected, a negative or a more powerful spirit can enter your body and then experience all his/her wants and desires through your body, while you wait outside scratching your astral head.'

'Do you know how to leave your body . . .?'

'You mean out-of-body travel? I shouldn't say so but I have had just a glimpse.'

'You do know how to get out of your body, right?'

Dada looked at me for a while and then He laughed.

He said, 'No, I don't', but He wouldn't look into my eyes.

'So your inherent sense of humility won't let you admit that you can do astral travel, which I understand, but is this how saints and Masters go and help Their lot?'

'Yes, yes, they go and help. They help disciples who may stay at far-off places. So many stories of Masters show how the Master materialized in a particular places miles and miles away from where the Master was physically residing, helped the disciple and returned into the body, without anybody being the wiser. I remember reading about the son of a Sikh Guru, who travelled in spirit form, went to Peshawar, finished his work, and came back into his body. There is the classic example of Shankaracharya. In those days, they used to have debates and the religion of the one who won the debate was considered victorious. In those days many belonged to Buddhism. Buddhism and Jainism are regarded as atheistic religions. They do not believe in the Creator. Shankaracharya was engaged in a debate with Mandana, a learned pundit. He could not win the debate. Mandana's wife came forward and started putting forward questions concerning sexual life. Shankaracharya was not aware of these things as he was unmarried. So Shankaracharya asked for fifteen days' time. How was Shankaracharya to get these experiences so that he could answer those questions? He told his disciples, "I am leaving the body. I am going to enter the body of somebody else and get these experiences. Keep my body intact. See that no one knows that I have left my body. My body will be dead; there will be no respiration."

'The disciples kept guard over the body day and night. Shankaracharya entered the body of a king who had just died. The body of the king became alive but it contained the soul of Shankaracharya. He lived with all the queens, got the experience he needed, and entered into his body again. The silver cord was intact. He met Mandana's wife on the sixteenth day and gave her all the answers. Everyone was astonished. He won the debate and Mandana became one of his favourite disciples. It is within a man's reach to keep the silver cord intact if he has reached that level, that spiritual height. He can keep his silver cord alive.'

I had a lot to say about Shankaracharya entering the King's body and 'gaining experience'. But Dada evokes such purity in even people like me that I did not want to talk about the 'flowers and the bees' in front of Him.

The kind of astral travel that Sai Baba of Shirdi did and which has been recorded is legendary. In ancient times, the noble king Vikramaditya was known to travel out of his body to help his people.

'So when you went out of body, what did you experience?'

'I cannot say, because during such an experience, you don't feel that you belong here. In my case it was just a glimpse, during the time I had the stroke. I have a faint memory of me being with Sadhu Vaswani. I know it was not a dream. I was with The Master and Sadhu Vaswani just turned His back to me and I got the message that I have to come back. My time was not yet done. I had to work here. I had work remaining. With Sadhu Vaswani stood Shanti. They both turned Their back to me. But the luminosity was tremendous. I have not seen the like of it anywhere. The form was there and the form was the same but the radiance was truly something else.'

'Have They manifested themselves in front of you?'

'I can feel the presence of the Master all the time. I don't feel that there is a distance between my Master and myself. And I actually feel that the work that is being done by Him. So I never have the feeling that I am doing the work.'

'Now was this experience that you had, this out-of-body experience, not a conscious effort to move out of the body?'

'It just happened. Because I never had a feeling that the Master was away from me, I have never felt Him leave me. As I have told you, when Sadhu Vaswani passed away, I quietly went to a room on the upper floor. Then I remembered the previous night, when I was pressing His legs, He had held my hand and said, "My child be by me! Be by me!" But after He passed away, as I told you, I could truly hear those words come back to me, as though He was loudly repeating those words, and the words came to me when I went to the upper room, which made me sure, very sure, that He was with me. He may have left the body but He was back with me. From that moment I have always had that feeling that I am not alone. But that is His grace.'

'Has He ever come in Your dream or anything of that sort?'

'Sometimes, sometimes yes. But this was not a dream.'

'I know Dada that You truly heard Sadhu Vaswani. But when He does come in your dreams, what is it for? Is it to give You a message or is it just to make You comfortable? Or give You a tight hug?'

'Some of the dreams are common, ordinary dreams and some of the dreams do have a message. For instance, I had a strange dream a long time ago in which Gurudev Sadhu Vaswani was taking me to a sprawling mansion. I was wonderstruck at the grandeur of the mansion. "Do you know how many rooms are there in this mansion?" Sadhu Vaswani asked me. "There are 365 rooms in it." Then the two of us stepped inside this mansion. As we approached a huge hall, the portals opened of their own accord.

'In the hall there were hundreds of pictures. Pointing to them, Sadhu Vaswani said, "My child, these beautiful pictures that you see are to be hung and displayed in each individual room. Jashan, pick a picture that you like and hang it on the wall." I looked at them and was enthralled by the one in which Sri Krishna was handing over a torch to Sadhu Vaswani as if to say, "Go and light the flame of My name in each heart." So I lovingly picked up that picture and hung it on one of the walls. And you will not believe it, but the painting spread itself and filled the entire room. A mystical experience indeed!

'But now that so many years have passed by, these dreams too have decreased. But that feeling is there, that consciousness is there. You know when we had begun the interview and I was coming to you, at that moment I had the feeling and I said to him, "Master, now it is for You to answer His questions, for I won't be able to do it."'

I sat quiet. I knew what had happened. I sat humbled and remembered how I too had prayed during those early days of our interviews, pleading with Sadhu Vaswani to come through and speak or make sure Dada communicated expressively.

'You know I too had gone to the Samadhi and told Sadhu Vaswani, "Your greatest disciple is not telling me quite a few things. So will You please make Him talk or You talk through Him." Since then I have felt You open up much more.'

'But I am not His greatest disciple. I seek to be the least of His little ones.'

'Yes. Yes. I am sure.'

'Well, He listened to both of us,' Dada said with a twinkle in His eyes. We began to chuckle. I knew for a fact that it was true. But it humbled me to realize that a great, noble Master had called out to His Master to be part of our conversations.

'Dada, when people are lying in a state of coma what is going on?'

'The soul is awake but the brain is asleep.'

'So the soul is aware of what is going on?'

'The soul is aware. Therefore whenever I hear that a person has entered a comatose state, I request people who are close to him to keep a recorder which plays the Holy Name of God, because the soul hears.'

'You also used to go visit those lying in a state of coma?'

'Oh yes, a number of times.'

'And if the person was being taken care of at home, you would advise for kirtans and bhajans. That helps the individual?'

'Yes. It works in both ways. I have seen recovery take place and I have also seen the soul leave the body peacefully. There have been many who passed away while we were doing kirtan for those in coma or when the person is about to leave the body. And one thing that I have observed is that if we keep on doing kirtan and the person is in a comatose state, when the person is about to pass away, the person opens his eyes. I have seen that I should say in all the cases that I have attended. At the last moment he opens his eyes. That is the power of the Name Divine.

'The Name Divine has inherent power, it has power of its own. Thus earlier, a Guru would initiate His disciple by whispering the Name of the Divine to His disciple. Now that power is to be heightened, is to be cultivated. The initiator can pass on the Name Divine to the one whom He is initiating but the one who is being initiated must give time and cultivate it. And thus empower the Name that has been given to him. Now that is what is missing today.'

'Nowadays thousands are initiated through the loud speaker.'

'Yes, I know. I don't know how such initiation works. I don't know.'

'There have been a lot of avatars, Maha Avatars, but what is so special about Shri Rama and Shri Krishna?'

'Even as there are saints at different levels even so Gods are at different levels. There are many Gods, there is not one God. Or you may say one God in many forms and they belong to different levels. Krishna and Rama, so far as the Hindus are concerned, are at the highest level which one can reach. Therefore Krishna says: Come unto me! Rama says: Come unto me! To those have achieved the state of realization, there is no difference between Krishna and Rama.'

'Now when you say these Gods or different avatars of God have their own levels, is this similar to the dimensions of Brahma called *Brahmaloka*, Vishnu called *Vishnuloka* and Shiv called *Shivloka*?'

'Each God has His own dimension. Now it depends upon whom you have worshipped while you were in the human body. Even as we have different states here and different governments, even so we have in the higher worlds, it's only a replica.'

'But our job is to go beyond all these dimensions too right, go right to the Source?'

'Yes, go far beyond all these dimensions to that Source.'

'To The Ultimate One.'

'Yes. The ultimate you cannot reach but . . .'

'But one has to keep trying. Because even these dimensions or these various lok have their own limitations?'

'Yes. Only The Creator of Creators has no limitation.'

'Talking about dimensions or loks, is that why our elders would say to believe in One and move only towards that One? So at least you know where you are going when you leave the body? Otherwise, if you believe in five, you could land nowhere.'

'Yes. But I believe that there is only One. That One will take the form of the deity whom you have worshipped.'

'When you talked about prana, when you are talking about the etheric double, you said it runs on the prana. You meant the life force, didn't You? What is the *kundalini* and the associated *chakras*?'

'I know very little of the kundalini because that is a different way of arriving at the goal. But the little that I know, the kundalini is the shakti, the power that each one of us has. It is asleep, it is to be awakened. Once it awakes, it rises up. But this process, they say, should be done under the supervision of a Master because a slight shift in the energy here or there may make a person lose his balance . . . physical, emotional, mental.'

'Because of the force of the kundalini?'

'Yes. Now when that kundalini shakti is awakened and moves in the right way and in the right direction, it goes to the crown chakra, the *sahasrara* and then man can create anything.

'Most of us are not aware of this primordial energy within us. This energy is invaluable. But unfortunately, in most people, it is consumed by kama, desire or lust. This energy takes time to form and reinforce itself. But man is impelled by his basic instincts to use his energy in satisfying his sexual urges; in fact, many people focus on developing this aspect of their sexual energy rather than concentrating on their spiritual energy. Their purpose is limited: it is nothing but the pursuit of satisfying sensual desires. What they fail to understand is this: if this fantastic energy is sublimated into creative, spiritual energy, it can work wonders for us!

'Let me explain to you how this energy is formed, so that you may understand how valuable it is. One hundredth of what we eat forms a drop of blood. One hundredth of each drop of blood is converted into bone material. One hundredth of the bone tissue forms the universal element. One hundredth of this universal element forms a drop of primordial/sexual /reproductive /self-producing energy.

'Just think how valuable this serpentine energy is! For a momentary physical pleasure, we waste this energy. This is why our minds are not at peace. I used the term serpentine energy with good reason. The Sanskrit word, kundalini, means coiled, like a snake.

'Kundalini energy is little understood by most people; even practitioners of yoga and meditation are not quite clear about it. However, it is mentioned extensively in Buddhist and Hindu literature.

'Traditionally, two ways have been recommended by teachers for awakening the shakti within us: active and passive. The active approach involves systematic physical exercises and techniques of concentration, visualization, *pranayama* and meditation under the guidance of a competent teacher. These techniques which are essentially based on the four main branches of yoga are sometimes referred to in this connection as kundalini yoga. The passive approach is perhaps allied to the path of self-realization through surrender: here, the aspirant lets go of all the impediments to the awakening, rather than trying to actively awaken the kundalini.

'Meher Baba, himself a spiritually awakened Master, tells us that kundalini shakti enables man consciously to cross the lower planes and ultimately merge into the universal cosmic power of which it is a part. He adds one important point: that the awakened kundalini is helpful only up to a certain degree, after which it cannot ensure further progress. It cannot dispense with the need for the grace of a Perfect Master.

'In India, kundalini energy and its awakening have been acknowledged by Masters like Sri Aurobindo, Swami Paramahamsa Yoganand and Swami Sivananda. The Theosophical Society has taken kundalini yoga to the West, where it's healing and transformative power have been acknowledged by eminent psychiatrists like Carl Jung. It must be stressed, however, that in Hindu spiritual tradition, awakening this tremendous spiritual energy has been associated with cleansing the impurities in our subconscious and focusing the mind on God as a means to attain liberation. If you wish to control and preserve this precious energy and to put it to the highest use, you should be wary of your thoughts. Every thought has its own energy. A positive thought generates positive energy which can be tremendously uplifting and peace giving. A negative thought produces energy which is unhealthy and disturbing. An important scientific rule is this: energy follows thought. As we often say: you are what you think; you achieve what you believe in. The energy your thoughts create, accumulate and work on the universal radar!'

'Celibacy may be very necessary to acquire psychic and paranormal powers, but how important is celibacy where spirituality is concerned?'

'In several cases celibacy is useful. But it is not essential. Celibacy, I think, is important because you have less to worry about and therefore can focus on spiritual growth without the need to compromise. If you have a family of your own, one gets trapped into situations which could take you from the path. But otherwise there is no compulsion. You can be a celibate and yet not be spiritual. Hitler was a celibate.'

'Yes, he was a vegetarian too.'

'He was a vegetarian too. Thus there is no spiritual reason for being a celibate.'

'But then why do so many sages insist on celibacy?'

'If you have children, naturally you get attached to them and that means a load of worry. There used to be a spiritual man of Iran, a *dervesh*, who used to say that so long you are a celibate you are walking on land. The day you marry, you enter into a boat and the day you give birth to a child, the boat sinks and you drown.'

Strange chap this dervish is, I mused. And what I found truly amusing was that not once did it even enter Dada's consciousness that in today's time and age there is no connection between marriage and celibacy.

'We have a lot of Prophets, Zarathustra, Guru Nanak Devji, Gods and Goddesses who were all married.'

'Yes. Sri Ramakrishna Paramahansa, who, though married, lived a celibate life. He used to say that if you are married, you are within a fort, you are protected. He used to encourage marriage. He said if you are a sanyasi, then you are out in the open and you can get attacked from any side. You rarely see a married man who has no worries.'

I wanted to tell Dada that whether you were married or not, everybody had their own issues. Yes, marriage could magnify the issues but could also magnify the joy in one's life. It was extremely subjective.

'Ok, let's get on to another subject. Why do we touch the feet of elders and Gurus? What is the real reason?'

'Dham are places of pilgrimage. It is said when you touch the feet of a spiritual person, it is as though you have been to a place of pilgrimage. It is believed that the eyes, the hands and the feet of a saint are places of pilgrimages.'

'So why do You stop everyone from touching Your feet?'

'Because I myself am in search of a dham and I am disciple too.'

'I think You should let your disciples decide that.'

'I have no disciples.'

'Ya right. Anyway, why are pilgrimages and going to dhams considered to be a very important part of one's spiritual journey?'

'In those early days, holy men, men of God, inhabited those places. It was not going to the place, but going to where that holy man lived that was important. But now it has degenerated. The rivers were considered sacred because holy men, truly powerful spiritual beings had taken a dip in those rivers.'

'There are a lot of Samadhis, holy tombs of Masters, who have left Their body. Does the holy tomb emanate vibrations of the Master?'

'The holy tomb itself may not produce vibrations but the people who go and visit, they give their vibrations to the tomb. And the more people go, the more charged the tomb becomes. Of course it also depends on the people who go. With what purity and love and faith they visit the Shrine of the Master. But it works both ways. The blessings of the Master comes on to them, but according to me, they are the ones who are charging the Holy Shrine too.'

'Most of the religious books have been written long after the Prophet has left the body. Do you feel the exact words and essence of the Prophet is there in the books? Because sometimes it could be centuries later that the words of the Master may have been penned down.'

'Even in the case of Jesus, the first Bible came out 100 years or later. It depends upon the reason and response that the reader gives to the Book. Now for instance the same book is given to you as it is given to somebody else. But, your response, the emotion that awakens within you, is of a higher quality than what it arouses in somebody else. Yes, one will never know what the Master has truly said but the essence of the Prophet or the Master should be present in the book and when one reads with love, devotion and the spirit of Oneness, that is what truly counts.'

'Because how people interpret and then manipulate the Holy Book has resulted in score of innocent people being killed all in the name of God. More people have died in the name of God than in the name of the devil.'

'Yes. This is our greatest tragedy that we have not even let the words of God through the Master remain untainted by our own personal agenda.'

'According to you, who is Jesus?'

'I regard Him as a Prophet. Jesus, Krishna, Buddha, Nanak, Zoroaster, Muhammad are all Prophets according to me.'

'Why are Shri Ram and Shri Krishna so different though they come from the same source, Lord Vishnu?'

'They represent different aspects of life. Rama came to teach us how we should live in the world, Krishna came to show us that be part of the world but do not get attached or tainted by it.'

'Do you believe They really existed the way they have been projected throughout history?'

'I believe that. I believe that They were there, but, because I have been a student of science, I also believe that there have been many additions. I believe that Krishna, as He is represented today, was not the Krishna of 5000 years ago. But I worship Him.'

'He is the most colourful God ever. And what about planets? Do you believe that the sun and the moon and the other planets have a serious impact on the lives of each individual?'

'I don't think so, but I do believe that the sun and the moon and other planets of the solar system create electromagnetic fields. Now you and I may have been born in the same maternity home or same room at the same time. But your destiny is different from my destiny because of this electromagnetism. You are born in a particular electromagnetic field, I am born in a different electromagnetic field. In fact this was what I was considering for my PhD. I wanted to work on this subject.'

'It would have been very interesting. It's not late yet for You to work on this subject.'

'Now all this doesn't matter to me. It is only Sadhu Vaswani. Another thing that interests me is to find out a fire that has no heat, just light. Fire which creates light without heat.'

'You think there is fire without heat?'

'I think so. It will be difficult to find. But I think so.'

'So what does an individual do to draw out the strength from the electromagnetic field and to protect himself or herself from may be the aggressive or negative aspect of the electromagnetic field?'

'We need an electromagnetic shield, what that is we have to discover.'

'Would prayer create such a shield?'

'Why not? But again prayer has its laws. We have to study those laws.'

'So when Laxman drew the spiritual boundary around Maa Sita to protect Her from any negative being, which is called the *Lakshman Rekha,* was He creating a shield of the electromagnetic force?'

'Probably yes. Ravana could not have entered, he would have got burnt. He knew that thus he had to use devious means to break that shield.'

'So may be in those days they knew the functioning of electromagnetic force.'

'Yes, it is quite possible.'

'When Zoroastrians say their prayers, we tie this holy thread called the *kasti* around our waist and our prayers mention that as I tie this holy thread around my waist, with this prayer, let there be a shield that surrounds and protects me from all evil, negativity and the malefic effects of the planets. So may be the ancient people knew all this.'

'Yes. They knew these things but they did not know the mechanics. Once we know the mechanics it will be a wonderful thing. But nobody pays attention yet to that aspect.'

'Is that why people are told to wear rings of certain gems on certain fingers?'

'Yes, as every gem has its own electromagnetic force and field. But one needs to have somebody study this in depth and come with conclusive scientific proof of the how, why and the what.'

'But most religions have insisted that first there was the word.'

'Yes. The Eternal expressed itself in a word. We Hindus believe that the word was "*Om*" and its resonation is there. That resonation is manifestation.'

'So all that we see and touch are the ramifications of the resonation.'

'Yes. There are teachers who will tell you to meditate on that resonance, Om . . . mmmm.'

'In many of your books, you have been very emphatic on visualization.'

'Because man has the power to visualize but man has for some reason or another not used that power. Even scientists tell you nowadays that man does not use more than ten per cent of the capacity of the brain.'

'Look at the mess we have made in 10 per cent.'

'I think the real mess has been made by not using the 90 per cent.'

'So what happens with visualization?'

'Either you change what is around you or you change yourself.'

'So positive visualization can change your environment or it can change you to go beyond your environment or at least accept it gracefully?'

'Yes, the way you handle it. But most importantly, the way you look at it.'

'Do affirmations work in the same manner?'

'There is a difference between affirmation and visualization. I believe that visualization is more powerful. When you picturize something, it is as though you are giving life to it. The other thing is more abstract.'

'But as we have been talking about karma, when you say certain things that are destined, would visualization be able to alter that?'

'Or alter you. Your attitude to what is happening is altered which virtually means you have altered your destiny or the way you have gone through that experience. It makes a lot of difference. I visited an old mother who suffered from back pain. It was terrible. She could neither sleep nor sit nor stand nor walk nor turn in bed but she never ever complained. And when I asked her, she said, "It must be my karma. I must have done something now but I am happy I am paying off the debt."'

'So one's attitude towards everything is most important.'

'Yes. If there were someone else in her condition, she would be complaining all the time.'

'So what you are saying is that as she accepted her lot gracefully, she could go through that experience in a more calm manner. Destiny had to play its part but the impact was far less than what was originally planned.'

'Yes, it is all about what is our attitude towards every situation and experience.'

'Dada, tell me, when a natural calamity takes place, like an earthquake or a tsunami, thousands of people die or suffer. Do they share a joint karma?'

'Maybe, but not always. There is individual karma and there is group karma. In Hindi they say, *karmoon ki gat niyari*. Karma is not arithmetic like two plus two equals four. It is very difficult to understand the working of karma but karma is and therefore we all should be careful of the thoughts we think, of the words we utter, of the deeds we perform. Whatever be their result, it is there. But it is difficult to say that this is due to karma and this is not due to karma. Nobody will be able to determine that.'

'Is the moment of death destined?'

'In most cases, yes. But in some cases it can be postponed.'

'What about Perfect Masters. Do They decide to leave as and when They want to?'

'A Perfect Master can decide when to leave the body. I believe that holy men of God do not have any predetermined period of existence. I believe the key is in Their hands. When they think the time is up, they depart. They are not governed by the law of karma. They are free liberated souls who choose to come to this earth again and again, for the sake of us, who are bound souls. There are two types of souls—the *badhas* and the *buddhas*.

'The buddha is the awakened one, the liberated one, the emancipated one. The badha is the bound soul. We are bound by the chain of our own desire, and it is we who are subject to the law of karma.'

'So The Perfect Masters rule the five elements and even time.'

'Yes. There was a Master who met me and told me that every morning, what we call the Lord of the *graha* or time spirit would come to Him and ask Him, "What are your instructions for the day?" He would instruct the graha and He told me this happens every morning and this man never lied in His life, so I believe Him implicitly. In the story of Pundalik of Pandharpur, we are told that Pundalik actually saw the river Ganga and the other holy rivers come to the ashram of a Sage where He spent the night and gave Him the revelation that He must respect and serve His parents. And He went back to serve His parents.'

'Isn't He the same person who told Lord Krishna, also called Lord Vitthal in Maharashtra, to wait on one spot as He couldn't attend to the Lord as He was pressing the feet of His parents? He slid a stone slab and told Lord Krishna to stand on that slab and wait till He had finished serving His parents.'

'Yes, that is why Shri Krishna is known as Vitthal in Pandharpur. Vitthal means the Standing One.'

'Dada in early times, Ayurveda and even astronomy were sciences and so profoundly accurate even though there were really no laboratories or scientific equipment for either studying plant life or studying the constellations and the movement of stars and the planets. But they knew everything and were so accurate.'

'The soul power is so tremendous that mankind can achieve anything. The stronger the soul power, miracles and inventions and predictions all are like parlour tricks.'

'How does one cultivate the soul? You have time and again said that one needs to cultivate the soul. How does one do that?'

'There are laws for strengthening the soul power. One of them is giving without expecting anything in return, not even a word of thanks. You do something to me, I immediately react. Likewise there are laws. Those laws, if followed, cultivate and strengthen the soul.

They unfold your soul power. The best of all is to bless those that insult you or harm you.'

'You keep mentioning this aspect of blessing those who insult or harm us. You said it could be the only way for grace to enter one's life and now you say it is also the best way to unfold one's soul power. But it is so difficult. One needs to really go beyond one's ego and ego has such a strong hold on most of us.'

'There is no other way. Love all selflessly. And those who are filled with anger and hate need our love more.'

'You think that is the most important quality of cultivating the soul?'

'Go and serve the person who has hurt you.'

'You want to go and boil the head of the person who has hurt you, not serve the chap. It is very hard.'

'Oh yes! In reality, you have to do what the ego tells you not to do and not do what the ego tells you to do. Zoroaster spoke of *Ahura Mazda* and *Ahreman*. In lay terms, God and the devil. Listen to the voice of God. Reject the voice of the devil.'

'And they are both within. He said it is all within each one of us. It all eventually boils down to what you have been saying since a while— practise silence and go within. I don't think this is going to happen unless we have a complete change of education at home and school. So it all boils down to spreading the right wisdom.'

'Yes. What will change the world is education and not politics. Governments come and go.'

'I believe that the Aryan philosophy, seen in the scriptures of the Sanatha Dharam, called Hinduism nowadays, and scriptures of Zorastrianism, both insist that gyan daan, spreading knowledge or imparting the right education, is the greatest of all daans.'

'Yes. What is sight to the body is wisdom to the soul.'

'Ok Dada, we digressed from astronomy and astrology.'

'Yes. Astronomy and astrology existed in those days, long before even glass was invented, forget scientific laboratories. In the nineteenth century, we had Dr Heinneman who tried all medicines on himself before administering them to others. He passed through severe tests himself. But nowadays these allopathic laboratories first test the medicines on animals. They call it vivo testing or vivisection to which animal lovers object rightfully, vociferously.'

'But then don't we all use those same medicines?'

'Now there are medicines which claim that it has not been tested on animals.'

Dada halted for a while. I remembered Piya talking about Dada's love for all beings.

'Earlier, when Dada used to take His daily walks, we would go to Koregaon park. Pune then was a small and a beautiful place. There was no traffic. The weather was fantastic. Thus, at 12 o'clock in the afternoon, we used to go for a walk. There are lanes in Koregaon Park which have trees lining both sides. Even now those lanes with those trees exist. You must have seen them. We used to call it *thandi sadak*. Cool streets. One day, a dog got crushed under a moving car and the car sped away. I don't think the driver even realized his car had hit the poor dog. We were walking and we saw this happening. Dada and all of us picked the dog and kept it on one side of the road under the shade of a huge tree. We knew the dog was dying. It was very badly hurt. So Dada started fanning the dog. He said, "Go bring some water." We had to enter somebody's garden to fetch water. It took a little time. Dada sat near the dog, fanning it with His handkerchief, because we did not have anything else with us. The poor dog was panting, gasping. Before the water could be brought, the dog passed away. Its eyes were on Dada the whole time. It kept looking at Dada as it passed away. We then took it to the side and buried it. We all could make out how deeply this incident affected Dada. He was silent for hours.

'Then there was another time, when we were in Hong Kong. That was years ago, sometime in the 80s. We were travelling in a car when we felt a bump. The road was rocky and we assumed the tire had gone over a stone or something. Later, somebody told Him that a cat had gone under the car. That was the big bump. Dada was so sad. He had been silent in the car and was unaware of even the bump. That night, He didn't eat His food. None of us could eat. How could we eat? We cannot eat if Dada isn't eating. There were so many people there. In those days, everybody used to come at the time of dinner. Everybody used to come at the time of lunch. We used to have after lunch sessions where Dada used to sit and talk and we would laugh and enjoy with Him. It was such fun. Everybody freely spoke to Him. That is how He got everyone close. So everybody had come and none of us ate. We were about sixty or seventy of us. All cramped up. Some people were sitting on the chair, the others on the sofa. Some were standing. Some stood next to Him. We used to be so cramped up. Even though they were small rooms, everybody loved to be there. I really miss those days. So none of us ate. Dada said that we must have a prayer meeting for the cat. So we had a prayer meeting. And then everyone dispersed.'

'What does He feel about what's going on now in the world? So many people are being killed in the name of various religions and for a man whose life has been so filled with compassion, it must affect Him?'

'You know what, He never questions God. He says this is a passing phase. Who knows? See, we don't know the complexities of karma, we don't know where we are. This is a transition period. He believes God is in charge and when God is in charge, let Him decide what's best for each one of us.'

'What gives Him real happiness?'

'Anything where pure love and blessing comes forth from the person helped gives Him immense joy. When somebody truly blesses you. When we provide artificial limbs to the physically challenged. Dada feels truly happy especially when the person is poor and now can walk and become independent. Or the free operations done every day in our hospital that restores vision. Or free heart operations. I can make out that all these things give Him true joy.

'Oh I forgot to tell about the fish incident. In Hong Kong, we were having a walk somewhere when we passed through a market and one could get the smell of fish. I never knew such kinds of fish even existed.'

'What were you all doing in a fish market?'

'No idea. Guess we took a wrong turn. I remember that wherever we went, there was a fish market.'

'You all are the most unsuited people to walk through a fish market.'

'I know. Anyway, the sea bank was close by. Dada saw that the fish were kept in very shallow water, barely alive. He went and bought a huge bucket of fish. We then hired a boat and took it into the sea and then released the fish in the water. Wherever we may be in the world, Dada would go and talk to the fishermen and try to convince them to take up another profession. Once we were in Malaga in Spain. He used to love to take walks on the beaches and sea fronts. Because the ocean is His first love, He loves to see the waves and can spend hours looking at the water. That is why we still go to Goa. He sits and watches the water. So Dada found a fisherman . . .

'He asked him how he would feel if someone catches him or his children and cuts them into bits and they had a long conversation. Dada will keep trying no matter how impossible a task it may seem. In Singapore, we saw a lady with two fishes in her hand. Dada said, "Why don't you put them back? I will give you the money." She said they are for her breakfast. The fish were still flapping their fins. She asked Him what difference it would make if she put one fish back as fishes are being caught by the score all over the world. Dada looked at her and said, "I do not know about the scores of fish being caught, but I do know your generous act will make all the difference to this fish. At least this fish will live." She understood and we gave her the money.'

Dada looked up at me and smiled.

'Dada, how practical is it for an individual in this time and age to really be a vegetarian? You may not eat meat as a meal, but shoes, belts, wallets and purses, even toothpaste and capsules, have a component of non-vegetarianism.'

'If you are really particular of the sanctity of animal welfare, then one would be particular of the items used in day-to-day life. For instance, there are vegetarian capsules where, I think, the medicines does not include animal substances. Now they have that green dot that tells you that everything you use in that product is vegetarian. The time spirit is in favour of vegetarianism. So it is growing. There was a time when India was totally vegetarian, in the days of King Ashoka. When Ashoka saw what happened in the Kalinga war, he became a Buddhist. He saw to it that there was no slaughter of animals. A king can do it. But if Ashoka was present now, in our times, I don't know if he would have been able to be as successful. We have adopted Ashoka's *dharma chakra* as India's symbol but we are not true to the spirit of Ashoka.'

'But even yogis and sages used to use animal skin to meditate or pray?'

'In most cases, those animals were the ones whom they had loved when they were alive. And they wanted that closeness to prevail. Secondly, these skins are water proof. In those days they sat on grass or mud and these skins would prevent the moisture from the ground seeping into His body, thus allowing him to meditate or sit.'

'Dada, being a vegetarian is not an act of spirituality but an act of compassion. Or do you think one's diet can make an impact on one's spirituality?'

'I do not know how much it can contribute, because there have been people who have been eating non-vegetarian food all their lives and yet have become holy. So it is a subject which needs to be scientifically researched. But it is believed that food has a direct effect on the temperament of the individual. Woodland Kehler, who was the president of the World Vegetarian Association, told me that he had an attack of paralysis. He was a very rich man, an aristocrat. He consulted some of the best doctors in the continent, but nothing seemed to have an effect on him. Someone suggested to him to try a change of diet. He told me that when he switched over to a vegetarian diet, not only did his health improve but his temperament also changed. He used to feel irritated and get angry over small things. But then as you pointed out, Adolf Hitler was a vegetarian too.'

'So basically, according to you, more than temperament and spirituality, being a vegetarian is the right way to express oneness with all of creation.'

'I don't think one has the right to kill anybody and anything for any reason and to do so to placate one's taste buds is certainly not a good reason.'

'Why is the cow revered and called a mother . . . *Gau Mata* . . . in India?'

'The cow helped sustain the lives of countless people. From one cow, families got milk, curd, butter, ghee (clarified butter), cottage cheese, butter milk. The dung of the cow was used to thatch homes and the floors and used as fuel and the urine was used as pesticide and also as medicine. So I think out of love, the cow got the status of a mother.'

'Most Gurus have an inner circle, close disciples who live with the Guru, serve the Guru . . .'

'Every Guru has His inner circle.'

'What is the significance of this inner circle, the *mandali*, as Meher Baba used to call it?'

'The Guru does not expect any gift of money or kind from his disciples. All that He wants is obedience. There are very few disciples who will give you cent per cent obedience. Obedience is either 100 per cent or 0 per cent. There was a man who said if my Guru gives me ten orders, I am able to fulfill eight of them and so I get 80 per cent marks. No, he gets a zero because he chose those eight. He became the final decider. There are very few people who give cent per cent obedience. They are the ones on whom the Guru can rely. Therefore, they are a class apart. The inner circle, those who were with Christ were called the apostles.'

'Being part of the inner circle is a double-edged sword because there is tremendous amount of jealousy directed towards them.'

'Yes. And from their own brothers. There are disciples who become jealous of the ones who are very close to the Guru. But they are not the ones who are prepared to obey the Guru.'

'Is it because of a karmic relationship the Guru and the individual shared that makes the disciple part of the inner circle?'

'No. The Guru–disciple relationship depends mostly on the grace of the Guru. It is above karma.'

'So it is a purely spiritual bond?'

'Yes.'

'But I have gone to a few ashrams where the so-called inner circle is quite dangerous. Why does the Guru allow that to happen?'

'You look at a particular thing from one aspect, another person looks at it from another aspect. The way the Guru looks at that group is different from the way we look at it. In the case of a number of spiritual groups you will find that the ones who are closest to the Guru are the ones in whom there are deep-rooted faults. But the Guru has a reason for keeping them close to Him. The workings of a Guru are best left to the Guru.'

'Who were *Sapta Rishis*, the seven wise sages?'

'Indian and Greek civilizations speak of the seven wise ones. I have not studied Them in detail. But They were and are revered for Their wisdom.'

'Number seven seems to be very significant spiritually . . . any reason for that?'

'The number five, seven and nine, these three are regarded as mystical. I do not know why. But one respects the wisdom of the ancient ones.'

'You have mentioned the seven colours of spirituality, the vibgyor of spirituality?'

'Yes. I used it more in the context of the seven colours that combine to make sunlight. I believe that even as the white light of the sun is built up of seven colours, the light of spirituality is composed of seven colours. In simple terms, it means imbibing and internalizing certain qualities associated with spirituality and putting them into practice to the extent possible in our everyday lives.

'For me, spirituality or a spiritual being has to have these seven qualities—truth, purity, humility, childlike trust, selfless service, practice of daily silence and love.'

'Dada, what is the difference between the three temperaments or gunas written in the Gita and in Ayurveda?'

'The gunas of Gita are different from the gunas of Ayurveda. The gunas of the Gita are *tamo, rajo, sato*. They relate more to the mind of man than his body. But the gunas of Ayurveda relate to the body of man.

'So sato or *satva* is purity or light. It makes the jiva or the soul or the individual eager for knowledge and virtue. But even light binds the jiva to the body, the flesh, when it causes attachment. There are scholars eager for knowledge: their joy is in study and scholarship.

But they develop an attachment to knowledge and will not easily renounce the scholars' way. And they do not cease to be egocentric. They have a tendency towards introversion, self-analysis, scholarship and thought. These become to them ends and are not the means to the ultimate transcendence of thought and scholarship. They are *sattvic*, but not God-centred.

'Think of Nietzsche. What a noble soul! In his private life, he was pure as a maiden. His admirers called him a saint. He protested against vulgar money-making. His soul was lonely, but it was not in communion with God. He was ego-centred, not God-centred. His thought eclipsed the Spirit. He despised the masses. He misunderstood Christ. He asked for leaders who would "deduce their rights" neither from God nor from the people, but who would "boldly rule in their own right, because they are stronger". Here is the difference between the scholar's knowledge and true enlightenment. Knowledge is ego-centred, enlightenment is centred on the spirit.

'In the West, there are many scholars of sattvic temperament but their concern is less with eternity and more with "future time" and "present time", with plans and programmes of reform and progress. In India, even after few centuries of Anglicization, the truth is still not forgotten that the final end of life is knowledge of God enlightenment, *mukti*, or emancipation from the bondage of matter and self. And so, even today, you may find men who in their middle age give up position, power, wealth and academic pursuit to become *jignasus*—seekers of enlightenment and seekers of God, and endeavour to transcend the sattvic life to a life of contemplation and one-pointed devotion to the Divine Reality.

'Rajo or *rajas* is energy, mobility, passion. Rajas is *trishna*. A thirst for life. It is passionate energy. It is the child of the strong desire and attachment. It binds the soul by activity. When greed or external restless activity predominates, it means rajas prevails. Zeal for work is the mark of the man of rajas.

'The man of rajas is always in the midst of struggle and work. He has a strong desire to assert and achieve. He struggles hard to show and establish his superiority over others. He goes about in life, not as a servant of Krishna, but as the proud lord of all he surveys. The man under the influence of rajas is the man of action, of initiative, of inordinate ambition and restlessness.

'The only way out of this pattern is to break the bondage of work through work. How? Make your work and offering to the Lord. Convert work into yagna, i.e. a sacrificial offering of love.

'*Tamo* or *tamas* is neither light nor energy, but lethargy, listlessness, delusion. Tamas is darkness: it is a delusive child of ignorance. It binds the soul by heedlessness indolence and sleep. When darkness and inertia predominate, you have a sure sign that tamas prevails.

'In the man of tamas, the forces of matter predominate and he lives like the lower animals. He eats, drinks and sleeps. He lives from moment to moment but in search of appeasing his bodily pleasure and hunger. He tries to satisfy his bodily appetites. He does not bother about the ideals in life. He is slothful, negligent, deluded and ignorant. Break the bondage of tamas by doing your appointed task, by fulfilling your dharma, by taking your place at the station of life, however humble or insignificant. Nothing is really insignificant. Remember, it is not to the giant oaks only that the wind speaks. The voice of the wind cometh also to the little blades of grass.'

'So what Gita tells you is that there are people who are lazy. They belong to the *tamasic*. There are people who are overactive—they achieve nothing but they are active. They are the *rajasic* people. Then there are sattvic people who are the ones who are peaceful and calm but most often caught up in their knowledge but very often far from wise. But the Gita does not approve of any one of them. The Gita says there is the fourth type known as *gunateeta*—someone who has gone above these three gunas. He is the master of these three gunas. If a thing is not to be done, he will not do it. If a thing is to be done, he will do it in a peaceful and calm manner.'

'And Dada, what is yoga?'

'Yoga is the journey back. We were with God and for some reason or the other, we got separated. I think I spoke of three journeys—one journey away from God, taking us away every passing day, further and further away from God. Then something happens and you wake up. You realize the futility of all you are doing. You take a U-turn and enter into the second journey, the journey back to God. But then there is the third journey of which people do not know. It is the journey in God. And God is the Limitless One.'

'How does one take the U-turn?'

'The causes are many. There are many ways to get awakened or take a U-turn. As we spoke the other day, a person may get a shock like the one that Raja Bhartrihari got when He gave the fruit of immortality to his wife, who gave it to her lover and in the end it reached a prostitute who gave it back to the King. Or a moment of awakening, as when a person goes to a satsang, hears a line of a song sung by a saint an it is like a lightning from the sky. He is awakened out of his slumber. U-turn is only the waking up of the sleeping soul.'

'Would it depend on one's karma to reach that level of shock or awakening or is it beyond karma?'

'Ruzbeh, I would like to believe it's beyond karma.'

'Ah yes, your favourite word—grace. But why would one person wake up and the other person not?'

'There is no why on the spiritual plane. It is only when you touch the spiritual plane that you get an answer to the why. There was a man, a chief minister to the king, who suddenly became a saint. Valiram was his name. He worked as a chief minister to the Mirs of Sind. So everyday there used to be a court, a *dewan*, where people and subjects gathered. The dewan was presided over by the Mir. As soon as the Mir was about to arrive, an announcement was made and all the people who attended the court stood up as a mark of respect to the Mir. They kept standing until the Mir sat on his throne. One day, while the Mir was passing, a scorpion got into the *shalwar* or coat of Valiram, and stung him. A scorpion sting is indescribably painful. But the poor man had to suffer because he couldn't stir. When the Mir went and sat on his throne, Valiram went to the bathroom, took off his shalwar and the scorpion, and moments later, wrote his resignation. He came to a realization, probably through the shock of being stung or being woken up, and told himself, "For years you have served the Mir and what have you got? Scorpion sting." He takes the resignation to the Mir. The Mir is crestfallen. He does not want to let go of Valiram. The Mir says, "I will double your salary if you want." Valiram says, "No, I don't want salary or anything." "Then what do you want? I will give you what you want." "You can't give me what I want as I want peace of mind." "That, my friend, I can't give you. But if ever you do find the peace of mind you seek, let me be the first with whom you will share it."

'Valiram leaves the court and becomes a seeker. He has sung some wonderful songs, songs of awakening. In his songs he says that one needs to awaken. "*Jaag jaag maan nindh na kariye! Aab to roshan hoya re!"* which can be translated as, "Now the sun is up, you are still sleeping." The sun is up means you have been born as a human. So, take advantage of it, wake up. "*Hire jaisa janam amolak, kodiya badle khoya re!*" which means, "A birth akin to precious jewels we have bartered for some lose change."'

'Dada, everybody keeps talking about detachment. What is detachment?'

'Detachment is being without desire, free from moha or kama. The root of all sin and suffering is attachment to things of the earth. True detachment is inner, so that if something is taken away from you, you don't feel it at all. You are the same. Your stability is not shaken.'

'That is easier said than done'

'Oh Yes! It is the most difficult thing. Most difficult because it is attachment that keeps us tied to this world. Most of us are trapped by our excessive attachment to our near and dear ones, our worldly pursuits, our possessions and power. Even procreation depends upon two people coming together and getting attached. If people were detached, there would be no procreation. So the continuity of the world depends upon attachment. Attachment, I think, is the greatest force that exists from the physical point of view. It must be transcended if we are to attain self-realization.'

'The problem is for most of us detachment is akin to being aloof from family, work, career, fun—everything that colours one's life.'

'Remember true detachment, which every spiritual book teaches us, is about not having a sense of attachment so far as your inner life is concerned, not outer. We have our satsang and sermons, *upadeshes*, to teach us this. Once a man was given the upadesh that a person who wishes to move on the spiritual path should grow in a spirit of detachment and should not be attached to anybody. And he was told: Your family is not your family and your children are not your children. So this man quietly went home and he told his family, "I have nothing to do with you all." He distributed that day's food to the beggars on the roadside. He didn't give anything to his family. Then it had to be explained to him that all this is just the inner aspect, it is not the outer aspect that should be blindly followed. That is why I said, true detachment is inner.'

'Because a number of people use detachment as an excuse to run away from their responsibilities. So many enter the path of spirituality because they can't face their own reality.'

'True. It is difficult to not be attached. We are naturally attached. If you have grown in detachment that is all that you have to do. There is nothing else you need to do. But in a natural way, I get attached to you. And when I get attached that attachment is real, it can't be fake. Why is it that the mind goes astray? Because of attachment. The mind has a hundred attachments. Therefore the very first work that the Guru does is to draw the disciple towards him in such a way that he forgets all other attachments. This is the difference between the Indian Guru and the Japanese Guru. The Indian Guru draws the disciple; the Japanese Guru will not let you come near him.'

'Why?'

'I don't know why, Ruzbeh. I have absolutely no idea why a Guru would not let His disciple come close to Him.'

'You think the Guru is scared of getting attached to His or Her disciples?'

'I wouldn't know. Once a disciple comes, knocks on the door of the monastery and wishes to be taken in as a disciple, he is told to get out as there is no place for him here. He comes again second time and a third time—that is what happens in Japan. There is an amusing story which you must have read somewhere about a man who is accepted as a member of a monastery but is told that he can only speak two words every three years. The rest of the time he has to spend in silence. So when the first three years are over, he goes to the abbot and tells him, "food insipid". Then he has to wait for another three years, and he tells the abbot, "bed hard". At the end of nine years, he comes and tells the abbot, "I quit". The abbot says, "I knew you would quit."'

We both chuckle. Dada's eyes twinkle. I realize I am going to miss Him. His innocence. His wisdom. His softness. His humility. His childlike aura, but most of all, I was going to miss His eyes that twinkle and sparkle when He laughs and smiles.

'Dada, when the Guru draws the disciple towards Him or Her, so that the various attachments of the disciple are diverted towards the Guru, it still doesn't take away the sense of attachment. The Guru has only diverted attachment from something else to Him or Herself.'

'Attachment has a place in spiritual life. Attachment to God, attachment to the Guru, are the very foundations of the path.'

Dada went silent. So I guess the Guru diverts all the distracted energies of His or Her disciple and directs it towards God, Goddess or Guru. So instead of many balls in the air, there is only one ball in the air, which becomes easier to juggle and also allows the disciple to focus on just one.

'Everybody does not have a Guru. How does one reach a stage of detachment if one does not have a Guru?'

'There is something very beautiful called negation. In Sanskrit it is called *neti*. Neti means . . . not this, not this, not this. The seeker wants to know the truth of life. But he has no Guru. He looks at the microphone—is the microphone God? No. Neti, neti. So he goes through everything with a question and after an unending process he arrives at the stage when the answer no longer is neti. But it is a long process. There will be innumerable mistakes on the way. Therefore, we usually say that having a Guru is the shortest and the easiest way to reach Him.'

'Dada who is a true *fakir*?'

'I was going through one of your two beautiful books titled *The Fakir*. And I have been asking myself, "What are the essential marks of a fakir?" A fakir must have these three qualities: One is called *zikur* (meditation), the other is called *fikur* (the repetition of the Name Divine) and third is *nafus* (control over oneself or one's lower self).

'What is the lower self? The base desires which we are so familiar with—lust, hatred, greed, egoism, jealousy, hatred, slander and several other vices. The fakir is supposed to control all these desires and live a life which is pure as the snow on the peaks of the Himalayas.

'Now zikur, meditation is essential for one to walk the path. Meditation leads to calmness, centredness and going within allows one to embrace one's True Being. Then there is fikur, the constant repetition of the Name Divine. It is from this word that the word fakir comes forth. So a fakir is essentially a man who with every breath of his being repeats the Name Divine.'

'Would you consider these three things essential for anyone who wants to walk the path of spirituality?'

'Not necessarily. But it so happens that these three qualities enter into the life of a pilgrim on the path. They automatically enter if you are on the path and most often settle in so silently that you are not even aware of them being within you. The pilgrim automatically wants to avoid idle talk; he goes within and he knows that the best thing in life is to converse with the beloved in the heart within. That is why my dear Ruzbeh, always live like a fakir.'

I entered the Samadhi Temple and put my head down on the cool marble. A few feet away stood our Sadhu Vaswani. I knew that in all probability this had been my last conversation with Dada where the book and documentary was concerned. Yes, Baba willing I would meet Dada, but the way I saw things, I would never be able to have such intimate talks with Him, for such lengthy stretches of time.

In Him I had found so many relationships—all rolled into one. Grandparent, parent, Master, friend, wise sage—somebody who was humility personified, childlike, with immense strength of will and yes, somebody whose entire being lit up when He spoke about His Master or when He laughed and smiled.

I realized that in Him I saw a complete era that was slowly and surely fading away, being replaced by noise, glitter and nonsense; the last of the giants left. I would miss the Kutiya and the devoted team, always present, always smiling, always respectful. It was a phase in my life I would always keep close to my heart and consciousness. I don't know if it was fate, destiny, or karma, whatever one may call it, but more likely it was the grace of my God, Goddess, Guru, that had got me this privilege and honour of spending such a surreal and beautiful time, most importantly, with a genuine human being, a saint, and a truly reluctant Master. I am sure I didn't deserve such an honour to spend so many blissful hours with Him.

But if there is anything that would leave footprints on my soul, it would be without doubt, how to try to be a disciple. I doubt there would be a perfect disciple like Him. I doubt it. But Dada had through His majestic humility shown me a pathway to aspire to be at least the dust beneath the dust of the feet of my Master, Sai Baba of Shirdi.

I, for a long time, lay my forehead on the cold marble top. Then I looked at Sadhu Vaswani. I was going to miss my regular conversations with this gentle sage. I folded my hands over Sister Shanti's folded hands. I thanked Them Both. I had asked Dada if my writing this book about our conversations was free will or destined. I knew the answer. It was neither. It was grace. Only God, Goddess or Guru's grace could have given me this honour, privilege and opportunity to write to interact with the greatest of disciples and the most reluctant of Masters, Dada Vaswani.

Leaving the Mission, I looked back and I saw Sadhu Vaswani, with His hand lifted up, one finger pointed skyward and I smiled. The finger of grace. I lifted my hand, one finger skyward and for a second I thought I saw a smile on the beloved face of Sadhu Vaswani.

Be blessed.

Jai Baba.

FROM THE SAME AUTHOR

Rabda: My Sai . . . My Sigh

Sai Baba in every breath . . .

Rabda has attempted suicide and chances are that he is going to die. Sai Baba of Shirdi enters the hospital room and awakens the spirit body of Rabda. The two, Master and musician, converse about life, death and everything in between.

Set in the present, *Rabda* takes the reader to the past, to when the Sai lived in His physical body. The life and philosophy of Sai Baba of Shirdi are revealed, often in his own words, and questions pertaining to Him and spirituality are answered. A powerful, spiritual read, *Rabda* is a journey you really do not want to miss.

Penguin Ananda
Spiritual Fiction/PB

FROM THE SAME AUTHOR

The Perfect Ones

The oneness family—their love, presence and protection with us all

When on a spiritual quest, what if you come to know that there are archangels, angels, perfect masters, saints, sages, celestial, terrestrial and physical beings who guide all seekers on the path? Like a parent leading a child. We call these guides the oneness family, the Perfect Ones.

The Perfect Ones is a collection of biographies written by spiritual guru Ruzbeh N. Bharucha about the hierarchical planes of the various spirit guides and how They are available to all those who seek. He talks about Their lives in the physical bodies; Their teachings and Their connect with other masters; Their love, presence, protection and oneness that engulfs all.

Written with love and from personal experiences with most of the Perfect Ones, this is a journey you don'

Penguin Ananda
Spirituality/PB